FACULTY WORK IN SCHOOLS OF EDUCATION

RETHINKING ROLES AND REWARDS
FOR THE TWENTY-FIRST CENTURY

Edited by
WILLIAM G. TIERNEY

State University of New York Press

Published by
State University of New York Press, Albany

For information, address State University of New York Press,
90 State Street, Suite 700, Albany, NY 12207

Production by Cathleen Collins
Marketing by Anne M. Valentine

Library of Congress Cataloging-in-Publication Data

Faculty work in schools of education : rethinking roles and rewards for the twenty-first
century / edited by William G. Tierney.
    p. cm. — (SUNY series, frontiers in education)
    ISBN 0-7914-4815-0 (alk. paper). — ISBN 0-7914-4816-9 (pbk. : alk. paper)
    1. Teacher educators—United States. 2. Education—Study and teaching
(Higher)—United States. I. Tierney, William G. II. Series.
LB1778.2.F32   2001
370'.71'173—dc21   00-036523

10 9 8 7 6 5 4 3 2 1

To my brothers and sisters-in-law,
Paul and Susan Tierney, and Peter and Carol Tierney,
for their friendship over the years.

Contents

Acknowledgments

I appreciate the help that Beth Lish, our superb administrative assistant in the Center for Higher Education Policy Analysis at the University of Southern California, and Jack Chung and Felicia Lee, my research assistants, provided in the compilation of this book. Support for research for this book has come from the Pew Charitable Trusts. I particularly appreciate the guidance that Ellen Wert, my program officer at the Trusts, has provided over the years. The Trusts are not responsible for the ideas in the text. Royalties for this book will go to the American Indian College Fund.

Introduction

Reforming Schools, Colleges, and Departments of Education

WILLIAM G. TIERNEY

"There is, to begin happily, a greater ferment throughout education now than has been evident for a very long time. There is more internal criticism than ever before, more pressure for reform, more support for raising standards, more actual change (though small), and more active interest on the part of academic faculty members, their scholarly associations, and government agencies. All this is a promise of better things to come."

What does it say about education that the preceding paragraph was not written by me, but instead was penned by James Koerner in 1963? Surely, the paragraph could have been written today—or in 1980 or perhaps 1970, though of course, it was also applicable over a generation ago. Schools, colleges, and departments of education seem to be in perpetual "ferment." Criticism always abounds. Quite frequently, there is talk of better things to come. At the same time, the hope of improvement is measured by a cynicism that all of this has been said before. Academe and schools of education always have been strange bedfellows and the promise of reform more often than not has run aground on the shoals of academic intransigence and confusion.

In the chapters that follow the authors point out the problems and challenges that face schools, colleges, and departments of education (SCDEs) as change agents try to reform them. Our premise is that calls for change often fail because reformers do not come to terms with the complex environments in which SCDEs exist. Some critics suggest, for example, that education faculty eschew research in favor of practice, but in doing so these critics often forget or overlook the research environment in which many faculty of education often work. Others argue that tenure should be abolished for education faculty but do not consider the implications for academic freedom. Still others say that

1

education would be better off if there were more part-time or practitioner faculty and assume that one institutional environment is similar to another.

The suggestion advanced in this text is that there are four competing issues that need to be considered that pertain to reforming the work, roles, and rewards for faculty of education. The goal of this book is neither to promote one particular agenda nor to suggest that reform is foolhardy. Indeed, the reader will discover that at times the authors have competing interpretations of a particular idea. Our point here is to develop as full-bodied a discussion as possible about SCDEs. The objective is to delineate the often-competing issues that frame the work of SCDEs so that as reformers suggest specific changes the dialogue will be more informed than usually takes place. In doing so, our hope is that comments such as those made by James Koerner above will no longer be idle conjecture, but instead will bring about long-lasting and meaningful reform. In what follows, I delineate the four issues that frame the book's chapters.

The Idea of Public Higher Education

Jeannie Oakes begins her discussion by talking about the public responsibility of schools of education in public universities. Perhaps no topic has garnered more discussion in legislatures, newspapers, and policy arenas than what the public expects of SCDEs. Oakes's outlines the roots of these ideas and considers why the university has fallen short of public demands. In particular she focuses on one of the largest articulated public state systems in the world—that of California—and offers a case study about the challenges that reform has presented to UCLA.

In some respects public higher education has had a murkier role to play in the United States than its K–12 counterpart. K–12 education certainly has had its share of critics and calls for privatization, especially of late. However, higher education has never been seen as a public good in the same way that K–12 education has been. Universal, compulsory primary and secondary school education is one of the cornerstones of America's public philosophy for over a century. In some respects, higher education has been seen as a privilege, but K–12 education as a right.

At the same time, as Oakes points out, the creation of land grant colleges and universities were seen as ways to create postsecondary institutions that were "of the people and for the people." State subsidies for public institutions, lower tuition, the GI Bill, and the creation of community colleges may all be seen as twentieth century examples of America's commitment to public higher education.

Teacher training and eventually other forms of educational preparation—special education, educational administration, home economics, and the like—

have played a central role in the elaboration of higher education institutions. UCLA began as a normal school as did countless other public universities. The transition from normal school to teachers college to state college to public university has occurred by and large in less than a century. The initial assumption was that elementary and secondary schools needed trained teachers. In this light, public higher education existed in part to respond to America's commitment to K–12 schools.

However, at the same time that the United States expressed a need for qualified teachers and created normal schools, there was also a demand for research and excellence in higher education. The creation of what were to become major research universities in the late nineteenth century— Johns Hopkins, Stanford, Chicago—also created a competing model for postsecondary institutions. On the one hand, then, were institutions whose primary mission was to train teachers and serve public demands; on the other hand, were universities who saw their roles as developing elaborated research agendas. Few saw these changes as contradictory or in competition with one another, but as Oakes points out, they are. Serving the public need for trained teachers and meeting the needs of schools and other educational bodies often is in direct competition with universities where research is the primary goal.

The Role of the University

Mary Kennedy and Yvonna Lincoln offer a counterpoint to Oakes's chapter. If the first topic that needs to be understood is what the public desires from education, then the second one reverses the lens and considers what those who work in colleges and universities think of their role. In her chapter Kennedy acknowledges that the public desires faculty in education to focus on more service-oriented activities, but she then turns to what the role of the university is, and ought to be. Her chapter is a philosophical consideration of the idea of truth as a regulative ideal and suggests that rather than faculty of education dropping the search for truth they should sustain and bolster it.

Yvonna Lincoln's chapter focuses on mission statements of universities. In essence, Lincoln takes the ideas of Oakes and Kennedy and asks: What do university mission statements tell education faculty about how to act? While she acknowledges that mission statements are not doctrinaire commandments that all must follow, she also argues that such institutional ideologies are symbolic commentaries that provide meaning for an organization's participants in general, and education faculty in particular. Perhaps not surprisingly to any one who works in the university, Lincoln finds that the statements are much more supportive of the kind of work that Kennedy suggests education faculty should do, than for what Oakes observes the public wants.

An easy response to Lincoln's chapter is to say, "Then universities should get their act together and change what they do to serve public needs." A corollary is that education faculty should do the same. If the chapter I have written had an epigraph to such a demand it might be, "Not so fast."

I do not so much disagree with Oakes, Kennedy, or Lincoln, but instead try to contextualize their points and highlight how different demands pertain to education faculty in different institutions. I utilize the National Survey of Postsecondary Faculty (NSOPF) as a way to gauge different patterns and then consider what these patterns might mean if the trends continue. I am reacting against the idea that "one size fits all," whereby all education faculties should move in lock step. I take seriously Lincoln's concern for mission statements and suggest that different institutions ought to be engaged in different kinds of activities. If the twentieth century has been a period of systemic assimi- lation where all institutions have drifted up a hierarchical ladder toward the mission of the research university, I argue, then the twenty-first century ought to be a period of systemic differentiation. Institutions need to carve out unique niches for themselves that set themselves off from one another.

If my call for differentiation is heeded, then education faculty face dif- ferent futures depending on the kind of institutions where they work. Sarah Turner's chapter looks at this issue by way of an economic analysis of pro- duction functions in schools of education. Her argument is that schools of education vary markedly in their production functions and associated cost functions; of consequence, there is wide variation in institutional responses to the changing educational marketplace.

Any book on a topic as full-bodied as education cannot cover every pos- sible policy issue that affects change. But these first two topics—the idea of public higher education and the role of the university—have as a backdrop the changing institutional contexts in the larger marketplace. The University of Phoenix is now the largest university in the United States. Distance learning is not some futuristic fantasy, but a reality. For-profit and corporate universities will be the fastest-growing postsecondary institutions in the next decade. One can no longer look at mission statements of land grant institutions, for ex- ample, in isolation; what Turner and my chapters attempt to do is point out how changing contexts impact on traditional colleges and universities and how schools, colleges, and departments of education will be framed. Nevertheless, one topic that demands further analysis is a consideration of exactly what for profits intend to do, how they do it, and how they might best be evaluated.

Faculty Roles and Rewards

In Oakes's chapter she points out the possibilities and pitfalls for faculty when they try to engage in work that differs from what Lincoln defines as the mission of the university. Although Oakes contends that alternative forms of scholarship are possible, she also is aware that it is fraught with contention. Assistant professors may be warned off engaging with the schools because their research productivity will suffer. Senior faculty may feel that such work is not prestigious. Indeed, Lincoln's argument in part is that if mission statements do not change, then reward systems will not change either.

In my chapter I also point out that different institutions have different demands. Part-time faculty, for example, are the fastest-growing sector of faculty in postsecondary institutions. There are those who will argue that such non–tenure track arrangements in SCDEs are a positive sign (Breneman, 1997; Gappa, 1996), but the authors frequently overlook the contexts in which such changes occur. Education faculty who work in a university that adheres to the kind of roles that Kennedy suggests will be ill served by an increase in part-time faculty. Simply stated, an organization that requires its faculty to do research will require research faculty. A college or university that wants its faculty to engage with schools and local organizations will need to rethink the promotion and tenure system.

Regardless of the intended changes, one area that is ripe for further investigation is how nontenure track faculty are treated, evaluated, trained, and socialized. James Hearn and Melissa Anderson tackle just that topic in their chapter on clinical faculty. Their chapter has a threefold purpose. First, they outline the extant literature and research on clinical faculty in schools of education. They then discuss ways one might improve the assessment and performance of clinical faculty and they conclude by considering what additional research needs to be done.

One irony with the recent arguments about tenure reform in general, and how education faculty should be rewarded in particular, is that the discussion has centered on traditional notions of faculty work and rewards while at the same time alternative work arrangements such as clinical faculty who work with contracts has not been investigated. Again, the overarching purpose of our book is not to say that SCDEs should or should not increase their non-tenure track faculty. However, we believe it is foolish to continue to argue over issues from a decontextualized and ahistorical stance. In this light, Hearn and Anderson are most helpful in sketching at least an initial framework for thinking about clinical faculty in schools of education.

If the Hearn and Anderson chapter treat one of the most recent and fastest-growing changes in the reward structure for ed faculty, then Philo Hutcheson returns the reader to one of the most enduring and historical of issues—that of academic freedom. Tenure came about to protect academic freedom. Hutcheson walks the reader through the general parameters of academic freedom and then considers what academic freedom has meant for education faculty. Since the American Association of University Professors (AAUP) has come into existence and kept records, Hutcheson is able to provide a case history of education faculty who faced problems that were defined as infringements on academic freedom. As might be expected, the reasons for dismissal are not that different from faculty in other disciplines and professions: procedural issues, charges of moral turpitude or political activity, and claims of fiscal exigency.

One might think of Hutcheson's chapter as akin to Lincoln's. Academic freedom is a central totem of the university. A commitment to academic freedom has as much symbolic and ideological value as it does strategic or legal. The implications for faculty in education are that they do not need to worry about avoiding controversies or speaking out on crucial issues of the day. Although such a freedom is imperative for all faculty, one might surmise for professors who are explicitly concerned in one way or another with public issues such as education, that academic freedom plays a critical role.

When roles and rewards structures shift, then of consequence, so too will the importance of academic freedom. Clinical faculty, for example, by definition do not have tenure, so their legal protection for academic freedom is absent. If education faculty move toward an explicit overarching engagement with schools such that the traditional roles of faculty are dropped, then will they need tenure since academic freedom may no longer be at the heart of their work? Again, Hutcheson and the other authors do not wish to argue one way or another, but we collectively assume that it is foolhardy to think about one important issue—the role of the university, for example—and not consider the implications for faculty roles and rewards. Change in one theme presages change in another.

Populations

Perhaps nowhere are such changes more apparent than with regard to who populates the enterprise. Who are education faculty? My chapter outlines how faculty in education compare to other disciplines and professions with regard to race, gender, faculty ranks, and institutional types. Hutcheson touches on the gendered nature of academic freedom by pointing out that during the retrenchment of the 1980s institutions often removed women professors before considering the removal of other male faculty members. He observes that of the eleven education faculty who were involved in court cases from 1980 to the present, nine of the dismissed education professors were women and only two were men.

Judith Glazer-Raymo continues this discussion by way of an extensive discussion about women's roles and work in SCDEs. Her argument is that women have occupied an especially vulnerable place in the academy in general, and this vulnerability can be seen with regard to education faculty.

Although women faculty are well represented in education, they still tend to occupy the lower academic ranks and receive less compensation than their male counterparts. Glazer-Raymo continues the trends of the other chapters by contextualizing issues such as tenure policies for women faculty. She also ties her analysis to Hearn and Anderson, and Hutcheson's, by pointing out that more women occupy non–tenure track positions in education than men; the implications are that these women do not enjoy academic freedom in a manner akin to their tenured counterparts. She trenchantly summarizes her chapter by pointing out that "women are less likely to gain tenure, receive recognition for their scholarship, be promoted to tenured full professors, and earn comparable economic rewards" (p. 20). Her point surely is not that tenure must be eliminated, but neither is it that issues such as tenure or the requirements for tenure should remain in place unquestioned and unchallenged. Instead, her chapter raises issues about how changes in the other themes will impact women faculty in education.

In the book's penultimate chapter James Antony and Edward Taylor focus on two crucial issues: graduate student socialization and the recruitment of minority faculty. Their argument is that although one finds African American faculty in the greatest numbers in education, there should be little cause for celebration. As I point out in my own chapter African American faculty are under represented in all disciplines; they just happen to have more faculty in education than in other areas. However, as with Glazer-Raymo's analysis, African American faculty tend to be clustered in the lowest occupational rungs in the profession.

Antony and Taylor's argument is that if the academy wishes to increase the number of minority faculty in education then one strategy is to focus on graduate student socialization. They conducted a series of interviews with African American doctoral students in education to demonstrate how the students conceived of a professional career. Most often, argue the authors, minority students find their personal, philosophical, and political views as incompatible with the norms of the academy. Minority students' concerns are multiple, and the authors explicate these concerns in order to think how those involved in graduate education might better train prospective faculty to meet the multiple needs of education faculty.

Their chapter, taken together with the other issues that are raised in the book, raise another point. However under represented minority faculty may be in education, or women, for that matter, what are the implications if education is given up as an area of study in research universities, as I suggest will happen in my chapter? If education faculty become primarily part-time or non–tenure track, and yet they account for one of the most diverse of subject areas, what kind of message is sent about the import of ethnic and gender heterogeneity? Again, the point is not to say that because women are relatively well represented in education that education as a field ought to remain the same. However, the time for blanket statements that are unhinged from related points ought to cease.

As I noted earlier, in this book we do not focus on every possible topic that pertains to education faculty. We do not, for example, investigate alternative credentialing arrangements or newly formed accrediting bodies, both of which may have significant impacts on education faculty. There are also interesting alternative tenure models such as charter schools of education that I consider elsewhere (Tierney, in press; Wong and Tierney, unpublished monograph). Nevertheless, the issues raised here are the central topics that form related challenges for those of us who desire to see change in education. As Arthur Levine notes in his summation, what these chapters point out are a variety of challenges and problems that demand action. A singular answer to the many problems that we pose may not be viable, but what is equally clear, as Levine concludes, is that to maintain the status quo will not work. Our argument throughout the text is that one ought not embark on change until thoughtful, accurate information exists. Our hope is that this provides just that.

References

Breneman, D. W. (1997). "Alternatives to Tenure for the Next Generation of Academics." *AAHE Forum on Faculty Roles and Rewards Working Paper Series*. Washington, DC: American Association for Higher Education.

Gappa, J. M. (1996). "Off the Tenure Track: Six Models for Full-Time, Nontenurable Appointments." *AAHE Forum on Faculty Roles and Rewards Working Paper Series*. Inquiry #10, Washington, DC: American Association for Higher Education.

Koerner, J. D. (1963). *The Miseducation of American Teachers*. Boston: Houghton Mifflin Company, p. 15.

Tierney, W. G. (in press). *Reforming Tenure in Schools of Education*. Phi Delta Kappan.

Wong, M. P. & Tierney, W. G. (unpublished monograph). *Charter Schools of Education: Challenges and Possibilities*.

CHAPTER 1

The Public Responsibility of Public Schools of Education

JEANNIE OAKES AND JOHN ROGERS

The central focus of public universities is a commitment to public institutions and solving public problems. That, at least, was the intention behind Congress's 1862 Act establishing the land-grant college. Turn of the century Progressive Era intellectuals such as John Dewey and Jane Addams similarly were hopeful that universities would marshal their "reason and research to improve the human condition."[1] This powerful legacy connects the intellectual and public missions of public universities. However, from the beginning, actual practice fell quite short. As Jane Addams noted in 1899,

> [A]s the college changed from teaching theology to teaching secular knowledge the test of its success should have shifted from the power to save men's souls to the power to adjust them in healthful relations to nature and their fellow men. But the college failed to do this, and made the test of its success the mere collecting and dissemination of knowledge, elevating the means into an end and falling in love with its own achievement.[2]

At the end of the twentieth century, public universities again are being called to demonstrate their public value, and contemporary critics echo Addams's concerns, if not her analysis.

Schools and departments of education are easy targets. Education is the largest public enterprise in every state, and the public requires both well-prepared teachers and sophisticated knowledge of schooling in order respond to a vast array of educational and social concerns. Concerns associated with demographic shifts, and the declining social conditions for children have dramatically escalated demands on schools; however, equally powerful social trends such as widespread cynicism about public institutions and the press for market-based reform have weakened public commitment to public schools.

These converging but conflicting social forces mean that faculties in schools and departments of education must search for opportunities to channel their universities' commitments to the public good—"reason and research to improve the human condition." Although many faculty in education are now struggling to meet the challenges of public education, most schools and departments are not well suited to support such efforts. For the most part, university programs of research and teaching do not respond directly to the needs of public education; neither have they forged strong connections with the profession and public that their schools and programs of education serve.

Integrating academic and professional work so that public problems guide the core work in faculties of education requires new conceptions of scholarship and of professional programs. The new conception of education scholarship must be driven, not only by the urgency of public problems, but also by a conviction that the nature of scholarly inquiry in education requires it. Integrating academic and professional work also requires a fundamental transformation of the structures and political arrangements within schools of education, between education schools and the rest of the university, and between the university and the public. This is no simple matter.

While there are many types of public institutions of higher education, this chapter focuses on public, landgrant universities and what this status implies for their role in public K–12 education. It takes the University of California as an exemplar, founded as a land grant 130 years ago. The past decade's crisis in California's public K–12 education system has turned the University of California again to its public roots and its public role, recalling old responsibilities and forging new meanings of the landgrant mission. Perhaps this is not surprising in a state where education has always been a central focus and in an institution where at least one of its major campuses, UCLA, began as a normal school. But given that national moods and movements often blow from West to East, the recent efforts by faculty in the University of California to transform its schools and programs in education in order to wed research opportunities with its public responsibilities may be instructive to others about the prospects of such efforts.

The University of California Case

The University of California's connection with its public was heralded by President Daniel Coit Gilman in his 1872 Inaugural Address:

This is the University of California . . . the University of this state. It must be adapted to this people . . . to the requirements of the new society and their undeveloped resources. It is not the foundation . . . of private individuals. It is "of the people and for the people" . . . in the highest and noblest relations to their intellectual and moral well-being. It opens the door of superior education to all.[3]

For most of the next one hundred years, this connection was enacted most visibly by developing a multicampus system that made higher education accessible to all geographic regions of the state and by providing technical assistance to the state's agricultural and mining industries. Gathering momentum over the last half century, the UC has forged its identity as a world-class research university.

In the past decade, UC's landgrant mission has been revisited by those concerned about the growing distance between the university and the public. Gilman's Inaugural was cited proudly when the current group of UC Chancellors reacted with outrage to California's Proposition 209 ban on affirmative action and the UC Regents' decision to prohibit race as a factor in UC admissions. Gilman's sentiments have been voiced by former University of California, Santa Cruz Chancellor Karl Pister in his work to help UC campuses to frame "outreach" efforts to counter the new restrictive admissions policies. Pister sees UC's current responsibility to improve public K–12 education as the proper twenty-first-century counterpart to its pivotal twentieth-century role in developing California's agriculture and industry. He argues that, today, this preeminent land-grant university must devote its enormous capacity to the state's undeveloped human resources, specifically to the education of its diverse and growing population of children.[4]

These are only a few instances of the growing interest in turning some of the university's attention toward the state's quite staggering educational problems. California schools, along with schools nationwide, face enormous challenges. By 2005, California's school population will be 12 percent larger than the 1999 population, with the largest growth among low-income children of color and English-language learners (currently 25 percent of school attendees). At the same time, a large proportion of the state's aging teaching force (currently one of six teachers is over age 55) is about to retire. The state will require more than 25,000 new teachers each year, and the greatest needs will be in poor urban and rural areas.

Projected demographic changes also call for a tremendous multicultural shift in teaching. California needs more teachers of color as well as teachers of all ethnicities who are well equipped with content knowledge and with pedagogies and attitudes appropriate for multilingual, multicultural classrooms. These teachers will need to understand and have a passion for working with the conditions of urban life and the special needs of low-income students. They will need cross-disciplinary training, knowledge, and expertise. They will also need the scaffolding university research to provide them with creative approaches to pedagogy and foundations for education policymaking. Finally, they will need university-school partnerships that build an education ecology comprised of a broad range of social and clinical, as well as educational, supports.

In sum, Californina schools and schools elsewhere must ready an increasingly diverse, increasingly poor student population to survive in and contribute to a society increasingly enmeshed in technological work, international markets, geopolitical tensions, and social complexity. To do so, these schools must move away from their emphasis on low-level skills and instead equip all children with problem solving abilities that are essential for productive lives and work.

Some efforts to reconsider the role of the University of California in meeting these educational needs have been visible over the past fifteen years. In the mid-1980s a systemwide committee, directed by then-UCLA Dean John Goodlad, called for the University to re-orient its schools and programs of education in order to direct systemwide and campus resources toward the improvement of K–12 schools. The report called for campuses to redesign programs that prepare professional educators. On some campuses, new initiatives reflected those recommendations, but overall, little changed. More recently, in 1992, UC's President charged a second systemwide committee specifically with recommending how the University could help strengthen the State's educational system. This most recent committee's work and the system's response to it provide useful insight into the University of California case.

The Vision—Blurring the Research/Practice Distinction

The 1992 committee began with a strong conviction that UC's education programs must act aggressively and get involved in building the capacity of the K–12 (or K–14) education system—responding especially to the state's rapidly increasing diversity, as well as the poverty and disruption that mark many children's lives. However, the committee was also sobered (but perhaps not surprised) by the limited impact of earlier critiques that proposed closing the gap between education schools and the practices and policies that affect so many of state's schoolchildren.[5] Addressing these disappointing results, the committee began with the view that for a great research university to work effectively with concerns about citizens' education and quality of life, it needed to embed these concerns into the core of its research mission. Hence, the university's public mission should neither be limited to teacher and administrator training nor relegated to the periphery as "public service." By way of analogy, just as the university has found intellectual and research challenges of the highest order interwoven in its technical scaffolding of the state's agriculture, mining, medical, and other enterprises, it could and must find similar intellectual and research agendas in its K–12 educational endeavors.

After much deliberation and drafting, the Committee issued its report in 1994. The report affirmed the significance of faculty's work in research, graduate education, and professional practice. It recognized the potential for a creative synergy of research, teaching, and the improvement of education policy and practice that UC's combined mission makes possible. Unlike the California State University (CSU) system, whose mission includes the preparation of the bulk of the state's educators, UC's role is to investigate, develop, and test new approaches to education and the preparation of educators. However, it also judged UC's programs of education to have fallen short. It offered the following recommendations to alter the structure and cultures of UC education schools to better support these roles in the context of the social responsibility of the public university.

The Charge to the Campuses

1. Reconfigure education activities at each campus in ways that integrate education theory, research, graduate education, and professional practice.

   - Reconfigure current resources and activities in education into programmatic units with clear missions that require the integration of research, teaching, and public service.
   - Revise definitions and specifications of professional preparation programs in education so that they become rigorous, long-term enterprises involving inquiry, as well as training and field experiences.
   - Strengthen the Ed.D. to emphasize its being a high-status, substantively rich professional degree with requirements that overlap with, but are clearly distinct from those for the Ph.D.
   - Redesign research-oriented Ph.D. Programs so that candidates engage in research apprenticeships in classrooms, schools, policy-making arenas, or other "real world" settings, in addition to providing analytic training in courses.
   - Establish long-term, equal-status, and mutually supportive relationships with key K–12 schools, community colleges, local districts, and other state and local education agencies that agree to work collaboratively on professional preparation and field-based research.
   - Expand the academic calendar for professional education and research degree programs to facilitate the full engagement of practitioner-students with research-oriented students and faculty research activities.
   - Establish differentiated staffing patterns that bring together senate faculty members and other professional staff and faculty in ways that model and promote the integration of theory, research, and practice at both the university and in the field.

- Allow for a limited number of extended, flexible appointments for education faculty members who hold joint appointments in education departments or programs and field-based centers.
- Maintain and increase the university grants program that currently encourages and supports problem-focused, collaborative inquiry between the university and the public schools.

2. Promote and support scholarship relevant to and valued in both the university and the schools.
   - Support collaborative, multidisciplinary research into "practical" educational problems.
   - Incorporate ongoing self-study and reflection.
   - Develop clear standards of education scholarship for merit and promotion of education faculty.
   - Develop mechanisms for enhancing broad communication between UC faculties in education and the professional and policy-maker communities.

3. Establish and support collaborative efforts across communities, institutions, and agencies that advance UC's mission in education.
   - Work hand-in-hand with those in other state universities, each contributing its own strengths and resources, to improve the preparation of educators.
   - Provide the structures and incentives that shift existing collaborative activities with the state education agency, K–12 schools, and community colleges into the core work of senate faculty, both in education and in the letters and sciences.
   - Establish new collaborative professional education programs between UC, the California department of education, and the K–12 sector that link the continuing professional development of educators and "alternative" routes for entry into the profession with senate faculty research and teaching.
   - Establish and maintain strong connections between UC and the K–12 and community college systems at the policy level as well as in programs and services.
   - Establish relationships between campus education schools and programs and community agencies that provide other health and social services to children and families.

4. Establish and support arrangements that promote collaboration *within* the university that advances its mission in education.
   - Establish academic exchanges with other departments and professional schools.
   - Establish interprofessional cognates for graduate students in education, health, and other social service fields.

- Work together on research and teaching programs in teaching the disciplines.
- Designate schools and programs of education as the intellectual and institutional homes for education extension and summer programs in the field of education, and as the clearinghouse for other university-based education professional development and school improvement projects.
- Education faculty and faculty in letters and science should join in research and community service projects in urban and rural schools.

5. Transform schools and programs of education into socially responsible learning communities.
   - Achieve racial, ethnic, and linguistic diversity and tolerance.
   - Initiate aggressive programs of financial and academic support to assist education schools to reflect the diversity of the state and nation in the composition of their faculties, staffs, and student populations.
   - Redesign the curriculum so that it reflects the racial, cultural, and linguistic diversity of the state and nation.
   - Mount aggressive efforts to provide greater financial aid for students in education schools and programs.
   - Restructure their schools and programs to support communities of learners.

To make these recommendations somewhat less abstract, the Committee developed several scenarios to illustrate how transformed education programs might look. While the scenarios' specifics varied considerably, they all pointed toward differentiated staffing patterns that bring together Senate faculty members and other professional faculty and staff; long-term collaboration with key schools, school districts, and/or state education agencies; revised definitions of professional preparation as a long-term enterprise involving inquiry as well as training; preparation programs for practitioners and researchers that blend classroom and "real world" experiences in meaningful ways; and simultaneous integration and functional differentiation among different units within the University and between the University and other educational and social institutions. Together the scenarios made more concrete the committee's conception of a seamless education profession—one in which the preparation of administrators, teachers, policy makers, and researchers overlaps significantly, and one that provides rich learning opportunities for both novices and seasoned professionals. The scenarios offered images of the university's institutional commitment to elementary and secondary education, and its own willingness to experiment and to investigate the outcomes of alternative approaches.

The Committee called on the UC Office of the President, campus Chancellors, and the Academic Senate to provide convincing leadership in adopting these recommendations and foster an institutional environment for the development and testing of alternative scenarios in education schools and programs. The Committee's hope that its report would prompt actions that prior, similar reports have not. It called for a readiness to integrate effective alternatives into their formal and core structures. The report called for a task force on each campus to design and report progress on their efforts to fulfill these recommendations. Without that solid commitment, the report argued, schools and programs of education will face serious limits to their capacity to fulfill the university's public responsibility.

The Rationale—An Expanded View of Scholarship

The current model of education scholarship that operates at the UC's mimics the form and substance of academic departments in the letters and sciences. It is understandable why this is the case. The status of the field of education within the university and rewards to individual professors have traditionally depended on conforming to this model. This tradition embodies old notions of separating thought (scholarship) and action (practice) and sustains enormous obstacles for UC faculty attempting to integrate academic and professional approaches to the field of education. The challenge, then, is for faculties to entertain new conceptions of learning where thought and action come together and to persuade their colleagues across the campus that such conceptions are legitimate.

An expanded conception of education scholarship must include both traditional types of research and new forms that more closely integrate the "practical" and "academic" in its approach to education problems. The Committee argued that juxtaposing the academic and the practical becomes less problematic when we recognize that scholarly inquiry in education, while not excluding basic, discipline-based research, necessarily integrates theory and research with practice.

The 1994 report made clear that, in the past few decades, education research, including that of UC faculty, has produced knowledge of great value for the conduct of education. As a result of education research, economists can now speak meaningfully about the role of education in economic development; sociologists can better specify race and class barriers to equal opportunity; organizational theorists have a stronger purchase on how schools and colleges work and the dysfunction of school bureaucracy; psychologists have made impressive strides in understanding learning in and out of school. UC faculty have made important inroads in our understanding of the processes of first-language loss and second-language acquisition; of the links among development, motivation, and learning; of the impact of school and classroom organization on educational opportunity and achievement; of the importance of classroom context on learning, and the technical requirements for valid and reliable information about student learning, to name just a few of numerous contributions.

Of course, we need to know much more, and we should pursue energetically research programs that will expand our knowledge in these domains. However, given what we have accomplished, we now need to do much more to generate knowledge regarding the practical application of theory and empirical findings. In part because the large pedagogical and social questions that impact schools and children do not lend themselves to tightly controlled experimentation, researchers must seek such knowledge via their engagement within schools, not by their disinterested view from outside. Further, both schools and researchers need multidisciplinary research in education that addresses more directly the problems of education policy and practice, illuminates effective new approaches to teaching, and helps practitioners comprehend the conditions of their work. Drawing on John Dewey, Ernest Boyer, and Ann Lieberman, the UC Committee has argued that an expanded vision of education scholarship is necessary, not only because of public urgency, but also because scholarly integrity demands it.

Roots in Dewey. Of course, this expanded conception of education scholarship is not new. In 1929, John Dewey argued in *Sources of a Science of Education*,

> The answer is (1) educational practices provide the data, the subject matter, which form the problems of inquiry. They are the sole source of the ultimate problems to be investigated. These educational practices are also (2) the final test of value of the conclusion of all researches. To suppose that scientific findings decide the value of educational undertakings is to reverse the real case. Actual activities in educating test the worth of the results of scientific results. They may be scientific in some other field, but not in education until they serve educational purposes, and whether they really serve or not can be found out only in practice. (32–33)

Echoing Dewey, then, the UC Committee argued that the value of connecting education research and practice go far beyond simply informing practice. Rather, as Dewey argued, social research also stands to benefit as a consequence of contact between the worlds of practice and research.

> It is not education alone that has suffered from isolation of thinkers in the social and psychological disciplines from the occurrences taking place in schools. Indifference to the latter, a hardly veiled intellectual contempt for them, has undoubtedly strengthened the rule of convention, routine and accidental opinion in the schools. But it has also deprived the sciences in questions of problems that would have stimulated significant inquiry and reflection. Much of the barrenness and loose speculation in the humane sciences is directly due to remoteness from the material that would stimulate, direct and test thought. (40–41)

Echoes in Boyer and Lieberman. Dewey's view of education scholarship is echoed in recent reexaminations of the nature of scholarship and the relationship among research, teaching, and service across academic departments and professional schools within universities. For example, recall Ernest Boyer's words in *Scholarship Reconsidered: The Priorities of the Professorate*, "What we urgently need today is a more inclusive view of what it means to be a scholar—a recognition that knowledge is acquired through research, through synthesis, through practice, and through teaching. We acknowledge that these four categories—the scholarship of discovery, of integration, of application, and of teaching—divide intellectual functions that are tied inseparably to each other" (p. 25).

Ann Lieberman invoked these ideas with specific reference to education in her presidential address to the American Educational Research Association in 1992 (Lieberman, 1992). Lieberman argued that education scholars must venture beyond traditional research to include three diverse, methodologically pluralistic, and context specific types of work: "studying school programs, events, practices, people, organizations, and particular cultures to better understand and describe the improvement of practice; creating new frames and strategies for thinking about, understanding, and acting upon this new knowledge; and building new collaborative structures and relationships between schools and universities that deal with specific or general areas of content and pedagogy, aimed at the transformation of research and practice" (p. 8).

Lieberman concluded, "The practice-theory connection is no better served than when it is lived. We can learn from as well as about practice. Our challenge is to create a community that educates all of us, those in the University and those in the schools, a community that expands our relationships with one another and, in doing so, our knowledge and effectiveness" (p. 11). In sum, then, not only the urgency of public problems, but also the nature of scholarly inquiry in education support a renewal of an integrated mission for the faculty in public university's schools and programs in education.

New Standards for Promotion and Tenure. The most cogent arguments for an expanded view of education scholarship mean little unless the university rewards faculty for work that simultaneously meets rigorous standards of scholarship and communicates clearly to practitioners and policy makers. Such work will sometimes (but, by no means always) depart from the form and substance of traditional basic research in letters and sciences. Thus, the UC committee argued that it is long past time for campus review committees to judge the work of professional schools, generally, and schools of education, in particular, by professional as well as traditional academic standards. On some campuses, their report suggested, it may be useful to establish a new structure for reviewing scholarship in professional schools. However, the committee also warned that structures alone are insufficient to set, communicate, promote, and sustain high and appropriate standards for such work. The primary objective is to develop both the commitment and expertise to make such judgments rigorously and with a clear understanding of professional school faculty's work. Education schools and programs, the UC Committee, argued need clear standards of scholarship for merit and promotion that make explicit the criteria for judging school-relevant scholarship and creative work and concerted effort to educate faculty reviewing bodies about the meaning and importance of these standards.

Five Years Later

As one might suspect, the 1994 report created only the tiniest ripple when it was released. The campus academic vice chancellors were briefed, as were systemwide academic policy groups. Most listened politely and moved on to the next item of business. However, on some campuses, the recommendations came at a time when the state's demographic transformation and schooling crisis could no longer be ignored. Some faculties were ready and eager to move, and the report gave legitimacy to their impulses and provided some images of what shape their movement might take. Other faculties took little notice.

Five years later, some tangible changes have taken place that integrate teacher education and work with schools (traditionally low-status activities on UC campuses) into faculty's research and graduate teaching, and faculty on many campuses (notably Santa Barbara, Santa Cruz, and Los Angeles) have sought and won major new grants that connect their research with K–12 policy making and school reform. For example, the Deans at UC Berkeley and UCLA drafted a statement asserting the essential role of UC in "working with California's schools to improve student preparation and achievement" and that an integral part of this role "must be significant programs for the pre- and post-credential education of teachers."[6] The Riverside campus has hired a new dean with a strong commitment to teacher education. At five UC campuses (Davis, Los Angeles, Santa Barbara, Santa Cruz, and San Diego), teacher education programs have been designated by the state as "experimental" programs where faculty research will inform state certification policies. The Irvine campus now requires that each new tenure-track faculty hire must commit to working with K–12 schools or in professional preparation programs, and Berkeley's faculty developed a set of guiding principles to help them integrate teacher education into the core of faculty work. San Diego's faculty is developing a "charter" high school that will be a research site, as well as a laboratory for teacher education. Nearly all of the campuses have initiated new collaborative efforts between letters and science departments and education aimed at developing stronger K–12 teachers or supporting curriculum projects on K–12 campuses.

In the past two years, these efforts have been given a substantial boost by the university's effort to replace Affirmative Action programs with "Outreach," defined, at least in part, as campuswide programs aimed at increasing the number of students of color who are eligible for university admission by improving K–12 schools in low-income neighborhoods. However, it remains to be seen whether this new campuswide attention will lead to the changes in core faculty work required to sustain this new direction.

Like other professional schools, education programs wrestle with competition between disciplinary and professional definitions of research, research methods and reports; they juggle campus-based forms of instruction and the kind of clinical practice best provided in natural field settings; and they struggle to balance their investments in the local and regional professional infrastructure with investments in state and national policy making. These issues are even more complicated for education schools because K–12 schooling is largely a public enterprise—in contrast to law, medicine, and business. Because of its public nature, improving the practice of education requires a process more akin to public inquiry and community building than it does to policy design and implementation. Given the diverse constituencies engaged in the education profession and the practice of schooling, this kind of community building is in itself an essential and extremely challenging enterprise for schools of education. While several faculties have worked to educate campuswide review committees, no campus has yet established a fundamentally more expanded view of scholarship that includes integrated research and practice.

Center X

UCLA's Center X provides a concrete example of the changes that have taken place and also illuminates the struggles faculty are encountering in this new work. Center X (Where Research and Practice Intersect for Urban School Professionals) began in 1994 in response to the education faculty's determination to connect its work more tangibly with Los Angeles's central city neighborhoods and schools. Center X was formed by merging under one mission and organizational umbrella the preservice M.Ed./credential teacher education program, six of the state-sponsored California Subject Matter Projects and related professional development for practicing educators, the UCLA Principals' Center, and the Ph.D. teaching and research programs of a handful of tenure-track faculty whose work on urban schools, teaching, and educational equity relate to race, class, culture, and language.

Mission-Driven Activities

Center X's work is grounded in a set of principles that include social justice, collaboration, and the integration of research and practice. Center X blends theory, empirical studies, professional preparation, and practice principally through its partnerships with schools in traditionally underserved urban communities. Members of these collaboratives are committed to work together over the course of several years to improve academic achievement for all children and to substantially increase the number of graduates prepared for college admission.

The Center X strategy is to develop and study pre- and in-service teacher education as rigorous, high-status, field-based inquiry that connects university faculty, teachers, and community members in urban Los Angeles area schools. Its preservice teacher education program engages novice teachers at schools where the faculty is involved in an inquiry-based approach to their work with low-income children of color. That way, rather than seeing the status quo of teaching and learning as the ideal, novice teachers experience a faculty engaged in serious inquiry about how schools can better serve low-income, language- and ethnic-minority students. Accordingly, teams of teacher candidates learn to teach in the context of a school community, supervised not simply by the traditional "master teacher," but rather by school faculty and a team of UCLA research faculty, clinical faculty, and doctoral students (most are preparing to be teacher educators and are conducting their own research on urban teacher education and school reform).

Within this collaborative context, Center X integrates coursework and field experiences over a two year period to prepare graduates to be professionals who endeavor to make public schools democratic public spheres, where all children—regardless of race, class, gender, or age—can learn what it means to be able to participate fully in a society that affirms and sustains the principles of equality, freedom, and social justice. All UCLA students specialize in cross-cultural language and academic development, and many earn bilingual certification in either Spanish or Korean. Year I begins with a comprehensive academic sequence comprised of the basic curricular requirements for the credential and the master's degree. First year students also participate in "novice" teaching at partner schools with racially, culturally, and linguistically diverse low-income student populations. During Year II, the program supports students as they become first-year teachers. Each student assumes a paid residency at a low-income, urban school while they simultaneously complete a program coursework and prepare and defend a portfolio for the M.Ed.

Overlapping with the preservice program, the Center X Outreach provides programs for continued growth and professional development of educators and parents in Los Angeles area schools and colleges with high populations of students from underrepresented minority groups. Programs in writing, literature, mathematics, history, science, and the arts aim to strengthen teachers' content background, develop a repertoire of teaching strategies, refine their understanding of reform in content areas, and develop their leadership expertise.

At this point, five tenure-track faculty have shifted their research programs into Center X, investigating a variety of questions about preparing and sustaining teachers in central city schools, and studying the impact of the collaboration on teaching and learning in the partner schools. It is significant that the specific research questions have emerged from the real and challenging issues of teaching and learning for low-income children in urban schools, and the research methods faculty employ attempt to reflect a synergy of cutting-edge research and practice that can produce useful lessons for other cities, universities, and schools. In addition to faculty research, six Ph.D. dissertations have been completed about the Center's work. Perhaps because this work focuses theory and empirical studies on the daily struggles of urban schools, faculty have won a number of government and foundation grants to support their research.

Today, the Center consists of about ninety very diverse colleagues. Research faculty include those with junior and senior standing on the tenure track, as well as visiting faculty and postdoctoral scholars. Clinical faculty (most are former or current teachers and school administrators) with doctorates teach courses in the M.Ed. program for our teacher candidates, provide nondegree professional development activities for practicing educators, and administer our credentialling process. Some lead Center X programs and courses on campus or in schools and district offices. The fifteen or so Ph.D. students affiliated with the Center provide a mix of support for the teaching programs and research.

Changing Structure and Culture

The Center X faculty have committed to the view—however idealistic—that schools and teaching for low-income, racially culturally, and linguistically diverse children can change, and that the university has a powerful substantive and symbolic role to play in that change. To accomplish this ambitious goal, Center X strives to be more than a peripheral "public service" of UCLA's Graduate School of Education and Information Studies. Rather, it works to foster both structural and cultural change in faculty's core work. Such changes—far more than the programs themselves or the individual accomplishments of faculty and students—provide indicators of whether or not the Center serves to integrate scholarship and practice. Three such structural changes have been the development of clinical faculty, the use of the

Center as a site for Ph.D. research and teaching apprenticeships, and the shifting of faculty research programs under the Center's umbrella.

Perhaps most striking has been the change in the role and status of clinical faculty. UCLA, like most research universities with credential and in-service education programs, had for years employed a cadre of "supervisors of teacher education" and as "directors" of "soft"-money projects. For the most part, those occupying these peripheral roles were without authorization to teach graduate courses and did not have faculty privileges, even though they had extensive professional experience, and many held doctorates. In the past two years, these positions have altered significantly. Those clinical faculty with doctorates now hold positions as "academic administrators"—a job title designed for those who administer and teach in academic programs, including programs at the graduate level. Some have been recruited by the department chair to teach courses outside the Center. All clinical faculty now draw their salaries from core university funds, and "soft" money supports the more transitory staff, events, and materials related to the work with teachers. Clinical faculty now participate in education faculty meetings, are eligible to sit on faculty committees, and they vote on all but personnel matters. Several have sought and won grants as principal investigators—a status formerly reserved for those in tenure-track positions.

Culturally, the Center strives to press the Graduate School to become what its faculty wants schools to be—caring, ethical, racially harmonious, and socially just. As such it attempts to model in the conduct of its work a constructivist approach to teaching, learning, and organizational life, and a "curriculum" that reflects the diversity of our society in all its aspects. It strives to re-create Los Angeles's rich diversity of language, culture, and race as it forms cohorts of students and groups of participating professional educators, and to mirror this rich diversity in our clinical and research faculty. To a large extent, this cultural change is palpable.

From the beginning, the Center X faculty worried that many forces would conspire against its ambitious social and educational agenda, despite its clear connection with the university's land-grant origins and mission. Faculty thought that, unless they established a solid principled grounding for the Center's work, they'd soon find themselves on the slippery slopes of efficiency and expediency. But, frankly, few have objected to the Center's mission of social responsibility; most colleagues and community members have applauded the Center's bold direction. But it's far less clear whether Center X is reshaping the culture around faculty rewards and promotion that sustaining the Center will require.

The substance of the Center's research has been applauded by faculty colleagues, manuscripts have been accepted by respectable academic journals, one faculty colleague won a Spencer postdoctoral fellowship to support his Center-based research, and most of the Ph.D. graduates have used their

Center X research and teaching apprenticeship to launch careers as teacher educators in research universities. However, faculty colleagues have been far less enthusiastic about the Center's research strategy that blends inquiry and practice. Junior faculty have been cautioned that their publication of research articles may proceed too slowly, and that they may get too bogged down in the "administrative" end of the Center's work. Moreover, nontraditional "forms" of scholarship—for example, work that aims at professional, rather than research audiences—has yet to stand the test of a cross-campus review. Two tenure cases and one senior faculty promotion will be heard in the next year. Time and considerable risk–taking will tell just how tolerant faculty will be of this major shift in the research culture.

Beyond Progressive Paternalism

The nation's current educational problems require a deep, research-based understanding and significant restructuring of the complex educational system in which teachers and students are embedded. Only universities have the solid public commitment, the rich research, development, and training capacity, and the necessary geographic dispersion to grapple with fundamental, systemic reform. The education professorate in public universities should provide a loud, clear, and edifying voice in the states' and nation's efforts to reconstruct education for an increasingly diverse group of K–12 students and an unpredictable future. However, it can be so only if the means and ends of our research and teaching, as well as our public service, contribute to developing the educational infrastructure—the sound education policies, highly skilled professionals, and better schools—that the public badly needs. The University of California case provides one example of how this work might proceed.

However, the public may not willingly accept this new definition of the public university's mission. Universities have not escaped the widespread cynicism about public institutions, heightened public scrutiny, or the widespread disfavor with education. In the past several years, policy makers and the public have increasingly questioned the social value of the university, particularly with regard to its seeming indifference to public problems. In the absence of a clear demonstration of relevance, increasing numbers of critics, including some educators and politicians, have advocated draconian changes in the University as a whole and Schools of Education in particular. Heightened expectations and demands to have universities produce knowledge that responds to social needs may force public universities to renegotiate their social contract with the professional and political constituents to whom must ultimately answer.

Moreover, public research universities have not typically responded to the needs or problems of poor and working people of color who often experience the work of the university as alien and alienating. This failure stems in part from a narrow understanding of the university's role in producing and sharing knowledge that may be traced to the Progressive Era. The reconstruction of university programs toward their public mission will require that faculties acknowledge the limits, as well as the great strengths, of the Progressive Era legacy. Three assumptions undergird much Progressive Era (as well as contemporary) rhetoric about connecting university knowledge to social betterment that public universities must move beyond: (1) That there is a broad public consensus on the meaning of social betterment (and hence on the meaning of social problems); (2) That social problems can be reduced to technical problems that are amenable to technical fix; and (3) That university-trained experts will invariably act in the general interests of society in addressing these problems. These assumptions ignore the diversity of publics that universities serve, the contentious nature of many urban problems, or the different perspectives and experiences of university trained professionals and urban residents. Further, by posing a paternalistic view of engagement with communities or "outreach" in which the universities "reach out" to communities rife with problems, these assumptions devalue local knowledge and hence distance the very publics the universities seek to engage.

To make our research universities public in the truest sense of the word, we argue that public universities must do more than apply university knowledge to public problems; they must invite communities into the life of the university. They must bring multifaceted publics together in dialogue with faculty and staff over what constitutes social betterment in the here and now and how this may be achieved. If urban research universities, in particular, are to sustain public support, they must find ways to direct the work of research and scholarship toward the concerns of these local publics. A public university of this sort is sure to be intellectually vibrant and far more attractive to the public in general, and particularly to poor and working class communities of color. If this analysis is correct, it questions the very foundation of the university's social research and teaching. It remains to be seen whether and how public schools of education will rise to this formidable challenge.

Notes

This paper draws on the combined work of members of the UC Advisory Committee for Planning Professional Programs in Education, especially Eugene Garcia, Hardy Frye, Irv Hendrick, Alan Hoffer, David Sanchez, Jon

Wagner, Willis Copeland, Burton Clark, Barbara Epstein, Karen Merritt, Bob Polkinghorn, and Ami Zussman.

1. Ira Harkavy and John Puckett, "Universities and the Inner Cities."
2. Jane Addams, "A Function of the Social Settlement" (1899).
3. Daniel Coit Gilman, Inaugural Address (Berkeley: University of California, 1872).
4. Karl S. Pister, "Improving Educational Opportunities," *San Diego Union Tribune*, April 2, 1998, Opinion page.
5. For example, Fraizer, William R. *The University and the Schools: Education Excellence, A Joint Responsibility.* A Report to the President from the Committee on Student Preparation. (Oakland: The University of California Office of the President, 1984); Gifford, Bernard et al., *Proposal by the Deans of the University of California Schools of Education.* Oakland: University of California Office of the President, 1986); Goodlad, John I. *The Role of the University of California in Precollegiate Education.* Report of the University-Wide Program Review Committee for Education (Oakland: The University of California Office of the President 1994); Pister, Karl S., *Report of the Universitywide Task Force on Faculty Rewards* (Oakland: The University of California Office of the President, 1991).
6. Ted Mitchell and Eugene Garcia, "University of California's Role in Professional Education for Teachers," Draft, March 1998.

References

Addams, J. (1899). *A Function of the Social Settlement.* Philadelphia: American Academy of Political and Social Science, pp. 323–345.
Boyer, E. (1990). *Scholarship Reconsidered: Priorities of the Professorate.* New York: Carnegie Foundation for the Advancement of Teaching.
Dewey, J. (1929). *Sources of a Science of Education.* New York: Horace Liveright.
Fraizer, W. R. (1984). *The University and the Schools: Education Excellence, A Joint Responsibility.* A Report to the President from the Committee on Student Preparation. Oakland: The University of California Office of the President.
Gifford, B. et al. (1986). *Proposal by the Deans of the University of California Schools of Education.* Oakland: The University of California Office of the President.
Gilman, D. C. (1872). *Inaugural Address.* Berkeley: University of California.
Goodlad, J. I. (1984). *The Role of the University of California in Precollegiate Education.* Report of the University-Wide Program Review Committee for Education. Oakland: The University of California Office of the President.

Harkavy, I. & Puckett, J. L. (1991). "Toward Effective University-Public School Partnerships: An Analysis of a Contemporary Model." *Teachers College Records*, 92 (4) 556–81.

Lieberman, A. (August 1992). "The Meaning of Scholarly Activity and the Building of Community," *Education Researcher*, 21(6), 5–12.

Mitchell, T. & Garcia, E. (March 1998). *"University of California's Role in Professional Education for Teachers,"* Draft.

Oakes, J. et al. (1994). *Education in Troubled Times: A Call to Action.* Oakland: The University of California Office of the President.

Pister, K. S. (1991). *Report of the Universitywide Task Force on Faculty Rewards.* Oakland: The University of California Office of the President: Oakland CA.

———. (April 2, 1998). "Improving Educational Opportunities," *San Diego Union Tribune*, Opinion page.

CHAPTER 2

Incentives for Scholarship in Education Programs

MARY M. KENNEDY

President John Kennedy once described the city of Washington as a city of Northern charm and Southern efficiency. In like manner, education programs offer students the intellectual status of agriculture and the financial prospects of philosophy. Education programs lack the intellectual traditions of the liberal arts, the financial rewards of medicine and business, the prestige of architecture and law, and the technical utility of engineering and computer science. Not surprisingly, education programs have always held a tenuous position in the academy. Two years ago, for instance, the University of Chicago decided to close its education department. The decision dismayed many educators, for Chicago is one of very few institutions that does have an intellectual history in education. But the decision was not noticed by many others.

Education programs have tried valiantly to conform to university norms. They emphasize theory and research more than folk wisdom and technique. They devise curricula that provide students with research findings—warranted knowledge—about child development, teaching techniques, methods for identifying handicapping conditions, and so forth. Yet despite these efforts, both students and alumni frequently complain that the research findings either do not work in the real world or are not relevant to pressing real-world problems. Teachers prefer craft knowledge, knowledge that is learned in the doing and is justified by experience. The tension—some would say incompatibility—between knowledge warranted through formal research methods and knowledge warranted through personal experience has always plagued education programs and has made it difficult for them to fit comfortably into institutions of higher education. On one side, they face constituents that prefer craft wisdom, and on the other they face their institutional homes: colleges and universities that value warranted knowledge. My task in this paper is to examine the role that research could and should play in education programs.

29

I chose to focus on the role of research in part because the value of research to educational practice is such a contested issue, and in part because research—or at least warranted knowledge—has traditionally played such an important role in the culture of higher education and in faculty reward systems throughout higher education. To the extent that past behavior is the best predictor of future behavior, we can reasonably expect these norms to continue to be an important part of college and university life in the future.

Every field of study has some unique qualities, of course, but every field of study in higher education must also find a way to accommodate the concerns and interests of that broader institutional context. In the sections below, I first examine the values and norms that characterize institutions of higher education in general, and then examine the values and norms that characterize education programs in particular. With these considerations in hand, I hope then to address the question of how faculty incentives in education might be altered to render the norms and practices of the education professorate more compatible with those of their institutional hosts.

Some Observations about Higher Education

American institutions of higher education are probably more various than those of any other country. They include technical institutes, community colleges, four-year colleges, large multiversities, and highly prestigious research institutions. The types of programs housed in these different types of institutions frequently reflect the institutional context. Medical and law schools, for instance, tend to reside mainly in more prestigious universities, agriculture schools mainly in public universities, and many vocational programs proliferate in community colleges. Education programs are especially populous in regional state universities, many of which evolved from normal schools. But education programs can appear in almost all the categories of institutions of higher education, and in fact do appear in some 70 percent of all institutions of higher education.

What, then, are the norms and values that are shared by these diverse institutions of higher education? Below, I outline several observations about academic values and incentives that seem to be shared by most institutions of higher education. Much of the discussion below outlines an idealized portrait of the university—what Rice (1986) called the socially constructed fiction of the university professor, and readers will be easily able to point out exceptions to these general observations. But these generally held values may help us understand why education programs have had such difficulty obtaining legitimacy in the academy.

Observation 1: A Central Role of Higher Education Is to Seek and Preserve Truth

Colleges and universities are widely recognized as places where people have knowledge, and in addition are often places where people create new knowledge through research. The centrality of knowledge to higher education leads to an acute awareness of the importance of truth and the meaning of truth (see, e.g., Shils, 1983). Institutions of higher education are places where Truth—with a capital T—is highly valued.

This is an important feature of higher education that is frequently taken for granted. But truth is not the only criterion that can be used to evaluate ideas— ideas can be also evaluated for their beauty, their moral integrity, or their practical utility. Indeed, outside of universities, most of us prefer ideas that pass all of these tests. That is, we prefer ideas that are attractive, useful, true, and just. Maxims like the golden rule are popular because they seem to meet all of these criteria. Still, in some walks of life some criteria are more important than others, and often societies develop special systems to assure that certain criteria are attended to. American society, for instance, has developed a legal system to evaluate the justice of various ideas, a market system to evaluate the utility of ideas, and a system of higher education to evaluate the truth of ideas. None of these systems is perfect, none is oblivious to the other criteria, yet each serves a societal role in reinforcing the importance of a particular criterion.

So in higher education, truth is the principal criterion, and research is the principal method used to evaluate the truth of ideas. Even in small colleges, where relatively less research is carried out, faculties still take pride in their role as arbiters of truth and defenders of truth. And they are expected to infuse their curricula and courses with warranted knowledge rather than superstitions, private beliefs, or personal experiences. We do not normally find, for instance, creationism taught in university biology departments, for creationism cannot withstand the rules of evidence and argument used by biologists. Nor do we find education professors teaching their students what to do if they encounter children who are possessed by the devil. The ideal of truth permeates virtually all decisions made by academics—decisions about what to study, what to teach, and how to advise novices in the field.

Because truth is a guiding ideal in virtually all sectors of higher education, it naturally enters into decisions about faculty promotion, tenure, and rewards. This is why all sectors of institutions of higher education—small colleges, large universities, teaching institutions, and research institutions— place such a high value on academic freedom, and this is why telling the truth is considered such a fundamental moral imperative in university communities. Other criteria are not entirely ignored in higher education, of course, but truth is an essential ingredient in college and university deliberations.

Moreover, the importance of truth has not been altered much by postmodernism. Despite the acknowledged difficulty of knowing what is really true, academic discourse still uses truth as a *regulative ideal* (Phillips, 1990), something to strive for in spite of the impossibility of being sure we've found it. Truth now joins other regulative ideals, such as honesty or loyalty, as ones we know we can never perfectly attain, yet we continue to strive for them and we continue to evaluate others according to how closely they appear to approximate these ideals.

Nor has the importance of truth been compromised much by the proliferation of professional schools within higher education. Indeed, professions as disparate as journalism, law, and medicine each have their canons, rules of evidence, and procedures for settling disputes. Nearly all professional schools make sharp distinctions between the academic portion of their program and the clinical portion of their programs, and while the clinical portions may expose students to other regulative ideals, the academic portions still tend to emphasize truth over other regulative ideals.

Observation 2: Institutions of Higher Education Promulgate Norms and Practices Designed to Enable Truth to Emerge

Since colleges and universities are concerned mainly with truth, they have developed an interrelated set of professional norms designed to increase the prominence of truth as a regulative ideal. Each field of study has its own canon, its own rules of evidence, and its own rules of argument for evaluating new ideas. Each field strives to sustain a marketplace of ideas and to assure public debate and evaluation of these ideas. Each has a system of peer review, of conferences that involved presentation and commentary, and of literature reviews and book reviews. Most major debates, particularly debates about the merits of particular research findings, are documented in journals that are housed in libraries for all to read.

The institutional environment in higher education is also important for much of this. Virtually all fields of study value academic freedom as a vehicle for ensuring that scholarly debate continues to thrive. And more than any other types of institution, colleges and universities honor academic freedom. In fact, most institutions of higher education also provide tenure systems that are presumed to ensure academic freedom. Finally, most institutions of higher education also support extensive libraries and Internet services that enable their faculties to keep abreast of the developments in their fields. Institutions take pride in the library resources they provide for their faculties. These institutional contributions increase even more the chances that new findings and new ideas will be widely available and open to debate and critique.

The important thing about this system is that it is a system. No one piece of it, such as the tenure piece or the library piece or the rules-of-evidence piece or the conference-presentation-and-response piece, would be adequate to sustain truth as a regulative ideal. But the combination of professional norms and practices has, for the most part, been successful in assuring that truth is the central criterion used by the academy to evaluate ideas. It cannot, of course, assure that frivolous or self-serving ideas are never put forward, but it can assure that such ideas receive strong critical review.

These canons, customs, and professional norms govern scholarly decisions not only in research but in teaching as well. We do not normally find, for instance, creationism taught in university biology departments, for creationism cannot withstand the rules of evidence and argument used by biologists. Nor do we find education professors telling their students what to do if they encounter students who have been possessed by the devil. The ideal of truth permeates virtually all decisions made by academics–decisions about what to study, what to teach, and how to advise novices in the field.

Although all avenues of academic work are designed to be regulated by truth standards, one of the most prominent and most controversial norms in higher education is the tendency to reward publications more than most other activities. Publication productivity contributes heavily to promotions, to tenure, and to salary increases. A recent study sponsored by the National Center for Education Statistics (Fairweather, 1993) indicates that time spent teaching, rather than conducting research, was *negatively* related to salary, *regardless of the type of institution*, while the career-long total number of publications was positively related to salary.[1] That is, faculty received higher salaries when they devoted more time to research than to teaching and when they had more publications. And the salary reward for research activities appeared not only in research universities but also in state colleges and universities and even in small liberal arts colleges. This pattern also dominated across a wide range of fields of study, including education.

It is tempting to suppose that this emphasis on research productivity somehow ultimately benefits teaching. Perhaps a direct involvement in research keeps one abreast of new developments and increases the likelihood that one's courses are based on the most warranted truths available at the moment. This argument is part of the socially constructed fiction of higher education, but as Hattie and Marsh (1996) have shown, there is no evidence to suggest that a reliable relationship exists between research activities and teaching activities. There are cases where the two activities enhance one another, cases where they compete with one another, and cases where they have nothing to do with one another. This is not to say, of course, that teaching activities are not concerned with truth, but rather that the task of creating new findings does not necessarily enhance the task of transmitting those findings to students.

Findings such as Fairweather's have created a great deal of controversy, for many interpret this reward system as discouraging faculty from attending to their teaching and from providing important public services. But how widespread, in fact, are these reward systems? Fairweather's study included only full-time, tenure-stream faculty, and according to the National Center for Education Statistics, tenure-stream faculty now comprise only 47 percent of all college and university faculty (NCES, 1997). Moreover, the distribution of these tenure-stream faculty across institutional categories also suggests that tenure-stream appointments are associated with research. That is, research universities have larger fractions of tenure-stream appointments than do comprehensive universities; comprehensive universities have larger fractions than liberal arts colleges; and four-year institutions have higher fractions than two-year institutions.

So tenure-stream faculty are more prominent in research-oriented institutions, and research productivity is an important contributor to the salaries of tenure-stream faculty. But tenure-stream faculty are rewarded for their research productivity across all types of institutions, not just in research-oriented institutions. Throughout the entire system of higher education, tenure is associated with independent scholarship. It appears more frequently in institutions that emphasize research than in other institutions, but it is associated with research effort and publications even in liberal arts institutions.

Observation 3: Despite These Efforts, Truth Is a Difficult Regulative Ideal to Sustain

Most people evaluate ideas against several criteria: their utility, their ethical implications, and their attractiveness, as well as their truth. That these other criteria are valued by society at large, and by university faculty as well, means that there are continual pressures on academics to take these other criteria into account. Three threats to the regulative ideal of truth are particularly salient in higher education: (1) public pressures to consider the ethics, utility, and attractiveness of ideas; (2) external funding for targeted purposes; and (3) ordinary human foibles and social communities within academic institutions. Each of these phenomena works in its own way to discourage the strong emphasis on truth as a regulative ideal.

Public Pressures to Consider Other Criteria. Ironically, to the extent that ordinary citizens become interested in university research, academic freedom may be threatened. This may seem an odd statement, because most of us wish there were more public interest in our work. But in recent years, we have seen instances in which ordinary citizens have become violent in their opposition to research in certain areas. They have acted against the use of animals in medical research and have vandalized laboratories where researchers are studying unpopular topics. Such activities can threaten the physical well-being of researchers, can be a strong deterrent to continuing a line of work, and can influence the decisions of research sponsors as well. Though physical threats are less common in fields of study such as education, the education professorate is not immune to public scrutiny. Indeed, ridicule of education programs has become almost a national pastime as lay commentators snicker smugly about the dismal failure of the new math curriculum of the 1960s, wonder about the wisdom of the mathematics standards of the 1990s, and complain about the attention teacher educators give to phonics or whole language instruction. And books such as Rita Kramer's *Ed School Follies* (1991) seem to make the best-seller list at least once a decade.

External Funding for Targeted Purposes. Large-scale investments in university research began during World War II, when the federal government sponsored several large research centers and laboratories in universities (Geiger, 1993). These research centers brought together diverse collections of independent researchers, often from multiple disciplines, to work on specific practical problems. The primary affiliations of these researchers were the research centers rather than academic departments. This funding arrangement continued for several decades, so that by the 1960s, universities had become highly complex organizations that were heavily funded. And, consequently, heavily dependent on external funding.

It was in the 1960s that education research centers were legislated and joined the already-complicated university structure. Like their predecessors, education research centers were housed in universities, but expected to engage in programmatic research that would ultimately have utilitarian value. Over time, individual grants for education research have virtually disappeared, so that mission-oriented research centers now constitute almost the entire research budget of the U.S. Office of Educational Research and Improvement.

As federal research funding has stabilized, and even decreased in some areas, corporate research sponsorship has increased, so that the trend toward large-scale, sponsored research has been sustained for nearly half a century. The problem is, these external research sponsors have brought new evaluation criteria with them—criteria that frequently consider the practical utility, morality or attractiveness of ideas as well as their truth. Erickson (1987) has noted that these external influences can have a number of subtle as well as more visible influences on research: they can bias the selection of research questions, selectively advance individual careers, selectively disseminate research findings, slant the acquisition and interpretation of evidence, and so forth. Viewing the same phenomenon in a more positive light, Gibbons et al. (1994) have noted several distinctions between traditional knowledge production and what they call "the new production of knowledge." It's not clear, of course whether there ever was a "traditional" approach to research, but the features of these new arrangements warrant attention: (1) It is done collaboratively by scholars from many different disciplines; (2) it is done to solve practical problems rather than theoretical problems; (3) it is large-scale and usually sponsored by external agencies; (4) the problems to be addressed are determined by the funding agency rather than by the scholars themselves; (5) the work is evaluated by society as a whole, presumably as represented by the funding agencies, rather than just by disciplinary colleagues; and (6) evaluation criteria extend beyond disciplinary considerations of methodology, evidence, and so forth, and include utility, relevance, and social value.

These developments can be viewed in two very different ways. On one hand, they could seriously erode the institution's commitment to truth and could erode the academic freedom of individual professors. To the extent that universities need funding, sponsored programs of research are likely to influence research agendas. As universities press faculty to generate more and more external funds, faculty in turn must learn to sell their ideas on the basis of their attractiveness, their utility, or their moral implications in addition to, or perhaps instead of, their potential truth value. Thus, the press for funding could seriously compromise the university's commitment to truth as its primary regulative ideal.

This is a real issue. State funding for universities has declined by some 32 percent in the past twenty-five years (Barton, 1997), and federal funds for research have also declined. Hook (1987) has argued that universities cannot sustain academic freedom without some public financial support, for without it they are at the mercy of special interests. The problem is exacerbated because of the excesses of past funding. Because universities have been so heavily capitalized in the past, they have invested in research labs and equipment, and have produced such a large supply of Ph.D.s, they must continue to raise new capital to sustain these programs (Massey, 1990). These financial pressures force universities to compete for money in a marketplace that may value the beauty, morality, and practical utility of ideas as much or more than their truth. Universities also become vulnerable to policy changes (Sommer, 1987), and many universities have entered the lobbying business to promote their own research priorities, thus encouraging research decisions to be made on political grounds rather than scholarly grounds.

Moreover, external sponsorship is not limited to large research centers. Another, relatively new source of funding in higher education appears in all types of institutions: the targeted philanthropical gift. Many institutions of higher education depend on financial gifts from alumni or other patrons. In the past, such gifts have tended to provide general institutional support. Recently, however, many such gifts have been targeted toward specific programs or specific curriculum offerings that match the concerns of their sponsors. And to the extent that universities become dependent on these gifts, they may compromise their academic freedom and their purchase on truth.

This combination of public oversight and external targeted gifts can result in a relative diminution of the salience of truth in the evaluation of ideas, and a relative increase in the salience of ethical, practical, and aesthetic considerations. Note, though, that these are *possible* outcomes, not necessarily outcomes we have seen. And in fact, some financial sponsors endeavor to restrict social and political values from their funding decisions by seeking guidance from university professors when establishing their research agendas and by drawing on university professors for peer review of proposals.

And there is some evidence that universities are protecting themselves and their regulative ideal from these external pressures. For instance, many of the faculty who work in large capitalized research centers are *not* part of the tenure system (Kruytbosch & Messinger, 1970). That is, universities appear to be distinguishing between their faculty-for-hire and their tenure-stream faculty. The most visible such arrangement in the field of education is probably at Johns Hopkins University, which houses the Center for Research on the Education of Students Placed at Risk (CRESPAR). Virtually all researchers in that center are supported by soft money and nearly all lack tenure-stream appointments. In fact, Johns Hopkins does not even have an education department in which to grant these researchers tenure.

Still, the strong presence of external sponsorship of college and university activities—not just research, but teaching as well—combined with increasing public oversight of these activities, raises important questions about the meaning of academic freedom and about whether or how academic freedom might be sustained in the future. The continuing and intensifying engagement of public, government, corporate, and philanthropic sectors of society in higher education suggests that the most important protection of academic freedom may not be the simple guarantee of job security that tenure provides, but instead may be the integrity of the university community itself and its ability to preserve a coherent and integrated system of professional norms and practices. For it is the academic community itself that ultimately regulates both the supply and the demand for ideas in the marketplace of ideas. This observation reminds us, however, of a third threat to truth as a regulative ideal.

Normal Human Foibles and Social Communities within the Academy. The concept of academic freedom carries with it a number of important assumptions. It assumes, for instance, that academic faculty function both as purveyors and as evaluators of ideas in a marketplace. It assumes that they define truth as their regulative ideal, and it assumes they try their best to actually use truth as their primary criterion when evaluating ideas. It does not assume that individual faculty members are without foibles, however. Nor does it assume they are error free. Indeed, the whole notion of a marketplace of ideas suggests that bad ideas will be put forward, but that eventually the best ideas will arise from the public scrutiny of, and debate about, new ideas.

The most troublesome assumption in this view of academic freedom is that individual faculty members make independent decisions in the marketplace. Just as economists assume each individual decision to buy or to sell a product is independent of all other decisions, so too the market metaphor for knowledge carries an assumption that each "purchasing" decision is independent of each other decision. In both economic and academic contexts, the assumption of independent decisions overlooks social interdependencies, fads, and other trends. Indeed, like other consumers, professors are members of social communities, and their judgments about the merits of ideas are influenced by their perceptions of the social standing of the author, by a desire to conform, a desire to keep up with the latest trends, a desire to increase their own social standing, and a desire to obtain the approval of their peers. The communal nature of academic life, intensified by tenure and the consequent necessity of forming life-long relationships with one's colleagues, can severely impair the marketplace ideal, both by altering the supply of ideas and by altering the demand for ideas.

One way this happens is that, because academic researchers are purveyors as well as buyers of ideas in the marketplace, they are motivated to try to sell their own ideas, for they receive a variety of rewards for their contributions to knowledge. The individual whose ideas are "bought" in the marketplace will accrue not only salary increases but recognition, professional status, perhaps perks such as a larger office, and perhaps new consulting contracts or new research grants. Academics, therefore, frequently work *against* the free exchange of ideas, preferring instead to promote their own ideas (Bartley, 1987).

Another way academic communities influence the free exchange of ideas is through specialization. Weinberg (1967) noted that specialization is a natural consequence of academic pursuits, for when the original problems that were established by a discipline are solved, new, more specialized problems develop. Consequently, university communities tend to become fragmented and problem oriented, whereas society as a whole is more mission oriented. As subdisciplines develop, less and less attention is given to the value of the knowledge of the larger community.

But specialization is only part of the problem. Small enclaves of academic specialties often create their own associations and journals, effectively developing "niche markets." Schools of thought work in parallel tracks, independently of one another, developing their own ideas and testing them in their own niche markets. These discrete niches of scholarship can greatly increase the speed with which ideas spread among members of the relevant communities, but they can also further isolate these communities from their larger community. Specialization reduces the likelihood that one's ideas will be seriously challenged by others, for specialists communicate only with other scholars who share their particular paradigm and operating assumptions (Bell,

1992). Consequently, specialization can create communities that are self-reinforcing, cohesive, less open to new ideas, and less likely to receive serious critique by members of other communities. To the extent that a scholarly field becomes fragmented into multiple niches, each with its own journals, its own rules of evidence, and its own community standards, it loses the competition among ideas that it needs to sustain a viable overall marketplace.

The problems of factions and of journal proliferation are especially acute in education, for education already contains many disciplines. It is studied by political scientists, sociologists, psychologists, economists, and anthropologists. In addition to these specialization areas, scholars housed in virtually all the disciplines can take an interest in education: mathematicians study the teaching and learning of mathematics, scientists study the teaching and learning of the sciences, English professors study the teaching and learning of writing and literature, and so forth. Interest groups such as Blacks, Hispanics, women, and Native Americans form communities of scholars who focus on the special problems of their demographic groups. To the extent that these many groups of scholars define their areas as specialized and as unrelated to one another, the field as a whole becomes splintered and the ideas within any given group do not receive scrutiny from any other group.

Academic communities also influence the supply and demand for ideas through tenure decisions. When new faculty are hired, the existing faculty must make decisions about which schools of thought they want represented in their local community. In fields such as education, where there is no clear "right" approach to study—no dominant paradigm—these decisions cannot be made using the potential truth-value of a candidate's ideas or research agenda. Instead, tenure decisions are made by *negotiation* among the existing faculty within the institution (Lewis, 1990). Instead of using truth as their regulative ideal, faculty in fragmented departments must resort to bargaining among factions—an essentially political process—to make decisions about potential new hires.

One of the most potent ways in which academic communities can manipulate the free exchange of ideas is through moral judgment,[2] a form of social condemnation that is particularly dangerous to academic freedom. Just as history has revealed a lot of murder and mayhem conducted in the name of religion, so has it revealed many instances in which civil liberties and individual rights have been curtailed in the name of moral authority. Frequently, communities that are bound together by their moral codes become intolerant of other communities or of their own members who do not conform to their moral codes. An extreme example of this occurred in the 1950s, when members of many different academic fields were ostracized if they did not demonstrate allegiance to the United States and opposition to communism. Arthur Miller's famous play, *The Crucible*, shows us how otherwise-sensible people can join a mass hysteria in the name of moral imperatives. Within the field of education, we find moral certitude permeating arguments about teaching reading, about sex education, about teaching evolution, and about how to represent Thomas Jefferson—a man who both authored our constitution and owned slaves—in our curriculum.

Even when moral judgments are not so severe, and when communities are not so tightly cohesive, social forces can stifle the free exchange of ideas, often in very subtle and invisible ways. Tierney (1993) has argued that moral judgments can suppress the ideas of people whose *demographic characteristics* differ from the dominant group, such as minorities or gays. Critics of contemporary higher education have argued that moral judgments can also suppress people whose *ideas* differ from the dominant group—those who are politically conservative, for instance. Though Tierney's argument comes from a politically liberal point of view and his counterparts' arguments come from a politically conservative point of view, both attribute the problem to community pressures to conform to a dominant view. What draws these diverse complaints together is that, in each case, the concern is that ideas are evaluated for their *moral implications* rather than for their truth value. In each case, disagreements have turned to disapprovals, and disapprovals, in turn, have stopped the conversation.

All of these possibilities stem from the fact that professors are human beings, and human beings are susceptible to numerous human foibles. In fact, these normal human tendencies may be exaggerated in university communities because of the ambiguity of the work and the lack of immediate and clear feedback. The uncertainties of scholarship, the difficulties of ascertaining the truth, and the constant threat of public scrutiny create severe insecurities, and these, in turn, heighten the need for social approval. The problem is, despite efforts to suppress their human tendencies, academic communities cannot buck human nature. Like all communities, members of the academy are susceptible to social forces—to the pressure to conform, the pressure to obtain status, and the pressure to impose moral judgments. Faculty members strive to sustain their regulatory ideal of truth, but they also struggle with their own human weaknesses. They publicly laud the benefits of a free exchange of ideas while privately trying to manipulate that exchange to promote their own ideas.

Social forces are hard to see: They are subtle, take many forms, and can be masked in a variety of subterfuges. Moreover, their very invisibility may enable them to pose a more serious threat to academic freedom than does public oversight or targeted external funding. And they pose a more serious threat to academic freedom than the potential removal of tenure does. Social forces cannot be avoided, yet they inherently threaten the free exchange of ideas in the marketplace.

That such social forces exist within academic communities, just as they do elsewhere, illustrates the importance to universities of protecting their complex web of professional norms and practices that support the regulative ideal of truth. And they illustrate why tenure alone is not an assurance of academic freedom. In fact, tenure may increase the pernicious influence of social forces by creating communities who know they will live together for the durations of their professional lives. If tenure existed without this full range of professional norms and practices, it could be the most misused professional perk ever invented. Without the full complex of professional norms and practices, tenure could become nothing more than a protection for a wild array of frivolous and self-serving ideas that are never evaluated or scrutinized.

The presence of these normal human foibles and social communities can serve to strengthen the resolve of universities to devise professional norms that encourage competition among ideas rather than conformance, that encourage *disagreements* but discourage *disapprovals*, and that depend on standards of evidence. The presence of these social forces is also one of the main reasons universities are chary of compromising their reliance on truth as their primary regulative ideal. Universities need the strong presence of truth as a regulative ideal and they need strong procedures for enforcing that ideal in order to control the behavior of their own community members.

Summary

Institutions of higher education are in a unique position in American society. They are society's principal institution for enforcing truth as a regulative ideal. In this sense, they compete with the legal system, which enforces justice as a regulative ideal, and with the marketplace, which enforces utility and beauty as regulative ideals. This general observation about higher education applies to a tremendously varied set of institutions—to those that are very small and those that are huge, to those that engage mainly in teaching and those that engage in research, to those that are independent, those that are publicly sponsored, and even, often, to those that are sponsored by religious groups. Despite the wide variety of institutions engaged in higher education, nearly all claim that their teaching and research activities are regulated more by considerations of truth than by considerations of beauty, justice, or utility.

American institutions of higher education have also devised complex systems of professional norms and practices that are designed to ensure that truth remains their primary regulative ideal. Even though the rules of evidence differ across fields of study, each discipline and each profession can be defined in part by its canon, its rules of evidence, and its rules of argument. These canons and rules are further supported by such institution-wide norms as academic freedom and tenure and by institutional support for libraries and Internet connections.

However, truth is a difficult regulative ideal to sustain. Members of the press, politicians, and the public at large can and do critique college course offerings and research agendas; government and corporate sponsors try to guide research directions with their grants; and philanthropists try to shape curricula and program development efforts with their gifts. The criteria used by these various nonacademic constituents frequently include the full range of regulative ideals. In fact, those that would shape the curriculum or research agendas of our colleges and universities frequently do so precisely because they want more attention paid to other regulative ideals such as utility or morality. Even apart from these external forces, though, academic communities are susceptible to the same human foibles that all social communities are susceptible to. Individuals seek recognition and prestige, seek to conform and to be accepted by others. Small groups form cliques that cling together and shun other groups with differing views. Fields of study become splintered into interest groups who no longer take an interest in the views of those outside their small circles. These social forces work in opposition to the broad academic norms that value open markets of ideas and public scrutiny of ideas, for each subgroup aims to manipulate the market toward its own interests.

Some of these threats to truth are new, but many are not. Indeed, *all* regulative ideals are routinely threatened, not only by other regulative ideals but by the ordinary human motives of self-interest and social acceptance. This is why societies create institutions to uphold these ideals. This is why institutions of higher education strive so diligently to maintain complex systems of professional norms and practices that will sustain their regulative ideals. Without these complex systems, the normal forces of human nature could quickly erode these ideals.

With this understanding of higher education in mind, let us now turn to the field of education, both as a field of study and as a profession.

Education as a Field of Practice and as a Field of Study

The foregoing analysis suggests that education departments might be more valuable to the larger academic community if they could help sustain the university's regulative ideal rather than threaten it. This means that education professors need to subscribe to truth as a regulative ideal; need to subscribe to agreed-upon standards of evidence; need to demonstrate a willingness to publicly critique and debate ideas; need to be willing to evaluate ideas on the basis of evidence rather than the beauty, utility, or moral attractiveness of the ideas; and need to be willing to disagree with, while not disapproving of, competing ideas.

The surface features of education programs suggest that they are complying with the norms of higher education. Like other professional programs in higher education, education programs are formed on the premise that knowledge from research can contribute to professional practice. Education faculty members are encouraged to conduct research because such knowledge is presumed to be useful to practitioners. Findings from research are codified into textbooks on the assumption that transmitting such knowledge to prospective teachers, counselors, and administrators will yield some benefit in their eventual practice. Courses are organized and offered to students—indeed, required of students—on the assumption that there is a knowledge base that can be articulated and transmitted to students and, further, that this knowledge base can contribute to their future practice: to their professional expertise.

Some 1,200 institutions—roughly 70 percent—of higher education institutions participate in this enterprise (Kluender, 1984), offering programs of study for students, developing program participation standards, completion requirements, and so forth. All fifty states participate in this system, outlining courses and curricula that they require for teaching certification. Textbook publishers participate in this system by publishing the texts that are used in all these courses. Funding agencies, both public and private, participate in this system, sponsoring research that they expect will add to the knowledge base and will be of value to practitioners.

Yet, despite the size, complexity, and expense of this undertaking; despite the widespread commitments of philanthropic foundations, state agencies, textbook publishers, and colleges and universities; and despite the apparently systemically entrenched, institutionalized, and embedded nature of education programs, there have always been skeptical questions about the need, value, or merit of these programs. When viewed from the vantage point of institutions of higher education that are continually striving to sustain their tenuous purchase on truth, several important observations can be made about programs of education studies.

Observation 1: Education Studies Are Perceived to Lack Practical Value

One might think that education studies would have an assured future in higher education simply by virtue of their income-producing potential. After all, more baccalaureate degrees are awarded each year in education than in any other area: 10 percent of college-educated women and 4 percent of college-educated men become teachers (Lanier & Little, 1986) and far more than that were prepared to teach. No other profession claims such a large proportion of the college-educated population.

Not only is education a remarkably popular pursuit, but education studies are frequently the "cash cows" of universities: They generate numerous student credit hours, yet receive relatively little funding from the university (Peseau, 1990). In fact, the funding weights assigned to teacher education are often lower than even liberal arts disciplines, which are presumed to need no special resources or equipment at all (Peseau, 1990).

Yet despite the volume of business generated by programs of education, the real value of these programs has always been challenged. Most adults, including teachers, view teaching as an extension of parenting, a line of work that either comes naturally or is learned in the doing. This received wisdom is widely held and remarkably resilient (Kaestle, 1992; Lortie, 1975). Within education programs, educational researchers reinforce this view by arguing that there is no evidence that teacher education programs contribute to teaching quality (see, e.g., Murnane et al., 1991; Hanushek, 1989). Policy makers subscribe to this view and regularly devise "back doors" into teaching, entries that avoid formal education studies—emergency certifications for teaching, alternative routes into teaching (Feitzritzer & Chester, 1992), and, most recently, charter schools, many of which are exempt from credential policies. These "back-door" policies are not limited to teaching. Many policy makers also believe schools would be better managed if more businessmen and fewer educators were overseeing them, for instance. Even though all states have official policies that require education credentials of people holding education positions, all states also have numerous exceptions to these policies and many advertise the exceptions as strengths rather than weaknesses in their policy portfolios (see, e.g., Cooperman, 1985).

In fact, even as students enroll en masse in teacher education programs, they themselves do not expect to learn anything from these programs. Many believe personal virtues such as caring are the most essential ingredients to good teaching (Kennedy 1998). Most also believe that they already have the personal qualities they need to be successful teachers (Book et al., 1983; Weinstein, 1990; Calderhead, 1991) and do not expect to learn much from their teacher education programs. Thus, they do not seek truth when they enroll in education programs; they seek the utility of a credential.

Finally, education alumni do not applaud their alma maters for preparing them for their practice. When asked, teachers nearly always express doubts about the value of their teacher education programs, believing that the most important things they learned about their work came from experience itself (Ryan et al., 1979). In a 1985 survey of practicing teachers, which inquired about the relative merits of fourteen different sources of learning, preservice teacher education was ranked second from the bottom (Smylie, 1989), while direct experience and observations of other teachers were rated highest. In other studies, novice teachers have indicated that they use very few ideas they received from their university courses (Browne & Hoover, 1990), and that the ideas they do use came from other sources (Clark et al., 1985).

As if to illustrate my point, a teacher recently wrote an opinion column about the University of Chicago's decision to close its education program. This teacher said he would not miss the University of Chicago Ed School— that it did not really offer much to teachers like himself. He further claimed that ed schools that are cut off from practice become arcane and irrelevant, that a good teacher training program acknowledges the importance of clinical faculty, and that a good ed school *recognizes that teaching is a craft, not a science.* "They respect and rely on the knowledge, judgement, and experience of practicing master teachers" (Bassett, pg. 35).

Observation 2: The Profession of Education Is Not Clearly Bounded

Most professions develop licensing policies that distinguish members from nonmembers, and most members make career-long commitments to their professions. The combination of restricted membership and life-time commitments to the field fosters strong professional identities and cohesive professional norms. Both of these aspects of professionalism have eluded education. A substantial fraction of the general population consists of former teachers or people who were certified but never taught, and a substantial fraction of practicing educators entered the field through alternative routes and so have received no formal preparation in education. The boundaries of educational expertise are further blurred by a presumption of expertise in the population at large for, as Carl Kaestle has noted, everyone has been to fourth grade, and that makes everyone an expert on educational matters (Kaestle, 1992).

To some extent, education must necessarily incorporate broad social participation, for it is inherently a social, political, and cultural activity. But broad social participation also has consequences that affect education programs within higher education. It renders education susceptible to fads, to overzealousness, to shifting political and social trends, and to shifting national moods. In contemporary education discussions, for instance, we find proposals to increase the role of technology in the classroom alongside proposals for cooperative groups and more authentic learning projects. We find proposals to increase teachers' subject matter knowledge and proposals to increase their knowledge of cultural differences. We find proposals to decentralize education into a system of competing charter schools and proposals to centralize the system through national standards and accountability mechanisms.

One result of broad social participation in education is that education ideas are more likely to be evaluated against regulative ideals other than truth. In a lay marketplace of ideas, ideas may be accepted on the basis of their truth, their attractiveness, their morality, or their utility. Arguments about the merits of education ideas may appeal to any combination of these criteria and may attract different adherents for different reasons.

Another result of broad social participation in education is that new educational ideas are as likely—some would say more likely—to come from outside the professional community as from within it. And their truth value is as likely to be rigorously evaluated by people outside the field as by those within it,[3] thus raising further questions about the need for granting education studies the status of a protected field of study within the academy.

*Observation 3: Education Studies Are Perceived to Lack Intellectual
Coherence*

Just as the practical value of education courses is frequently questioned,
so too is its intellectual value. Critics of education routinely cast aspersions
on education courses as shallow, technical, or unwarranted.

One problem is that education faculty often lack the resources needed
to evaluate the truth of education ideas. Relative to other, higher-status
domains, funding for education research is remarkably low (National Academy of Education, 1991). As a result, participants in education discussions
and debates frequently lack a strong empirical basis for the ideas that dominate their discourse. Because of the small funding base for research in
education, even those ideas that are empirically justified tend to have relatively thin warrants compared to warranted ideas in more well-endowed
fields. The lack of funding also encourages educators to lower their standards for warranted knowledge.

Another problem is that education ideas are frequently, and rightly, evaluated for their utility, morality, and beauty as well as for their truth, and the
presence of these other ideals threatens the university's tenuous grasp on truth
as its central regulative ideal. Education is a public good and consequently
education ideas must be evaluated against all of society's regulative ideals,
not just against a criterion of truth. Education is inherently a moral enterprise;
it is inherently a utilitarian enterprise; it is inherently an aesthetic enterprise;
it is inherently a cultural, social, and political enterprise. Education faculty
cannot function realistically without considering these criteria when evaluating education ideas. They cannot argue about the truth of educational ideas
without also considering their ethical consequences, their attractiveness to the
public, and their utility. Yet once they enter these value-laden arenas, they
tend to splinter into groups that reflect different moral stances rather than
different areas of specialization. Their disagreements quickly turn into disapprovals. And to the extent that they shun scholars or ideas because they
disapprove of them, they distort the supply and demand for ideas in the
marketplace and create social forces that threaten their own academic freedom and that can threaten the already-vulnerable regulative ideal of the larger
academic community.

Yet another problem is that, because education is a public good, new
ideas are continually being devised to accommodate shifting social norms and
political trends. Education researchers therefore face a rapidly changing panoply
of ideas that need to be evaluated, many of which are generated outside the
academy. The continually changing set of ideas gives a feel of fad and fan-
cifulness to the field, which does not sit well with critics who expect to see
slow, painstaking progress and methodical evaluation of ideas. The cacophony

of voices involved in education debates adds to the impression that the field is in intellectual disarray.

Moreover, the education professorate frequently appears to be as susceptible to fads as the general public is. Education faculty have variously advocated competency-based education and constructivism, vocational education and a strong academic curriculum, more use of technology and more attention to interpersonal relationships in classrooms. Education faculty enter into curriculum wars with fervor, as different camps produce research to argue for different educational strategies and most employ moral certitude to discredit their opponents. They often seem to promote fads and to disparage fads as quickly as politicians do, and their advocacy often has no more empirical basis than the advocacy of the general public. Relative to other domains within the academy, education professors appear to give little attention to the truth value of ideas.

Finally, education is a multidisciplinary field, and there is no single paradigm that unifies the field even when members limit their attention to the truth value of ideas. Education cannot be characterized by many of the descriptors often used to characterize professional fields: a shared body of professional knowledge, a shared paradigm, a shared set of professional norms. Instead, the field houses widely disparate forms of expertise, each of which relies on its own canons, rules of evidence, and rules of argument. Educationists can be lawyers, economists, psychologists, historians, sociologists, or anthropologists. These differences mean that even if education had a more substantial funding base, and even if it could focus more narrowly on the truth of its ideas, educators would lack an agreed-upon system for arbitrating disputes about ideas, beliefs, values, or justifiable knowledge.

To complicate matters even more, some of their disagreements arise from the fact that educationists evaluate research *methods*, as well as research findings, against the full range of regulative ideals. That is, it is not uncommon for education researchers to criticize others' research methods on moral grounds, not just on evidential grounds.

All of these things, then, create a sense of intellectual chaos and a sense that anything goes. The absence of agreed-upon rules of evidence and argument, the faddish nature of the field, the presence of regulative ideals other than truth, and the presence of isolated subspecialties working in parallel but using different terminology, methods, and rules of evidence, and the routine use of moral certitude to judge schools of scholarship—all of these things combine to discourage a regulative ideal of truth. Wilson (1986) made a similar argument when he suggested that the absence of clear standards in education, combined with an egalitarian value system, invited relativism and discouraged intellectual challenge.

Observation 4: Programs of Education Studies Are Not Clearly Defined

Programs of educational studies differ from most other professional programs in that they do not have complete control over their student's curricula. Some professions, such as medicine and law, control their students' curricula by locating the professional program entirely at the graduate level. Others, such as engineering, remain at the undergraduate level but still control their students' entire curriculum, even offering their own liberal arts courses (literature for engineers, ethics for engineers, etc.). Some professions, such as journalism and teaching, control only a small fraction of their students' curriculum and depend on the core disciplines for a substantial share of their students' professional preparation.

Teachers are not educated solely, or even mainly, in education programs, but instead are educated mainly in liberal arts programs. Teachers take the same lower-division general studies courses that are required of all university undergraduates; prospective secondary teachers select for their majors and their minors the academic subjects they hope to teach, and prospective elementary teachers typically study a wide range of subjects, including courses in music, geography, science, history, and literature. Usually, after most of these courses are taken, and before students participate in their clinical internships, prospective teachers take courses in educational studies. The number and variety of their education courses varies considerably from one campus to the next and can constitute anywhere from 15 to 40 percent of these students' total undergraduate curriculum.

That teacher education programs are spread throughout the university leads to a continuing tension between education departments and disciplinary departments, each of whom feels some responsibility for the students' overall program, and each of whom believes that the other side is using up too much valuable space in the students' overall curriculum. The animosity between education faculty and liberal arts faculty has a long history, replete with claims by liberal arts faculty that teachers need more subject matter and less education courses (Borrowman, 1965) and claims by education faculty that there is a knowledge base specific to teaching that teachers need to know (see, e.g., Haberman, 1985; Reynolds, 1989).

Because most of teacher education occurs outside of education programs per se, the character of the total teacher education program varies with the character of institutions of higher education as a whole. That is, teacher education programs can exist in open enrollment institutions as well as highly selective institutions, in religious institutions as well as public institutions, in research-oriented institutions as well as in liberal-arts-oriented institutions (see Tierney, this volume, for more on this issue). In part because education studies are so fragmented and ill-defined, they readily take on the character of these different host environments. They adapt to open-enrollment institutions by offering remedial courses in basic skills, for instance. They adapt to religious institutions by increasing their attention to the moral issues in teaching, and they adapt to research-oriented institutions by moving to the graduate level and emphasizing research. Education programs are especially prevalent in regional state colleges and universities, many of which evolved from normal schools, and in these institutions, education programs are frequently huge, producing hundreds of graduates each year.

Across these different types of institutions, the views of education faculty about the nature of their field, and about their role in that field, are almost nonoverlapping. Though education professors may feel some kinship with education faculty from similar institutions, they rarely feel kinship with education faculty in different types of institutions. In fact, education programs are so different across different types of institutions that members of any given group often believe that education programs do not properly belong in the other type of institutions. Because the content and character of education studies varies so much from one institution to the next, the field lacks a clear identity and a clear intellectual core that could justify its place at the academic table during financially competitive times.

Summary

In the context of higher education, education programs are a huge enterprise. Institutions of higher education graduate more people who intend to teach than intend to enter any other single profession. Some 1,200 institutions of higher education offer programs of educational study, more than they offer degrees in any other professional field. Every state is involved in the governance of education programs, defining both program accreditation standards and teacher licensure and certification standards. Thousands of students participate in education programs. In addition to those who actually teach, thousands of college and university alumni are former teachers or were prepared to teach, even if they never actually taught.

Despite the size of this enterprise, the practical value of education programs is a highly contested matter. Students entering these programs believe their success will depend more on personal qualities such as nurturing or enthusiasm than on professional knowledge, and alumni believe that their most valuable professional knowledge was acquired through experience rather than from their professional courses. State policy makers, even as they promulgate regulations requiring students to take courses in education, simultaneously create loopholes that allow teachers to enter the profession without taking these very required courses.

As a profession, education also lacks a coherent professional identity. Virtually any member of society can be an active participant in education debates, either as a parent, as a former teacher, or simply as a concerned citizen. Many teachers have never been formally prepared to teach, and many nonteachers have been formally prepared to teach. The ambiguous boundaries of the field, coupled with a naturally broad social participation in education discourse, greatly expands the number and variety of education ideas that are on the table at any given moment and increases the relative importance of regulative ideals other than truth in educational discussions.

Moreover, the intellectual value of formal educational studies is a matter of debate. Education research lacks the funding that more prestigious professions are able to garner and consequently cannot provide the kind of warrants for its knowledge that other professions depend on. Further, education researchers hail from a wide range of disciplinary backgrounds and consequently do not have a common paradigm, common rules of evidence, or common rules of argument. The lack of substantial evidence, combined with the variety of regulative ideals that are used to evaluate education ideas, makes the field appear to lack intellectual rigor. That appearance is exacerbated by the fact that education professors frequently participate in these public discussions in the same manner as the general public does. They become advocates for ideas, use moral certitude to eschew the ideas of others, and often base their arguments on regulative ideals other than truth. These qualities of education studies threaten the professional norms of their institutional hosts, which aim to sustain truth as their central regulative ideal.

Finally, education programs lack clear definitions. Education programs exist in a much broader variety of types of institutions than almost any other professional field. They appear in very large and very small institutions, in very selective and very open institutions, in religious, private, and public institutions. Like chameleons, they take on the character of their many host institutions, so much so that education professors often feel very little kinship with faculty in different types of institutions. The lack of shared norms and values across programs further erodes the ability of education professors to offer a coherent set of intellectual norms that justifies the entire enterprise.

The Problem of Fit and the Future of Education Programs

Much of the discussion above assumes that the goal for education programs is to retain their seat at the academic table. Certainly there are other goals education faculties might pursue. Certainly there are other goals that politicians or other constituencies may have for education programs. But if we assume that education studies belong in institutions of higher education, then we need to find ways to improve the fit.

Moreover, none of my observations about the nature of education programs, or about the nature of higher education institutions, is likely to change in the near future. Universities will continue to face both financial constraints and threats to their purchase on truth as their primary regulative ideal. They will likely try to resist these pressures by increasing their insistence on academic freedom, tenure, and such superficial indicators of scholarliness as publications and citations. The socially constructed fiction that guides their work may become more and more fictional, but it will nonetheless guide them and guide their judgments about the merits of marginal programs such as those in education. At the same time, the field of education will continue to be the subject of political, moral, and utilitarian debates and education programs in higher education will continue to attend as much to these other regulative ideals as they do to truth, thus threatening the integrity of their host institutions.

I can imagine two futures for institutions of higher education. In one future, they sustain their position as society's primary arbiter of truth and they manage to at least partially control the many external and internal threats to this ideal. They might even find ways to enhance their regulative ideal so that academic communities do an even better job of promoting a marketplace of ideas. In the other future, public, political, market, and internal social forces overtake the academy. Programs become more and more tied to the goals of external constituencies, budgets become more and more dependent on gifts and grants, and ideas come to be evaluated more for their utilitarian value or moral implications than for their truth. Academic communities become more fragmented and compete for resources rather than for truth, thus further inhibiting the free exchange of ideas.

If the second future obtains—that is, if institutions of higher education are overtaken by a market economy—education studies are not likely to fare well, for they have no visible utilitarian value and no visible constituency demanding them. Very few corporations and foundations invest in education, and those that do tend to be more interested in reform than in research.

Viewed in this way, education studies are more likely to survive in a traditional higher-education environment than in a market-driven higher-education environment. Despite their past difficulties in establishing credibility in that environment, they have somehow been able to remain at the table, the University of Chicago's education program notwithstanding. If past performance is a predictor of future performance, we might predict that education studies will remain in universities as long as universities are able to sustain their traditional value system.

To depend on such a future would be risky, however, for even if many institutions are able to sustain their traditional values, they will likely do so with smaller budgets, and institutional budget cuts frequently threaten marginal programs such as education. Even in the best of times, the disparity between the norms of the education professorate and the norms of the broader higher-education community raises questions about education's legitimacy in an academy that uses truth as its regulative ideal. The question of whether education faculty can engage in work that better satisfied their higher educa-tion hosts, then, is an important one.

The Potential for Incentives to Change Education Practice

To assure their place at the academic table, education programs would need to either (1) provide a curriculum that is perceived to be more useful to their professional constituent groups (2) adopt a set of professional norms and practices that produce an intellectual climate that better matches their host institutions' regulative ideal, (3) or both. In making this argument, I do not mean to suggest that either of their constituency groups is correct. That is, it is not clear that prospective and practicing teachers are correct to reject for-mally warranted knowledge in favor of craft knowledge. Nor is it clear that universities are correct in the norms and practices they have adopted to sus-tain truth as their regulative ideal. There are reasons to believe that both of these groups are living in socially constructed fictions. Still, these groups exist, they employ their fictions to evaluate the merits of education programs, and their regard for education programs has a great deal to do with the eventual survival of these programs. Their regard for education programs has led Tierney (this volume) to be remarkably pessimistic about the potential for education programs to remain in very many types of higher-education insti-tutions.

There are many arguments afoot these days to merge these two goals—not just in education studies, but across the university, so that all fields of study can produce a kind of scholarship that is both intellectually justifiable and practically valuable. One of the most widely cited is Boyer's proposal to infuse the full range of academic activities with scholarship, so that academic faculty have not only a scholarship of inquiry but also a scholarship of teach-ing, a scholarship of service, and a scholarship of interdisciplinary integra-tion. Certainly education would benefit from such an orientation toward its work, and Oakes (this volume) provides a very detailed discussion of the organizational implications of trying to promote serious and scholarly inte-gration of research, teaching, and service.

But translating ideas such as these into functioning incentives for faculty is more easily said than done, for two reasons. One problem is that outcomes from nonresearch activities are difficult to define and consequently difficult to apportion rewards for. As universal as teaching is, each instance of it is nevertheless local: Standards of performance can vary from institution to institution, from department to department, and even from course to course within a department. Even though the individual teacher may find the work rewarding, and may be convinced that he or she sees evidence of quality throughout the work, that evidence is not readily visible to faculty peers. Faculty judge one another's teaching more by hearsay from students than from any formal evaluation mechanisms, although Lincoln (this volume) argues cogently that this need not be the case.

And service is even more local. One faculty member may spend half an hour advising a state legislature and have far-reaching consequences on policy while another spends weeks mired in the organizational politics of a local school, only to make marginal changes in that local system. Is one of these efforts more socially valuable than the other? Is one more scholarly than the other? Even if two faculty members put forward the same amount of time on the same type of activity, how can peers evaluate the relative scholarliness of one person's work over that of another? Again, the judgments faculty make of one another's work frequently are based on hearsay from the field, not from the sort of indicators that can translate into salary increases.

So institutional rewards tend to accrue to publications more than to teaching or service largely because publications—especially those that are peer reviewed and cited—provide publicly visible indicators of intellectual integrity. The difficulty—or at least the perceived difficulty—of generating publicly defensible indicators of scholarship in teaching is a universal problem in higher education, but the difficulty of defining indicators of scholarship in service is even more troublesome, and more pertinent to education programs, for they are under more pressure to engage in public service than are faculty in most other fields.

The second reason these ideas are difficult to translate into practice is that those reward systems which could be manipulated are probably not the most powerful incentives guiding the activities of individual faculty members. It has been thirty years now since Robert Merton (1968/1973) pointed out the Matthew effect in research, but his point is still an important one. Merton noticed that national recognition tends to beget more national recognition. Those with national recognition are more likely to have their next articles read, more likely to receive further research grants, more likely to be invited to present keynote speeches, more likely to receive credit for new ideas that may have come simultaneously from several sources, and more likely to be given credit for multiple authored publications. National recognition provides an intellectually stimulating lifestyle as a "jet-set researcher" who frequently speaks at conferences, sits on prestigious national panels and advisory boards, whose advice is sought by government agencies, who can more easily acquire grants to study topics of his or her own devising, and so on. National recognition creates a lifestyle that faculty can find appealing enough to justify working hard to sustain. The incentives for maintaining such a lifestyle are likely to be far more motivating than are the formal institutional rewards of salary increases that colleges and universities can offer to try to manipulate faculty behavior.

Though Merton did not address other lines of work, we can easily imagine the same principle applying to teaching and to service. Good works that are recognized by others also generally beget more good work and a reward-ing lifestyle that derives from its recognition. Faculty who achieve recogni-tion as good teachers are likely to be motivated to continue improving their teaching and to develop a rewarding lifestyle associated with teaching, while those who obtain recognition for providing valuable services to their field or their community will be motivated to continue these services and to continue improving these services. As Finkelstein (1984) has noted, academics are motivated more by intrinsic qualities in their work than by external rewards. For many education professors, longtime commitments to troubled schools can result in a rewarding lifestyle, in which the university partner has a certain special status in the local institution, in which local educators and parents express appreciation, in which real-world benefits can be seen to the work, and so forth. Perhaps this work is as intellectually stimulating as that of the jet-set researcher, and perhaps it is morally satisfying as well. In each line of work, though, the incentive for carrying on comes from a whole composite of events—the overall lifestyle—not just from the specific salary incentives that the institution proffers.

In fact, one aspect of education work that is particularly rewarding for education faculty is reform, which can provide both moral satisfaction and intellectual stimulation. The history of education is replete with reform move-ments, almost all of which have been motivated by strong utopian visions (Tyack & Cuban, 1995). Reform movements are generally political move-ments, promoted by interest groups, and they can yield a lifestyle that is morally satisfying, idealistically justified, and recognized and rewarded by others. But the moral certitude that frequently accompanies reform move-ments is also responsible for many of the wars that characterize educational discourse—the reading wars, the mathematics wars, the bilingual education wars—and it can have a pernicious effect on the regulative ideal of truth. When moral certitude is the primary motivator, disagreements quickly develop into disapprovals and truth is less likely to be the primary regulative ideal.

Essential to the pursuit of truth are social norms that promote intellectual disagreements while discouraging moral disapprovals, that promote competi-tion among ideas and the use of standards of evidence to test ideas, and that promote rigorous scrutiny of new ideas against standards of evidence and argument. What is needed in education is not an incentive system that re-wards teaching or service over research, for education faculty can already find rewarding lives in all three of these activities even apart from the rewards their institutions might offer. What is needed instead is a way to promote *scholarship* in these different activities. This is particularly difficult in edu-cation, where the inherent nature of education requires that ideas be evaluated for their morality, their utility, and their beauty as well as for their truth, where reform is routine and where the moral certitude associated with reform can itself yield a rewarding lifestyle.

Notes

1. Other variables that Fairweather found to be important were seniority, status of the field as a whole, and being a male. This last variable is addressed in detail by Glazer (this volume).

2. Because I am constantly pitting the moral implications ideas against their truth value, readers may suspect that I am opposed to morality. I am not. However, I am aware that morality is often a tool to force conformity and can be a dangerous threat to individual liberities in general and to academic freedom in particular.

3. This was part of the argument made by the University of Chicago when it decided to close its Education program in 1997. Many believed that they saw better scholarship about education coming forth from other fields (economics, sociology, etc.) than was coming forth from education departments per se.

References

Bartley, W. W. I. (1987). "The Market in Ideas and the Entrenchment of False Philosophies." In R. E. Meiners & R. C. Amacher (eds.), *Federal Support of Higher Education: The Growing Challenge to Intellectual Freedom*. New York: Paragon House.

Barton, P. E. (1997). *Toward Inequality*. Princeton, NJ: Educational Testing Service.

Bassett, J. (1997, November 12). "The University of Chicago Will Not Be Missed." *Education Week*, p. 35.

Bell, D. (1992). *The Culture Wars: American Intellectual Life*, 1965–1992. WQ (Summer).

Book, C., Byers, J., & Freeman, D. (1983). "Student Expectations and Teacher Education Traditions with which We Can and Cannot Live." *Journal of Teacher Education*, 34(1), 9–13.

Borrowman, M. L. (1965). *Liberal Education and the Professional Preparation of Teachers*. Teacher Education in America: A Documentary History. Home shelf.

Boyer, E. L. (1990). *Scholarship Reconsidered: Priorities of the Professorate*. Princeton, NJ: Carnegie Foundation for the Advancement of Teaching.

Brookhart, S. M. & Freeman, D. J. (1992). "Characteristics of Entering Teacher Candidates." *Review of Educational Research*, 62(1), 37–60.

Browne, D. & Hoover, J. H. (1990). "The Degree to which Student Teachers Report Using Instructional Strategies Valued by University Faculty." *Action in Teacher Education*, 12(1), 20–24.

Calderhead, J. A. M. R. (1991). "Images of Teaching: Student Teachers' Early Conceptions of Classroom Practice." *Teaching and Teacher Education,* 7(1), 1–8.

Clark, D. C. et al. (1985). "Perceived Origins of Teaching Behavior." *Journal of Teacher Education,* 36(6), 49–53.

Conant, J. B. (1963). *The Education of American Teachers.* New York: McGraw Hill.

Cooperman S. & Klagholtz, L. (1985). "New Jersey's Alternate Route to Certification." *Phi Delta Kappan,* 66(10), 691–695.

Erickson, D. A. (1987). "Government Distortion of the Study of Education." In R. E. Meiners & R.C. Amacher (eds.), *Federal Support of Higher Education: The Growing Challenge to Intellectual Freedom.* New York: Paragon House.

Fairweather, J. S. (1993). "Faculty Reward Structures: Toward Institutional and Professional Homogenization." *Research in Higher Education,* 34(5), 603–623.

Feitzritzer E. & Chester, D. (1992). *Alternative Teacher Certification: A State-by-State Analysis.* Washington, DC: National Center for Educational Information.

Finkelstein, M. J. (1984). *The American Academic Profession: A Synthesis of Social Scientific Work Since World War II.* Columbus: Ohio State University Press.

Geiger, R. L. (1993). *Research and Relevant Knowledge: American Research Universities Since World War II.* New York: Oxford University Press.

Gibbons, M., Limoges, C., Nowotny, H., Schwartzman, S., Scott, P., & Trow, M. (1994). *The New Production of Knowledge.* Thousand Oaks, CA: Sage.

Haberman, M. (1985). "Can Common Sense Effectively Guide the Behavior of Beginning Teachers?" *Journal of Teacher Education,* 36(6), 32–35.

Hanushek, E. A. (1989). "The Impact of Differential Expenditures on School Performance." *Educational Researcher,* 18(3), 45–51, 62.

Hattie, J. & Marsh, H. W. (1996). "The Relationship between Research and Teaching: A Meta-Analysis." *Review of Educational Research,* 66(4), 507–542.

Hook, S. (1987). "Intellectual Freedom and Government Sponsorship of Higher Education." In R. E. Meiners & R. C. Amacher (eds.), *Federal Support for Higher Education: The Growing Challenge to Intellectual Freedom.* New York: Paragon House.

Kaestle, C. F. (1992). *Everybody's Been to Fourth Grade: An Oral History of Federal R&D in Education* (Report 92–1). Madison WI: Wisconsin R&D Center.

Kennedy, M. M. (1998). *Learning to Teach Writing: Does Teacher Education Make a Difference?* New York: Teachers College Press.

Kluender, M. M. (1984). "Teacher Education Programs in the 1980s: Some Selected Characteristics." *Journal of Teacher Education*, 35(4), 33–35.

Kramer, R. (1991). *Ed School Follies: The Miseducation of America's Teachers*. New York: The Free Press.

Kruytbosch, C. E. & Messinger, S. L. (1970). "Unequal Peers: The Situation of Researchers at Berkeley." In C. E. Kruytbosck & S. L. Messinger (eds.), *The State of the University: Authority and Change*. Beverly Hills, CA: Sage.

Lanier, J. E. & Little, J. W. (1986). "Research on Teacher Education." In M. C. Wittrock (ed.), *Handbook of Research on Teaching* (3rd ed., pp. 527–569). New York: Macmillan.

Lewis, D. (1990). "Academic Appointments: Why Ignore the Advantage of Being Right?" In S. M. Cahn (ed.), *Morality, Responsibility, and the University: Studies in Academic Ethics* (pp. 231–242). Philadelphia, PA: Temple University Press.

Lortie, D. C. (1975). *Schoolteacher: A Sociological Study*. Chicago: University of Chicago Press.

Massey, W. F. (1990). "Financing Research." In R. E. Anderson & J. W. Meyerson (eds.), *Financing Higher Education in a Global Economy* (pp. 41–56). New York: Collier Macmillan.

Merton, R. K. (1968/1973). "The Matthew Effect in Science." In N. W. Storer (ed.), *The Sociology of Science: Theoretical and Empirical Investigations*. Chicago: The University of Chicago Press.

Miller, A. (1953/1976). *The Crucible: A Play in Four Acts*. New York: Penguin Plays.

Murnane, R. J. et al. (1991). *Who Will Teach? Policies that Matter.* Cambridge: Harvard University Press.

National Academy of Education. (1991). *Research and the Renewal of Education*. Washington, DC: National Academy of Education.

NCES (1997). *The Condition of Education*. Supplemental Table 60-1. http://nces.ed.gov/pubs/ce/c9760d01.html.

Peseau, B. (1990). "Financing Teacher Education." In W. R. Houston, M. Haberman, & J. Sikula (eds.), *Handbook of Research on Teacher Education* (pp. 157–171). New York: Macmillan.

Phillips, D. C. (1990). "Subjectivity and Objectivity: An Objective Inquiry." In E. W. Eisner & A. Peshkin (eds.), *Qualitative Inquiry in Education: The Continuing Debate* (pp. 19–37). New York: TC Press.

Reynolds, M. (ed.). (1989). *The Knowledge Base for Beginning Teachers*. Elmsford, NY: Pergamon.

Rice, R. E. (1986). "The Academic Profession in Transition: Toward a New Social Fiction." *Teaching Sociology*, 14, 12–23.

Ryan, K. et al. (1979). "My Teacher Education Program? Well . . . : First-Year Teachers Reflect and React." *Peabody Journal of Education*, 56, 267–271.

Shils, E. (1983). *The Academic Ethic*. Chicago: University of Chicago Press.
Smylie, M. A. (1989). "Teachers' Views of the Effectiveness of Sources of Learning to Teach." *The Elementary School Journal*, 89(5), 543–558.
Sommer, J. W. (1987). "Distributional Character and Consequences of the Public Funding of Science." In R. E. Meiners & R. C. Amacher (eds.), *Federal Support of Higher Education: The Growing Challenge to Intellectual Freedom*. New York: Paragon House.
Tierney, W. G. (1993). "Academic Freedom and the Parameters of Knowledge." *Harvard Educational Review*, 63(2), 143–160.
Tyack, D. & Cuban, L. (1995). *Tinkering Toward Utopia*. Cambridge: Harvard University Press.
Weinberg, A. M. (1967). *Reflections on Big Science*. Cambridge, MA: MIT Press.
Weinstein, C. S. (1990). "Prospective Elementary Teachers' Beliefs about Teaching: Implications for Teacher Education." *Teaching and Teacher Education*, 6(3), 279–290.
Wilson, J. (1986). "The Teaching Profession: A Case of Self-Mutilation." *Journal of Philosophy of Education*, 20(2), 273–278.

CHAPTER 3

Resisting Reform

Tenure, Productivity, and the Public School Crisis

YVONNA S. LINCOLN

Background

Despite two decades of calls for public school reform—calls that came both before (Clark & Guba 1977) and after *A Nation At Risk* (1983)—and despite obvious relationships between public schools, public school teachers, and teacher training programs, colleges of education appear, at least to a skeptical public, to be singularly unresponsive to the needs of either the public schools or other emerging audiences. In this paper, I discuss several reasons for this seeming impasse surrounding the apparent unresponsiveness toward new college clients, such as public and charter schools; new college audiences such as families (especially those who might be affected by the so-called "full service schools" and interprofessional education efforts); the demands for school or teacher education reform; and school-university partnerships and collaborative efforts. Then I compare current promotion and tenure policies from four universities that currently graduate some of the largest classes of certified teachers in the country. I identify and explicate three major disparities in the education college/public school nexus; and finally, I suggest some alterations in the promotion and tenure process and reward structure that might both positively influence college culture, and at the same time, be responsive to emerging missions.

Reasons for Unresponsiveness

As a famous line from the popular contemporary movie, *Field of Dreams* goes, "If you build it, they will come." The same can be said of promotion and tenure and faculty reward systems; the systems having been built, faculty are simply responding to them. Lagon (1995) argues, in fact, that faculty are simply acting from classical "rational choice" theory: to wit, the incentive system of tenure, in particular, creates a force field where faculty would be acting irrationally to do other than to publish, and specifically, to publish for scholarly journals and other scholars in their disciplines, rather than to engage in improving their teaching, or participate in public service. Lagon (ibid.) argues, further, that the publication-over-teaching ethic is part of a larger culture that creates and fosters a "two-tier system," in which the "lower tier consists of the work–horse teachers, called upon to offer more classes, with larger enrollments" and the "upper tier, which is accorded greater prestige, . . . populated by star researchers who are paid more for often teaching less" (p. 207).

The worst difficulty engendered by this two-tier system, Lagon goes on to argue is that "the highly developed professional disciplinary norms of the tenure system create conformist, not innovative, behavior" (1995, p. 207), the results of which are publications directed toward quantitative and "arithmetic norms," rather than quality or utility. In short, a system is created wherein publications are *counted rather than evaluated* for their innovation, creativity, or utility, and rarely or never read by those outside the academy who might need them most. Lagon concludes that

> On the formal level, tenure appears to be the bulwark of academic freedom. It appears to protect the tenured from losing their job for writing or teaching something others disagree with. Yet in reality, tenure may create a culture enforcing conformity. John Stuart Mill suggested in *On Liberty* that the greatest danger to individual freedom is not government power, but the conformity enforced by social stigmatization. (1995, p. 208)

Tierney (1997) has a slightly different focus on the role and structure of culture. Lagon's conclusion is that "Tenure probably *cannot* be eliminated. It is like social security. One might discuss the danger of system failure, but once entered and expectation of benefits are created, change is difficult" (1995, p. 210, emphases in the original). Tierney constructs a much more positive view of academic culture and the possibilities for positive change. He notes that

> Tenure is an organizational structure that supports a central cultural belief of those of us in the academy—academic freedom . . . if we are to deal adequately with the organizational problems that colleges and universities face, then we must do so by focusing on the cultural framework in which academe is situated. (1997, p. 17)

For Lagon, a limitation on change is the culture; for Tierney, the only possibilities for change lie in deliberately changing the culture from within. It remains to be seen whether the prevailing culture can be changed, but clearly, there are many places in which the dialogue might be entered (Tierney 1999, in press; Lincoln 1999).

Assuredly, disciplinary presses are critical to the equation of tenure, productivity, and academic reform. Sadly, Lagon is nevertheless correct in his description of a tenure system that relies more heavily on counting publications than on evaluating them for their creativity and usefulness (1995), as many more senior faculty would admit than deny. Equally clearly, proposals for "differentiated staffing" (i.e., where some are hired to teach, and some to engage in research) have come about in higher education, willy-nilly, because of the creation of Lagon's "two-tier" system; because of the hiring of an increasing number of teaching scholars not on the tenure track (Hornig 1980; Finnegan 1994; Cole 1993; Bess 1990; Clark & Corcoran 1986); and because the work of teaching is often "assigned" to women, while men are "assigned" the "mental labor" of research and scholarship (Park 1996). Differentiated staffing is not a *plan* for accomplishing the teaching and undergraduate education work of research universities; rather, it is the outcome of nearly fifty years' worth of a struggle for excellence in research prestige, and a growing (at least, until recently) federal research budget.

More important, however, is not whether institutions maintain a culture that permits disciplinary norms to dictate the roles of faculty. The question is, rather, What is it about the promotion and tenure policies of universities that so negatively affects public perceptions of institutions, and threatens to unravel entirely the bank of goodwill and trust in colleges and universities (Harvey et al. 1994; Harvey & Immerwahr 1995a,b)? This problem is not new; Byse and Joughin (1959) took up the issue following the "shameful excesses of the McCarthy era," and the Commission on Academic Tenure redebated the issue of tenure in 1973, providing recommendations that sound strikingly contemporary (see, e.g., Tierney 1997). Likewise did Bardwell L. Smith and his associates (1973) deliberate on the meaning of tenure. Menand and his colleagues recently reasserted the necessity of academic freedom for faculty (1996), although by placing it in a framework of professional ethics rather than legal protections.

So what is it about tenure that so grates on the nerves of those who are not members of the academy? Authors outside the academy see the demand for abolition of tenure to reside in a growing disillusionment with economic opportunity for college graduates; in the resentment against supposed lifetime contracts in a context of corporate downsizing and middle-income wage earners' insecurity about their own futures; in a larger social call for accountability aimed at public institutions (whether schools, governmental agencies, or public institutions of higher education); in "sticker shock"—the rising tuition costs of higher education, which more adequately reflect the actual price of a college education; and in misinformation, disinformation (e.g., Sykes's [1988] *Profscam*), and lack of intimate knowledge of the structure of the academic world (Netherton 1996; Harvey et al. 1994). In part, some of these forces can be addressed via more concerted efforts to help the public understand what colleges and universities do (i.e., their multiple missions); how colleges and universities contribute to economic growth in their regions and states (i.e., the direct link between the knowledge higher education generates, and economic growth that ensues); and how institutions of higher education, particularly those in the public sector, intend to respond to accusations of deadwood protection and nonaccountability. It seems it is in the latter arena in which many of the suggestions for positive reform around tenure and productivity arise, and where institutions have the largest opportunity for influencing public perception. How might this be done?

Major Disparities in the University/Public School Nexus

Colleges of education, like law schools and colleges of medicine, and unlike English or history departments, have clearly identified, and newly emerging, client groups who should profit from the research and development work undertaken in university contexts. But the promotion and tenure policies of such colleges are less responsive to professional clients than to the larger university cultural milieu, which is rooted in disciplinary norms. Promotion and tenure policies, in particular, seem grounded in a culture of physics or astronomy far more than grounded in public schools, teaching-learning processes, or in public service. Thus, a first step would be to address the promotion and tenure policies that give the appearance of being less than responsive to professional client groups.

Second, new missions and audiences are arising from a new social science that seeks to link the amelioration of social ills (poverty, social disorder, crime, a permanent underclass, racism, and lack of economic opportunity) to the roles which schools fill in communities, especially roles that attempt integration of community social services, and press the public schools toward being a focal point of community action (see, e.g., Corrigan 1999, on interprofessional education and full-service schools). Public schools and schooling enjoy (or shrink from, depending on one's point of view) high visibility from policy makers and the public alike, and are increasingly seen to be both the site of social pathology, and the promise of extended social and economic opportunity. Between the view of schools as critical for creating opportunity, and research that calls for cost containment via providing social services for the entire community in one location, it is families, rather than individual children, that are emerging as appropriate clients of public schools.

In combination with other social and governmental pressures for change (e.g., the debate over a national curriculum, the debate over a national achievement test), contemporary demands on public schools have created new and more insistent claims on education faculty. The question is whether or not such claims can be addressed well, if at all, under current promotion and tenure policies.

In 1978, I argued that the answer to that question was no (Lincoln & Guba 1978). Deans and department chairs are in an extremely uncomfortable paradox with respect to their faculties' willingness or ability to respond to emerging missions. On the one hand, if deans encourage their new, young, untenured faculty to engage in public school collaborative work, such faculty are likely to be "sacrificed" at the time of promotion and tenure. On the other hand, it is quite difficult for deans to get tenured, senior "stars" to engage in such work, because it currently shows up rarely in merit pay decisions, and because, as Tuckman (1976) points out, having developed one set of successful skills (research, publication, entrepreneurial activity around grants and contracts), faculty are not likely to abandon those skills and begin anew re-creating the kinds of skills required for the gritty, time-intensive, and inexorably slow processes of school change and school reform. The major hope, then, of responding to both accountability demands, and of simultaneously engaging in the demanding work of culture redirection, lies in reformulating tenure policies. In the instance of colleges of education, that may additionally mean preparing careful and closely reasoned arguments for the larger institutional community.

What Do the Data Show?

As a way of grounding the foregoing arguments in actual sites and practices, I collected the college promotion and tenure policies from four colleges of education that graduate some of the highest numbers of certified elementary and secondary teachers in the country. All four examples are land-grant institutions, which assures that they are at least somewhat comparable along several programmatic dimensions (i.e., they are likely to have the same kinds of programs and professional schools, including agriculture, engineering, and strong components in the hard sciences, as well as large colleges of education), and that they will have, by state charter, a public service mission. What follows is a description and analysis of what the four sets of published criteria for promotion and tenure show.

Tenure Policies

Landgrant Giant University

Landgrant Giant University is a major university encompassing not only the typical landgrant schools and colleges, but also a college of human health, a law school, and national recognition for its philosophy and political science programs, among others. It also has one of the most "open-ended" of the promotion and tenure policies, and faculty are put on notice that their teaching work and student focus are critical in any summative evaluations. The university-wide statement on "appointment, reappointment, tenure and promotion recommendations" is mandated to be incorporated into "departmental and unit copies of the *Faculty Handbook*," and is recommended for distribution to the faculty. The *Recommendations* begin with a prelude that reads:

> Faculty at this research-intensive land-grant university must infuse cutting edge scholarship into the full range of our teaching programs. At [Landgrant Giant University] faculty are expected to be both active scholars and student focused, demonstrating substantial ability to promote learning through our on-campus and off-campus education and research programs. The essence of scholarship is the thoughtful discovery, transmission and application of knowledge that is based in the ideas and methods of recognized disciplines, professions, and interdisciplinary fields.
>
> Assessment of faculty performance should recognize the importance of *both* teaching and research and their extension beyond the borders of the campus as part of the outreach dimension. Assessment should take into account the quality of outcomes as well as their quantity, and also acknowledge the creativity of faculty effort and its impact on students, others the University serves, and on the field(s) in which the faculty member works.... Collaborative scholarly efforts, cross-disciplinary activities and the integration of scholarship in the creation, application and dissemination of knowledge also should be recognized as relevant dimensions of faculty performance.
>
> ... Each tenure recommendation should be based on a clear record of sustained, outstanding achievements in education and scholarship across the mission consistent with performance levels expected at leading research-intensive, landgrant Universities of international scope. (emphasis in the original)

Landgrant Giant University's promotion and tenure recommendations make a clear, open commitment to students by stating up front that faculty are expected to "promote learning" both on-campus and off-campus. The signals that teaching will be important, and will be evaluated, are unmistakable. Furthermore, Boyer's (1990) nomination of the scholarship of teaching and application is also clearly spelled out, as pointed reference is made to "infus[ing] cutting edge scholarship into the full range of our teaching programs." Further commitment to a philosophic "marketplace of ideas" may be derived from the comments regarding how an individual's scholarship is framed: with "the ideas and methods of recognized disciplines, professions and interdisciplinary fields ... [and] that it be deeply informed by the most recent knowledge in the field, that the knowledge is skillfully interpreted and deployed, and that the activity is carried out with intelligent openness to new information, debate and criticism."

The criteria hint broadly that excellent teaching is not enough; excellent learning should be the result. When the criteria state that "assessment should take into account the quality of outcomes as well as the quantity . . . "it might be reasonably inferred that student learning is now on the table, and that some accountability will be assigned for that learning (and possibly for other student outcomes). How such learning will be assessed is not discussed in this document, but presumably other documents exist that discuss and exemplify how student achievement will be appraised.

Two features of this statement are crucial. (The statement has not been repeated in its entirety, but any portion of the document that relates to criteria have been provided.) First, "collaborative scholarly efforts" and "cross-disciplinary activities" are to be recognized as "relevant dimensions of faculty performance." At no place in the document is there any caution that collaborative efforts must be sorted out for individual contributions. Collaborative scholarly efforts are merely taken for granted as one noteworthy aspect of faculty performance. Consequently, faculty may assume that creating cross-disciplinary or collaborative work groups will not be penalized, but rather, will be rewarded as a meaningful work mode.

Second, nowhere in the document is specific reference made to work with client groups such as public schools, practicing teachers, or in partnerships between the university and other educational agencies. Some conclusions may be drawn from both the statements that are made, and those that are not:

1. This college has moved past the tenure policies of twenty years ago in recognizing that the multiple perspectives brought to bear on problems is more critical than sorting out who made which contributions on a journal article.
2. The university has actively moved to link excellence in teaching with student learning outcomes. Whether or not this is done well, nevertheless, a written policy commitment exists to the connection between teaching and learning.
3. The time-honored dictum of "excellent in one activity, and acceptable in two others" has obviously been superceded on this campus. Excellence in *both* teaching and research is mandatory for continuing appointment at a tenured rank.
4. Both on-campus and off-campus programs are included in the evaluation of faculty for tenure. Often, off-campus programs and extension courses are given short shrift in evaluating programs, the distinct inclusion in this document recognizes both the time commitment and the distant clientele of the university's programs.

5. While the document makes strenuous efforts to include reference to the various forms of scholarship, and moves far beyond most promotion and tenure criteria statements in declaring teaching to be a primary mission, nevertheless service is acknowledged but partially obscured by the focus on research and teaching. Furthermore, no mention is made of faculty outreach efforts to schools, teachers and school districts. As a result, one conclusion that can be drawn is that partnership and collaborative efforts with public schools are either not factored into decisions about tenure, or are negotiated separately in individual appointments.

Upstate Landgrant University

Upstate Landgrant University has a long and distinguished history, having been one of the early postcolonial institutions created. It maintains a fully justified reputation for technical programs of national importance, but it is also well-regarded for many of its social science programs, and has been frequently viewed by parents and students as "one of the Ivies," even though it is not an Ivy-League school. The guidelines for the college of education contain the following criteria:

> The successful candidate is expected to be outstanding . . . in one of the three functions of the college—teaching, research, extension—and proficient in a second. In addition, the candidate's performance as a student adviser and the quality of the contributions to the department, the college and the relevant disciplines or professions are expected to be above average.
>
> . . . The evidence presented should be appropriate to the individual's assignment. Regardless of the primary area(s) of responsibility, i.e., teaching, research, extension, individuals must show evidence of creativity or scholarly activity. The contribution should be within the focus of the department and college. The relative importance and significance of the areas to be considered will vary with the type of appointment. . . .
>
> **Teaching.** Teaching is broadly defined in the college and this breadth should be taken into consideration when evaluating an individual's contributions as a teacher. In addition to classroom teaching, which can range from large lectures to small classes, individuals also deserve recognition for their efforts in advising students, supervising theses, providing guest lectures, and conducting seminars. . . .
>
> **Research.** In the evaluation of an individual's contribution to research and scholarship, consideration should be given not only to accomplished empirical research of a substantive or methodological nature, but to all other contributions to the conceptual framework or knowledge base of the discipline. . . .
>
> **Extension.** Does the material presented in the individual's program keep pace with developments in the field? Emphasis should be placed on the dissemina-

tion of university research (both of others and the individual), and use of appropriate delivery methods, innovative ideas and techniques and evaluation of program effectiveness.

Upstate Landgrant University is quite clear that research and scholarship are critical in the tenure process, but this institution is more willing to accept "proficien[cy]" in a second area than Landgrant Giant University. As the criteria make clear in the statement regarding the mandate of individuals to "show evidence of creativity or scholarly activity" regardless of their primary area of responsibility, tenure candidates had probably better assume a requirement for research and scholarship which has national recognition. In fact, in questions used to guide decisions about promotion and tenure, the criteria outline three:

- What has been the impact of the individual's contribution to the discipline or field?
- What research support has been awarded for the candidate's research, particularly when such awards are based on a peer review process?
- Where the applied research is conducted by teams rather than by individual scholars, some means of judging the faculty member's individual research contributions to a joint project should be provided.

As the reader can see from the last statement, there is little to commend the somewhat precarious process of creating collaborative efforts, especially if a candidate knows that he or she must somehow disaggregate such joint work at the end of the probationary period.

Under "extension" (this university's term for public service), some forms of public service work are spelled out. For instance, several possibilities for extension work include "requests for consultation by non-extension agencies and organizations (for example, Assembly and Senate Committees; federal, state, and local agencies; trade associations; community organizations)." Nowhere are public schools mentioned, nor is the sort of long-term partnership or collaborative work being pioneered around the country recognized as a possibility in the statement of criteria for promotion. Thus, the college of education at Upstate Landgrant University has no specific focus that could be determined on an emergent client group of some visibility.

Several lessons can be gleaned from a close reading of this promotion and tenure document. First, excellence in one mission, and proficiency in a second are required for promotion and tenure—so long as the first assignment is research. This reading, of course, is highly consonant with criticisms hurled at higher education for placing research over either teaching or service. It provides an accurate reflection of the research and scholarship culture that permeates major Research 1, public institutions, wherein faculty may be good teachers, but they had best be strong researchers first and foremost. Second, recognition of the college's commitment to schools by dint of their mission in teacher education is mentioned only indirectly, as "federal, state and local agencies." One hypothesis is that, as in many landgrant institutions, the norms and modes of the hard science colleges (engineering, agriculture, physics, etc.) overwhelmingly dictate the missions and criteria for judgments regarding tenure in all other colleges, regardless of their particular status vis-à-vis professional client groups. A third concern that may be raised in the analysis of this document is whether collaborative efforts may not only not be recognized, but may, at least for junior faculty, be ultimately penalized. The necessity of later dissecting creative and scholarly work for its individual contributions may be more trouble than it is worth. Individuals who have worked in truly collaborative partnerships and groups realize that individual contributions may be more complicated and challenging to disassemble than tenure committees make it seem. Group creativity, group thinking, group writing is a slow and laborious process, but sorting out who said what, when, and with what effect is sometimes nearly impossible. Consequently, two critical dimensions of emerging understandings about client groups and working relationships are either ignored or undermined in this particular document. Long-term collaborative relationships with schools are not explicitly recognized or rewarded, and major disincentives for collaborative research and scholarship are clearly asserted.

Grasslands Landgrant University

Grasslands University has a well-known and widely respected college of education, and its faculty regularly assume positions of leadership both in the state, and in national disciplinary and research organizations. It has several well-known departments, and nationally visible faculty. The college's most recent promotion and tenure document was approved by the faculty in 1995, and revised in 1997, so issues have been revisited and either amended, or reratified. The college of education appears to be influential in setting its own definitions of promotion and tenure criteria, apart from the influence of the traditional engineering-agriculture focus of many landgrants.

> . . . College faculty prepare others to be scholar-practitioners and so must themselves be scholar-practitioners who improve the quality of practice in education and related fields and who participate in the college community in reflective and effective ways.
> The characteristics of a faculty member who successfully embodies the scholar-practitioner model include the following:
>
> • consistently engages in scholarly activity which is defined as the construction, integration, application and communication of knowledge.

- functions as an active, reflective learner who as a teacher promotes active and reflective learning among students.
- conducts research that is informed by professional practice and relevant to improvement of that practice and/or that provides important conceptual frameworks that guide new research programs and/or development of theory.
- manages an integration of the scholarly role such that each element informs the other (i.e., communication of knowledge is informed by valid research findings; discovery or creation of knowledge is guided by important practice or professional issues; service activities are aimed at making a difference in practice by disseminating and evaluating innovations).
- pursues scholarly themes in a programmatic manner.
- provides leadership in the definition of and resolution of important issues facing her or his professional field.
- contributes effectively and reflectively to the college community through means such as the following:

  - contributes to the department, college and university governance and program development.
  - works collaboratively with colleagues.
  - mentors students to support their development as scholar-practitioners.
  - applies for external funds to support research projects and students.
  - engages in activities that support the valuing of cultures and equity efforts for all members of the university and larger communities.
  - carries out activities that provide valid information to the department, college and university for program evaluation and development.

Several features of this statement are noteworthy, and signal new understandings of the role of the college in contemporary social contexts. First and foremost, readers will note that faculty roles specifically mention the duty of preparing "scholar-practitioners," so both the student who is preparing for a position of scholarship, and the one who is preparing for a role in a practitioner setting are recognized. This recognition grounds faculty duties somewhat in the settings in which their students will work. Second, because of this role vis-à-vis students, it becomes now incumbent on faculty to model the appropriate professional behaviors: "so must [they] themselves be scholar-practitioners who improve the quality of practice in education."

Third, the definition of scholarly activities, characterized as "the construction, integration, application and communication of knowledge," closely parallels Boyer's (1990) configuration of the various forms of scholarship, and thus reflects the newest and broadest thinking about the forms of scholarship in the field. In combination with the injunction to "function as an active, reflective learner who . . . promotes active and reflective learning among students," tribute is also paid to Schon's (1983) "reflective practitioner," the practitioner who engages in double-loop learning, and specific connection is made to student outcomes attached to the scholarly role.

Fourth, the injunction to "conduct research that is informed by professional practice" grounds scholarly inquiry in field-based problems. This, in turn, might be construed as inviting faculty to become involved in schools and schooling practices (or other professional practices that relate to education, e.g., higher-education practices). This interpretation is buttressed by another characteristic, which enjoins the faculty member to "provide leadership in the definition of and resolution of important issues in his or her professional field." In particular, the injunction to provide "resolution" might suggest that faculty efforts to create working relationships with public schools would be welcomed and evaluated positively.

Fifth, the description of the scholar-practitioner as an individual who "manages an integration of the scholarly role such that each element informs the other" is a unique statement. It suggests that faculty need to reflect on their various roles, and find or create linkages between them such that coherence can be discerned, and a programmatic focus traced. It also suggests that compartmentalization, such as is often seen when faculty divorce their research selves from other tasks and roles, is discouraged as inappropriate and unprofessional. This injunction to a more seamless professional life is also unique in that it could be construed as supporting faculty in their attempts to locate a balance between roles (teaching, research, and service) by having those roles interact and abet each other.

Sixth, the encouragement to "work collaboratively with colleagues" suggests that multi-, inter-, and cross-disciplinary efforts will be treated for what they are: significant approaches to inquiry and teaching that will be respected. Nowhere in the document is there reference to parsing collaborative efforts in order to assign bits and pieces of responsibility to a candidate under review. While this practice may continue at Grasslands Landgrant University, it is neither recommended and encouraged, nor is it required.

Seventh, the specific injunction to "engage in activities that support the valuing of cultures and equity efforts for all members of the university and larger communities." This statement echoes that of Landgrant Giant University's statement on criteria that indicates a tenure candidate is meeting goals that "relate most closely to institutional contextual factors": "Progress of the unit toward achieving and maintaining diversity and recognition of diversity in the unit's definition of quality." Of the four institutions, these are the only two which specifically recognize and reward diversity and equity activities, and which make specific mention of "valuing of cultures" as criteria for successful candidacy in tenure decisions.

What can we infer from this particular statement of promotion and tenure criteria? Grasslands Landgrant University has a college of education that views itself as quite independent from the disciplinary presses of the hard sciences, agriculture, and engineering. The faculty have developed their own criterion statements regarding excellent performance, and have, if not specifically mentioned school-university partnerships and collaborative efforts, at least indicate that such activities would fit within any one of several criteria for success. Further, it is clear that antiquated notions of differentiating between specific contributions of individual authors to collaborative inquiry efforts is neither required nor advocated. It would accordingly be a short step from this statement of tenure criteria to one that specifically recognized and stimulated university-school partnership and collaborative efforts on the part of faculty.

Sunshine Landgrant University

Sunshine Landgrant University has a large teacher-education program, reflecting its popularity as a university close to year-round recreational areas, the phenomenal growth of the sunbelt regions of the country in the past two decades, and the quality of its teacher education programs. It is in a region where high populations of African Americans and Hispanic-origin cultures mean wide representation of diversity in the students, if not the faculty.

Its agricultural and veterinary medicine programs are highly ranked, as are its wildlife and fisheries programs; and its medical school and related biological and microbiological research programs and facilities are well-funded and recognized nationally. The University has taken a leadership role in studying and seeking to maintain the state's unique biodiversity and ecological features, and is often at the forefront of debates between maintenance and restoration of the state's wilderness areas, and pressures from sportsmen, hunters, and developers, who see the wild areas as opportunities for economic growth.

The college of education has, for many decades, been at the forefront of the effort to development and sustain, through ongoing consultancy and programming help, the community college movement. The college has also, fairly consistently, housed and supported several national and international journals in a variety of education disciplines.

The "Criteria for Tenure and Promotion" for the college of education state that:

> The performance of candidates is evaluated in three areas: teaching, research and scholarly activity, and professional service. The performance of candidates is expected to be outstanding in two areas and satisfactory in the third. . . .
>
> The [collegewide] Committee applies somewhat different criteria depending on the level of promotion involved. An individual applying for promotion from assistant to associate professor is expected to have established a state and regional reputation and to have demonstrated the productivity of an emerging scholar. A candidate applying for promotion from associate to full professor is expected to be a mature scholar who has established a national reputation.
>
> Evidence of quality teaching is drawn from a variety of sources. It is expected that the candidate's student evaluation scores will be well above the

means for the department and college. Unsolicited commendations from students, colleagues, and other professionals in the field are valued. The development of new courses, instructional materials, and syllabi are reviewed. Awards for teaching are also considered. Organizing and conducting credit or non-credit workshops for practicing professionals are also recognized. Other activity directly related to teaching also may be considered.

A variety of evidence is reviewed that relates to the candidate's scholarly productivity. Examples of evidence the committee may consider includes: books, monographs, and chapters in publications directly related to the faculty member's meetings [*sic*]. Other evidence includes articles in juried periodicals. Articles in non-referee publications which are appropriate to the candidate's field receive consideration. Successful grant proposals and the subsequent effective management of grants and research projects are valued.

Professional service also receives consideration within the college. It includes service within the college and university and leadership in local, state, regional, national and international professional organizations. It includes services contributed to school and other educational institutions, as well as government agencies. Evidence of effective professional service includes leadership roles in professional organizations documented by election or appointment to offices, by awards, or the documentation of particularly significant roles played by the faculty member. It is also demonstrated through recognized contributions to department, college and university committees. Special value is attached to those committees that deal with unusually complex or highly sensitive matters.

In summary, the College Promotion and Tenure Committee views the credential of each individual recommended for promotion within the context of the criteria related to teaching, research and service.

With respect to teaching, an interesting item is the criterion that says that "organizing and conducting credit or non-credit workshops for practicing professionals are . . . recognized." This would suggest that such workshops as in-service programs and special training sessions for principals, school district administrators, curriculum specialists, or other school-situated personnel would be considered evidence in the tenure decision. A second form of recognition for work with schools is in the research and scholarly activity criteria statement, where the document points clearly to "articles in non-referee [*sic*] publications which are appropriate to the candidate's field," which will "receive consideration." At many institutions, publications that are not in refereed journals receive little or no consideration; thus, this statement leads me to conclude that articles written for practitioners, in nonrefereed journals, would be valued insofar as they contribute to both improving practice, and ongoing communication with one or more practitioner fields. The press to publish in only or primarily refereed publications is, as a result, lessened, while at the same time, encouragement to directly address professionals outside the academy is given some weight in the tenure decision.

With respect to service, the criteria statement explicitly includes and values "services contributed to schools and other educational agencies." Therefore, the possibility exists that school-university partnerships and collaborations may be established, recognized and valued in the tenure deliberations. Accordingly, in three different places in this promotion and tenure document, teaching with or in schools, publishing in nonrefereed (likely, practitioner) journals, and service to schools are straightforwardly stated as possible activities for faculty members that will be considered positively in tenure decisions.

The conclusion I draw is that this land-grant university is open to responses to public schools (in particular) that may help to meet needs of one sort or another. This is considerably more open than many promotion and tenure documents, and could be viewed as moving toward declared responsiveness to an important client group: public schools and public school teachers and administrators.

Four Institutions, Four Different Policies

The four institutions chosen were chosen because they graduate a large number of certified teachers and administrators, and because they have faculty who tend to be highly visible in national professional organizations. As the quotations from their promotion and tenure documents show, the colleges demonstrate varying degrees of openness to missions that are less focussed on research, and more client-centered. Some mention virtually nothing of such missions, while others refer obliquely or directly to such work and its value within the mission of the college. Nevertheless, as open as at least two of the institutions are to external clientele, none of the documents specifically mentions the role of Professional Development Schools, school-university partnerships, or university-school collaborative efforts.

Additionally, only two of the documents specifically refer to (university) student learning outcomes as a part of the tenure deliberations. Grasslands University and Landgrant Giant both reference teaching associated with student outcomes, or the preparation of students who are "reflective practitioners" and learners. But the specific inclusion of one or more external audiences (for example, school and other local education agencies), and the primary internal audience—for example, students—of a college sends a clear signal that such audiences will be provided opportunities for feedback and have a significant place in the mission statement. In that sense, two of these documents can be regarded as moving toward the sensitivity to learners and external clients and thus the accountability that the public seems to be demanding. It seems clear that for some institutions, at least, the tenure system is as Lagon described it: internally referential, and almost wholly based in disciplinary and academic concerns, rather than client and community concerns.

The next question might be, What would a promotion and tenure system look like if it embodied public commitments to at least these two central clients—university students, and schools?

Possible Alterations in Promotion, Tenure, and Reward Systems

At least three different locations in the promotion and tenure process, and the reward processes, might be specifically revised to make clear professorial accountability for student learning and for external professional groups and sites where partnerships might bring about a more satisfactory state of affairs: (1) specific attention to students and student outcomes in the evaluation of teaching; (2) pointed recognition and reward of efforts in the public schools; and (3) posttenure review policies that reward individuals whose successful collaboration with public schools results in positive outcomes for schools, teachers, children, and/or learning.

The first, evaluation of teaching in conjunction with evaluation of student learning, will require a major rethinking of the way in which teaching itself is evaluated. Typically, the backbone of teaching evaluations have been student "happy sheets"—some form of institutional Optiscan form that is completed at the end of the semester (and occasionally, midsemester and semester's end). There are problems with the reliability and validity of such processes, not the least of which is the uneven ability, or even the inability, of students to gauge accurately what they know, whether or not it has been delivered appropriately (i.e., in a manner which befits the content), and what appropriate teaching methods might be. Nevertheless, a committee working in an institution with which I was doing some work many years ago—the Blue Sky Committee—was charged with developing creative and useful ways beyond student evaluation forms for appraising and refining teaching. The committee, working in a highly creative way, devised over forty sound recommendations for judging various aspects of the teaching process. I retain the list today of recommendations today simply because I am nonplussed when faculty say they can think of few ways to evaluate teaching ability or quality. I often throw out suggestions when faculty say they can think of no further ways to judge their own or their colleagues' efforts in the classroom or in mentoring—all from the Blue Sky list of twenty years ago.

The second, revision of tenure requirements to include the specific recognition of and reward for partnering with local schools and districts, may be the most difficult. Such partnerships might include anything from such programmatic coordination as extended field experiences programs for preservice teachers to complex school-university collaborations on field-based action research projects, from Professional Development Schools agreements, to reform-oriented partnerships. Two things are difficult about such revisions:

the political process of getting such revisions approved and through the administrative hierarchy, especially in Research 1 institutions, and the absolute absence of any formal criteria for judging such efforts when they are undertaken.

Both issues present difficulties, but education deans with some understanding of what public criticisms of higher education are, and with enough gumption, can work with their teacher education faculty (and others) to create space and time for such work. The development of criteria, however, presents a difficulty of another order. At present, many collaborative and/or partnership efforts are undertaken by senior faculty, individuals who do such work as a kind of professional and social commitment. Many of them expect little in the form of rewards, settling instead for the satisfaction of doing such work, and for a little released time. Consequently, no one has had to think systematically about how such work is judged, or what hallmarks might exist for exemplary practice in this kind of work. But if this work is to become one activity that satisfies scholarly activity or service commitments toward promotion, tenure or a reward system, then criteria must be developed by which this work may be fairly judged. This is a crucial point where "blue sky" thinking by faculty, *preferably in conjunction with those with whom they seek to partner or collaborate*, could begin to make collaboration less ad hoc and idiosyncratic.

Finally, posttenure review is upon us. While some institutions have elected to enact posttenure review systems as a way of demonstrating their commitment to accountability, not all posttenure review policies were fortunate enough to become policies in such an open or positive environment.[1] Nevertheless, posttenure review policies leave open the possibility of "performance contracts" (Tierney 1997), which might permit faculty members to renegotiate their original dependence on narrow versions of teaching, research and service into more open missions with new and emerging clientele, including school-university collaborations. In this way, without significant upheavals to ongoing research or teaching programs, the cultures of colleges of education might evolve toward where public expectations were well met by faculty's public commitments and institutions' internal reward systems.

Notes

1. At my own institution, for instance, Board of Regents members, upon hearing of "deadwood" in departments, wanted to move toward their immediate dismissal. Public statements issued by various members of the Board indicated they believed that as many as 20 percent of faculty could be gone within a year. When informed that they were not empowered to hire and fire at will, they immediately moved to create a posttenure review policy.

Fortunately, the specific outlines of such a policy were left to the faculty to devise (the result of some sure-footed political maneuvering and savvy), and the faculty arrived at a policy that is primarily developmental in focus.

References

Bess, J. L. (1990). "College Teachers: Miscast Professionals." *Change*, 22: 19–22.

Boyer, E. L. (1990). *Scholarship Reconsidered: Priorities of the Professoriate*. Princeton, NJ: Carnegie Foundation for the Advancement of Teaching.

Breneman, D. (1997). "Voluntary Incentives to Forgo Tenure." New Pathways Working Paper #14. Washington, DC: American Association for Higher Education.

Byrne, J. P. (1997). "Academic Freedom without Tenure?" New Pathways Working Paper #5. Washington, DC: American Association for Higher Education.

Byse, C. & Joughin, L. (1959). *Tenure in American Higher Education: Plans, Practices, and the Law*. Ithaca, NY: Cornell University Press.

Chait, R. (1997). "Innovative Modifications of Traditional Tenure Systems" *New Pathways Working Paper*, # 9. Washington, DC: American Association for Higher Education.

Clark, D. L. & Guba, E. G. (1977). *Final Report: A Study of Teacher Education Institutions as Innovators, Knowledge Producers, and Change Agencies*. National Institute of Education Project No. 4-0752. Bloomington, IN: Indiana University.

Clark, S. M. & Corcoran, M. (1986). "Perspectives on the Professional Socialization of Women Faculty: A Case of Accumulative Disadvantage?" *Journal of Higher Education*, 57(1): 20–43.

Cole, J. R. (1993). "Balancing Acts: Dilemmas of Choice Facing Research Universities." *Daedelus*, 122(1): 1–35.

Commission on Academic Tenure. (1973). *Faculty Tenure*. San Francisco: Jossey-Bass.

Corrigan, D. (1999). "New Visions to Guide the Development of Family-Centered, Community-Based, Special Education Training Programs for the Next Millennium." Keynote address at the *National Conference on Learning in the Twenty-First Century*. Sponsored by the Office of Special Education Programs and the U.S. Department of Education. Washington, DC. Sept. 8–10.

Fairweather, J. S. (1996). *Faculty Work and Public Trust: Restoring the Value of Teaching and Public Service in American Academic Life*. Boston: Allyn & Bacon.

Finnegan, D. E. (1994). "Segmentation in the Academic Labor Market." *Journal of Higher Education,* 64: 23–24.

Grogono, A. (1994). "Tenure the Teacher: Let Research Be Its Own Reward." *Educational Record* (Winter): 37–41.

Harvey, J. & Associates. (1994). *First Impressions and Second Thoughts: Public Support for Higher Education.* Washington, DC: American Council on Education.

Harvey, J. & Immerwahr, J. (1995a). *Goodwill and Growing Worry: Public Perceptions of American Higher Education.* Washington, DC: American Council on Education.

————. (1995b). *The Fragile Coalition: Public Support for Higher Education in the 1990s.* Washington, DC: American Council on Education.

Hornig, L. S. (1980). "Untenured and Tenuous: The Status of Women Faculty." *Annals of the American Academy of Political and Social Science,* 448: 115–125.

Illinois State Board of Higher Education. (1993). *Enhancing Quality and Productivity in Illinois Higher Education: Faculty Roles and Responsibilities.* Springfield, IL (pp. 29).

Lagon, M. P. (1995). "Rational Choice: The Prevailing Incentive System in the Field." *Perspectives on Political Science,* 24(4): 206–210.

Licata, C. M. & Morreale, J. C. (1997). "Post-Tenure Review: Policies, Practices and Precautions." *New Pathways Working Paper,* #12. Washington, DC: American Association for Higher Education.

Lidstone, J. E., Hacker, P. E., & Oien, F. M. (1996). "Where the Rubber Meets the Road: Revising Promotion and Tenure Standards According to Boyer." *Quest,* 48: 200–210.

Lincoln, Y. S. (1999). "Talking Tenure." In W. G. Tierney (ed.)., *Faculty Productivity: Facts, Fictions, Issues.* New York: Garland.

————. & Guba, E. G. (1978). "Reward Systems and Emergent Missions: Higher Education's Dilemma." *Phi Delta Kappan,* 59(7): 464–468.

Menand, L. (ed). (1996). *The Future of Academic Freedom.* Chicago: University of Chicago Press.

Netherton, R. (1996). "How the Public Sees Higher Education." *Currents,* 22(5): 10–11.

Ohio State Legislative Office of Education Oversight. (1993). *The Faculty Reward System in Public Universities.* Columbus, OH (p. 22).

Park, S. M. (1996). "Research, Teaching and Service: Why Shouldn't Women's Work Count?" *Journal of Higher Education,* 67(1): 46–84.

Primary Research Group. (1997). *Restructuring Higher Education: Cost Containment and Productivity Enhancement Efforts of North American Colleges and Universities.* New York: Primary Research Group.

Schon, D. (1983). *The Reflective Practitioner: How Professionals Think in Action.* New York: Basic Books.

Sid W. Richardson Foundation Forum. (1997). *Restructuring the University Reward System.* Ft. Worth, TX: Sid W. Richardson Foundation.

Smith, B. L. & Associates. (1973). *The Tenure Debate.* San Francisco: Jossey-Bass, Inc.

Sykes, C. J. (1988). *ProfScam: Professors and the Demise of Higher Education.* Washington, DC: Regnery Gateway.

Tierney, W. G. (1997). "Tenure and Community in Academe." *Educational Researcher,* 26(8): 17–23.

————. (ed.). (1999). *Faculty productivity: Facts, Fictions, Issues.* New York: Garland.

Tuckman, H. P. (1976). *Publication, Teaching and the Academic Reward Structure.* Lexington, MA: Lexington Books.

U.S. Department of Education: National Commission on Excellence in Education. (1983). *A Nation at Risk: The Imperative for Educational Reform.* A Report to the Nation and the Secretary of Education. Washington DC.

Wales, B. A. (1996). "Tenure Issues in American Higher Education: An Overview." (ERIC No. ED 400 771.)

CHAPTER 4

Faculty of Education in a Period of Systemic Reform

WILLIAM G. TIERNEY

As discussions continue about the need to reform the roles and responsibilities of faculty of education, it is helpful to know the present state of education school faculty. One ought not simply call for more part-time faculty, for example, if the current data indicate that part-time faculty are ineffective. It is also helpful to know how faculty in education differ from their colleagues in other professional schools or those in the humanities, liberal arts, and sciences. Without such data it is premature to suggest that one or another direction should be taken with regard to faculty roles and rewards in schools and colleges of education. Once a profile exists of the professorate it is then possible to discuss how to address the kinds of concerns that have been raised about what society needs from education school faculty and what professors of education might be able—and willing—to deliver.

It is interesting that there is very little research that outlines what education faculty do, or how different roles are changing. The text I mentioned in the introduction by James Koerner (1963) was a treatise on how the training of teachers needed to change. Judge's report (1982) about graduate schools of education, for example, was a philosophical study of the role of education schools in research universities. Clifford and Guthrie's book (1988) discussed the myriad problems that "education schools" face and proposed solutions. More recently, Timpane and White (1998) and Goodlad (1990) have considered different facets of educational reform and how Schools of Education might be reconfigured to meet current demands. To be sure, commissions such as the Holmes Group and reports such as *A Nation Prepared: Teachers for the Twenty-First Century* tackled what schools of education should be doing; more often than not, however, there was next to no discussion about what the faculty should do. That is, curricular changes have been proposed, and the dismantling or creation of one or another program has been suggested, but there has been virtually no discussion about the professorate. Any discussion of the professorate that existed was philosophical, rather than data-driven (Glazer, 1974).

We also have seen preliminary studies that consider the role of clinical faculty in education (Bullough et al., 1997; Cornbleth & Ellsworth, 1994), but we have had little hard data to compare changes over time. Perhaps not surprisingly, the most systematic portraits of the education professorate have derived from reports generated by the National Educational Association (NEA) (November, 1997; September, 1996; September, 1995). The multitude of other work is internally generated documents for an institution that is usually considering program closure. Such documents generally do not go beyond the confines of a particular campus unless an institution with the prestige of the University of Chicago closes its education program (Bronner, 1997).

Accordingly, this chapter outlines central characteristics of faculty of education. Rather than investigate the historiography of education schools—what was—or analyze what other studies have suggested education schools should become—what should be—I consider "what is" with regard to faculty who think of themselves as professors of education. The data derive from three sources. First, the National Study of Postsecondary Faculty (NSOPF) has provided a wealth of information about different variables pertaining to faculty life in general, and faculty of education, in particular. Second, visits to twelve schools of education took place in 1998 and 1999; a purpose of the site visits was to understand the different classification schemes that were being initiated. And third, sources such as the American Association of University Professors (AAUP), the NEA, and the American Association of Colleges of Teacher Education (AACTE) have developed documents or have data banks that are useful for the purposes of this paper. Nevertheless, as will be discussed below, gaps exist in what is known about faculty of education. The chapter also addresses only indirectly some of the fastest-growing areas in the education profession—for-profit providers, proprietary institutions, and non-campus-based organizations that certify teachers and conduct other tasks normally assigned to faculty in education.

The paper has four parts, including a discussion. I begin with a discussion about where the field of education is located within colleges and universities. The second part is an analysis of personal characteristics of the professorate—age, gender, ethnicity, and the like. The third part considers the classifications that exist for education faculty, and I discuss the work they do. In the fourth part I turn to a consideration about what the implications of these data are for the future of the education professorate.

My purpose is twofold. I first wish to outline broad characteristics of faculty in education, and I then shall suggest possible ramifications of these characteristics. In doing so, this chapter is an "essay" in the root sense of the word—a trial of some ideas. My goal surely is not to suggest that particular characteristics of education faculty predetermines how change will take place in different organizational units, but rather to think about how such characteristics presage various futures for faculty who think of themselves as professors of education.

Structural Typologies

Institutional Types

In general, with one significant exception, education faculty are found in virtually all kinds of institutions: research universities; liberal arts colleges; private and public institutions; small-, medium-, and large-size institutions. The majority of faculty work in public institutions, and state universities in particular.

Depending on how one classifies education, one might argue that education is more prevalent in the broad panoply of postsecondary organizations than other areas of inquiry. That is, in 1992 there were 50,860 faculty who thought of themselves as working in education; by comparison, there were 26,775 engineering faculty, 83,299 faculty in the multiple disciplines of the humanities and 68,534 social scientists in various fields. What is interesting to note is that obviously on some campuses education faculty are akin to a department, or even a program within a department. In this light one is more likely to see a faculty of education on a campus than anthropology, sociology, or economics. Similarly, as a profession, one is more likely to find education represented on a campus than engineering or law.

The site where education faculty are most often not found is in community colleges. On the one hand, this may not be so surprising insofar as other credentialed professions such as medicine and engineering are also absent from community colleges. On the other hand, as I discuss below, as discussions continue about how to integrate community college work more closely with four-year institutions, one wonders how prepared community colleges will be if they are asked to assume a greater role in teacher preparation.

Unit Configurations

One reason it is hard to obtain accurate data on education faculty is the array of areas in which they work. True, the majority of faculty are in schools and colleges of education, but even within these units there are combinations of faculties that may have little to do with education. A school of "education and nursing" exists on more than one campus, for example, as does a "college of health, education, and social work." Library science and information technology also have been joined with education on some campuses.

82   WILLIAM G. TIERNEY

Instructional Faculty and Staff in Four-Year Institutions

1992	Instructional faculty and staff	Part-time (%)	Full-time (%)
All programs	511,166	67.1	32.9
Agriculture/home econ	11,016	88.0	12.0
Business	45,865	63.0	37.0
Education	50,860	59.2	40.8
Engineering	26,775	76.1	23.9
Fine arts	47,581	56.5	43.5
Humanities	83,299	64.5	35.5
Natural sciences	101,995	78.1	21.9
Social sciences	68,534	70.1	29.9
All other fields	75,241	58.9	41.1
1987			
All programs	451,545	73.7	26.3
Agriculture/home econ	12,022	84.0	16.0
Business	42,304	67.7	32.3
Education	40,765	78.0	22.0
Engineering	26,189	79.9	20.1
Fine arts	48,516	56.9	43.1
Humanities	81,872	74.2	25.8
Natural sciences	95,911	78.0	22.0
Social sciences	57,925	81.7	18.3
All other fields	46,041	63.1	36.9

Source: National Study of Postsecondary Faculty (NSOPF).

Faculties also may be a department or division that are housed in any number of areas; education exists on one campus in a college of liberal arts, at another institution in a college of human development, and at a third institution in a college of urban and regional issues. At smaller institutions there may be a lone faculty member who thinks of him- or herself as in education, although he or she works in departments such as psychology, philosophy, or public administration.

Again, such a configuration is a bit at odds with other professions and disciplines. One generally sees engineering, law, and medicine as stand-alone schools or colleges. One certainly might find a department of business administration or nursing (especially in smaller, private institutions), but such units do not exist to the extent that one finds educational programs. The initial portrait, then, is of a faculty that are institutionally spread out more widely and have greater unit diversity than their professional counterparts or colleagues in traditional disciplines in the social sciences and humanities.

The Work of Education Faculty

The majority of faculty are involved with some variation of teacher education. Educational psychology had experienced a rise in the number of faculty after World War II, although now these areas are in a slightly downward trend. Special education, higher education, counselor education, and physical education are four additional specializations, although as noted above, these areas of inquiry are not necessarily assigned to a school of education. Counseling may be lodged in psychology or social work, for example, and physical education may be in a relatively new type of school—recreation and leisure studies. Fifty years ago home economics was a staple in education, and today it is rarely found in an educational unit—or under that name.

There are also pockets of faculty who think of themselves as in education, although they more aptly might be considered methodologists, historians, philosophers, or a multitude of other specialized areas of inquiry. These faculty might be entirely devoted to intellectual pursuits, such as the sociology of education, or to purely applied work, such as business education. Some faculty think of themselves as having little to do with practice, and others see their work as exclusively oriented toward effecting change in schools.

The point here is that the definition one uses to say that he or she is a faculty member in education is a bit looser than one finds in other areas. The field of education throughout the twentieth century has been interdisciplinary and a mixture of applied and theoretical orientations. To be sure, other professions and disciplines also have interdisciplinary or multiple foci. One might find a philosopher on a medical school faculty, or a traditionally trained psychologist on a business school faculty. But the portrait begins to emerge of education as perhaps more polyglot than others—in type, structure, and function. Such hybridity offers distinct challenges and possibilities during a period of change.

Personal Characteristics

Gender

Full-time faculty of education are about evenly split between men and women. In 1992 52.7 percent of the faculty were men and 47.3 percent were women. As Glazer-Raymo discusses in her chapter, over time the field has experienced a significant swing toward the inclusion of more women faculty. In 1987, for example, males accounted for 59 percent and women for 41 percent. Thus, in only a five-year period women increased their representation by over 5 percent.

In 1987 and 1992 education had more women faculty than any of the other fields that had been surveyed by NSOPF. If one looks at all program

TABLE 4.2
Gender of Full-Time Instructional Faculty and Staff in Four-Year Institutions

1992	Full-time faculty and staff	Male (%)	Female (%)
All programs	405,783	70.4	29.6
Agriculture/home econ	9,698	77.3	22.7
Business	28,885	76.4	23.6
Education	*30,127*	*52.7*	*47.3*
Engineering	20,381	94.2	5.8
Fine arts	26,874	67.3	32.7
Humanities	54,093	62.2	37.8
Natural sciences	79,633	83.3	16.7
Social sciences	48,030	73.9	26.1
All other fields	44,346	68.4	31.6
1987			
All programs	414,832	75.3	24.7
Agriculture/home econ	10,104	68.6	31.4
Business	28,630	77.3	22.7
Education	*31,812*	*59.0*	*41.0*
Engineering	20,915	96.6	3.4
Fine arts	27,628	70.9	29.1
Humanities	60,781	74.1	25.9
Natural sciences	74,852	84.0	16.0
Social sciences	47,324	80.2	19.8
All other fields	29,042	77.0	23.0

Source: National Study of Postsecondary Faculty (NSOPF).

areas in four-year institutions in 1992 women account for 29.6 percent or 18 percent less than in education. The closest field in terms of proportional representation for women in 1992 was the humanities, where women accounted for 37.8 percent of the faculty.

Race

Education, as Antony and Taylor observe in chapter 9, has the highest proportion of black faculty of any field; 9.2 percent of the education faculty were African American in 1992. Asian/Pacific Islanders are more underrepresented in education than in any other field. Only 1.2 percent of the education faculty are Asian/Pacific Islander, whereas fields such as engineering and the natural sciences have 19 percent and 9 percent respectively. Hispanics are relatively evenly distributed across different faculties, with humanities at 3.9 percent, the social sciences at 2.2 percent, and education at 2.1 percent.

TABLE 4.3
Race of Full-Time Instructional Faculty and Staff in Four-Year Institutions

1992	Full-time faculty and staff	American Indian (%)	Asian Pacific (%)	Black (%)	Hispanic (%)	White (%)
All programs	405,783	0.4	5.7	4.9	2.3	86.8
Agriculture/home econ	9,698	0.8	2.7	4.1	1.6	90.8
Business	28,885	0.6	5.9	3.7	1.4	88.5
Education	*30,127*	*0.5*	*1.2*	*9.2*	*2.1*	*87.1*
Engineering	20,381	0.2	19.0	3.0	2.5	75.3
Fine arts	26,874	0.5	2.6	6.1	2.7	88.2
Humanities	54,093	0.3	3.4	4.2	3.9	88.3
Natural sciences	79,633	0.3	9.0	3.6	1.7	85.3
Social sciences	48,030	0.4	3.2	5.5	2.2	88.6
All other fields	44,346	0.3	3.4	6.3	1.7	88.4
1987						
All programs	414,832	0.8	5.2	3.2	1.9	89.0
Agriculture/home econ	10,104	1.7	1.9	1.7	2.3	92.4
Business	28,630	1.5	8.7	3.7	0.9	85.2
Education	*31,812*	*1.1*	*1.2*	*7.0*	*2.4*	*88.3*
Engineering	20,915	0.0	14.2	0.5	1.7	83.6
Fine arts	27,628	0.6	1.0	4.2	1.4	92.8
Humanities	60,781	0.8	1.8	2.8	4.0	90.7
Natural sciences	74,852	0.6	7.2	1.8	1.6	88.8
Social sciences	47,324	0.5	3.8	4.1	2.0	89.6
All other fields	29,042	1.3	1.8	4.9	1.2	90.8

Source: National Study of Postsecondary Faculty (NSOPF).

When one compares the 1987 data with the 1992 data we find a small drop—from 2.4 percent to 2.1 percent of Hispanic faculty in education. Conversely, there was an increase in black faculty from 7 percent to 9.2 percent. There is no change in the representation of Asian/Pacific Islander faculty, and a small decrease of Anglo faculty from 88.3 percent to 87.1 percent. There was a similarly small decrease in Native American faculty from 1.1 percent to .5 percent. Overall, it is fair to conclude that minority representation in the field of education is relatively robust when compared to other fields, although Asians appear to be underrepresented.

Age

Faculty in education are getting older. In 1987 the average age was 48.2 and in 1992 it was 49.9. Similarly, in 1987 over 10 percent of the faculty were under 35; in 1992 only 4 percent of the faculty were. Two-thirds of the

WILLIAM G. TIERNEY

TABLE 4.4

Age Distribution of Full-Time Instructional Faculty and Staff in Four-Year Institutions

1992	Full-time faculty and staff	Avg. age (yrs.)	Under 35 (%)	35–44 (%)	45–54 (%)	55–64 (%)	65–70 (%)	71+ (%)
All programs	405,783	47.9	8.4	30.6	34.8	21.4	4.0	0.8
Agriculture/ home econ	9,698	49.8	8.0	23.3	34.6	27.8	4.4	1.9
Business	28,885	47.5	8.5	32.1	34.9	18.5	5.4	0.6
Education	*30,127*	*49.9*	*4.0*	*24.3*	*40.8*	*25.8*	*4.8*	*0.3*
Engineering	20,381	47.5	12.9	31.9	25.4	24.3	4.8	0.6
Fine arts	26,874	47.9	7.8	31.2	35.2	21.8	3.7	0.4
Humanities	54,093	49.3	7.1	23.3	39.4	25.1	4.2	0.9
Natural sciences	79,633	47.9	8.1	31.8	33.6	21.3	4.3	0.9
Social sciences	48,030	47.9	8.3	30.7	35.8	20.9	3.7	0.8
All other fields	44,346	47.6	9.8	30.3	34.5	20.2	4.0	1.2
1987								
All programs	414,832	46.9	10.8	31.8	32.9	20.6	3.7	0.3
Agriculture/ home econ	10,104	46.7	11.8	27.9	39.4	18.1	2.8	0.0
Business	28,630	45.3	13.4	37.5	28.7	18.6	1.9	0.0
Education	*31,812*	*48.2*	*10.4*	*26.2*	*32.6*	*28.0*	*2.7*	*0.2*
Engineering	20,915	48.1	12.1	25.1	30.6	29.3	2.5	0.4
Fine arts	27,628	45.7	13.0	32.8	36.2	14.4	3.1	0.5
Humanities	60,781	49.2	6.1	25.6	36.7	26.8	4.5	0.4
Natural sciences	74,852	46.5	9.2	34.4	35.9	17.7	2.6	0.3
Social sciences	47,324	47.2	8.8	34.7	32.4	19.5	4.2	0.4
All other fields	29,042	46.4	12.6	34.6	28.0	18.4	6.1	0.3

Source: National Study of Postsecondary Faculty (NSOPF).

faculty in 1992 were between the ages of 35 and 54, and in 1987 slightly over 60 percent of them were. Five percent of the faculty in 1992 were older than 65, compared to 3 percent in 1987.

When compared with other fields we find that education has become the field with the oldest faculty. Whereas in 1987 the humanities had an average age above that of education, and engineering rivaled education's average, in 1992 education had become the field with the most senior faculty. Only agriculture/home economics' age of 49.8 came close to education's average. The average age for all faculty was 47.9, or two full years younger than that of education. Engineering had the highest percentage of faculty under 35 with 12.9 percent.

Some of these facts are not particularly surprising. Education historically has been a popular choice for minority graduate students and women. One may wonder about the lack of Asian faculty and what, if anything, the implications are of a field that continues to experience shifts in gender and racial makeup.

Perhaps of greater surprise is the graying of the faculty. There are three distinct issues here. First, those who are most senior are frequently those most vested into the system and least likely to accept changes in workload, roles, and responsibilities. Second, there were fewer faculty in the ranks where traditionally leaders come from—those individuals between thirty-five and fifty-five. And third, the lack of faculty under thirty-five suggests that fewer job openings exist and/or fewer individuals desire the educational professorate as a career choice.

There are, of course, multiple ways to look at such data. A sense of renewal and new ideas may be diminished when fewer younger scholars join the ranks. One might argue, however, that an increase in senior faculty is a good factor during times of turbulence and change; they can provide history and insights that younger faculty may not. Others might suggest that regardless of whether having additional younger or older faculty is good for the culture and structure of the organization, it surely suggests significant changes. Senior faculty do different tasks than junior faculty. If the faculty is aging, what does that suggest for faculty roles?

Classifications

Full-time/Part-time

In 1987 78 percent of education faculty were full-time; in 1992 that percentage had dropped to 59.2. Except for the fine arts, which had 56.5 percent full-time faculty, education as a field had the smallest percentage of full timers. There was no clear trend of what had happened to faculty in all of the fields that were surveyed over a five-year period although the majority of fields had seen an increase in part-time faculty. However, no other field had the drop in full-time faculty that education experienced.

In addition to tenure line assistant, associate, and full professors, there are many other terms and ranks that are found in schools or departments where education exists. Here are some of the most common titles:

Research Professor at the assistant, associate, or professorial level is an appointment of a person with primary responsibilities for research, but he or she may also have teaching and service duties; the appointee may or may not be tenure track. Salaries are generally commensurate with tenure-line faculty.

Adjunct Professor at the assistant, associate or professorial level is an open-ended appointment of a person of substantial professional caliber who is given a semester or yearly contract to teach a course or series of courses;

the appointee is not eligible for tenure, and salaries are generally less than that of tenure-line faculty.

Clinical Professor at the assistant, associate, or professorial level is for individuals who generally are public school superintendents, principals, or teachers. The term is very loose in meaning and varies from institution to institution. Salaries are generally less than that of their tenure-line peers.

Instructor is a position for a junior faculty member who generally holds at least a master's degree. A significant number of instructors are part-time; they are appointed for one year or less, and may be renewed. Sometimes there is a time limit on how long an individual might be renewed at the instructor level. Salaries are generally less than that of their tenure-line peers.

Lecturer is a position for an individual who will give a series of lectures or courses in a particular professional or disciplinary field; the appointee is not eligible for tenure. Salaries are generally less than that of their tenure-line peers.

Visiting Professor is a full-time appointment generally for no more than six years. The appointee is not eligible for tenure. The title "visiting" is limited to persons who hold professorial rank and usually are on leave from another institution. Salary determination varies a great deal.

Faculty Ranks

In 1992 26.2 percent of education faculty were assistant professors, 32.5 percent were associate professors, and 26.3 percent were full professors. Accordingly, education had a smaller percentage of full-time faculty as full professors than any other field. Agriculture and engineering had 44.6 percent and 39.5 percent of their faculty as full professors; the closest field to education was business where 26.5 percent of its faculty were full professors.

Conversely, education had more associate professors than any other field. The ranks of assistant professors of education were in the middle of all of the fields that were surveyed. Business had the highest percentage of assistant professors with 31.2 percent and the humanities had the least with 21.7 percent. When compared with 1987 we find that in 1992 there were more associate professors and fewer full professors. Given that the composite of educational faculty is that they are also getting older, the data suggest that an increasing proportion of faculty are lodged at the associate level.

Tenure

In 1992 78.5 percent of full-time education faculty were on the tenure track; five years earlier 79.4 percent of the faculty were on the tenure track. These numbers are similar for faculty in most other disciplines and professions. There is a slight trend downward over the five-year time horizon so that there are fewer faculty in tenure line spots in 1992 than in 1987.

TABLE 4.5
**Academic Rank and Type of Full-Time Instructional Faculty and Staff
in Four-Year Institutions**

1992	Full-time faculty and staff	Full professor (%)	Associate professor (%)	Assistant professor (%)	Instructor/ lecturer (%)	Other (%)
All programs	405,783	33.9	26.5	27.0	9.8	2.8
Agriculture/ home econ	9,698	44.6	24.6	21.9	6.6	2.3
Business	28,885	26.5	30.2	31.2	10.0	2.1
Education	*30,127*	*26.3*	*32.5*	*26.2*	*11.3*	*3.7*
Engineering	20,381	39.5	30.4	25.2	4.4	0.5
Fine arts	26,874	33.3	27.7	23.6	9.9	5.5
Humanities	54,093	36.1	25.8	21.7	13.4	3.0
Natural sciences	79,633	41.6	25.0	23.2	7.1	3.1
Social sciences	48,030	40.2	26.0	26.3	6.1	1.4
All other fields	44,346	32.1	24.0	28.3	12.1	3.5
1987						
All programs	414,832	36.8	26.9	25.7	8.6	2.0
Agriculture/ home econ	10,104	45.9	26.6	19.4	7.8	0.3
Business	28,630	24.9	24.9	33.0	14.1	3.1
Education	*31,812*	*32.3*	*25.5*	*26.8*	*12.5*	*2.9*
Engineering	20,915	45.0	28.2	23.0	3.8	0.0
Fine arts	27,628	28.6	29.0	28.7	7.7	6.0
Humanities	60,781	42.5	26.7	20.6	8.5	1.7
Natural sciences	74,852	43.2	27.6	21.2	6.9	1.1
Social sciences	47,324	41.7	28.6	25.0	2.9	1.8
All other fields	29,042	32.0	25.2	26.2	12.5	1.1

Source: National Study of Postsecondary Faculty (NSOPF).

One point that is important to note here is that when combined with the changes from full- to part-time status, one finds a movement toward fewer tenure-line faculty in schools of education in 1992 than in 1987 when compared with part-time and non-tenure-track faculty.

Faculty Work

Time on Tasks

Education faculty spent 53.8 percent of their time on teaching activities in 1992. The remainder of their time was taken up by research (13.1%), administration (16.5%) and "other activities" (16.2%). Faculty in other fields

TABLE 4.6

Tenure Status of Full-Time Instructional Faculty and Staff in Four-Year Institutions

1992	Full-time faculty and staff	Tenured (%)	On tenure track (%)	Not on tenure track (%)	No tenure in program (%)	No tenure at institution (%)
All programs	405,783	55.5	23.5	12.4	4.5	4.1
Agriculture/ home econ	9,698	72.4	19.3	4.1	3.5	0.7
Business	28,885	51.5	29.9	10.4	3.6	4.5
Education	*30,127*	*54.9*	*23.6*	*14.1*	*4.7*	*2.7*
Engineering	20,381	61.8	27.5	6.0	1.4	3.3
Fine arts	26,874	52.9	22.1	9.7	3.4	11.9
Humanities	54,093	59.9	18.7	11.6	5.5	4.3
Natural sciences	79,633	63.7	21.4	9.0	3.1	2.8
Social sciences	48,030	63.4	23.0	8.5	2.5	2.7
All other fields	44,346	49.1	25.7	13.6	6.8	4.8
1987						
All programs	414,832	58.5	23.9	8.9	3.9	4.7
Agriculture/ home econ	10,104	75.3	16.8	4.9	2.6	0.4
Business	28,630	42.9	36.7	11.5	3.6	5.3
Education	*31,812*	*60.5*	*18.9*	*12.5*	*3.6*	*4.5*
Engineering	20,915	61.8	29.9	4.5	2.4	1.2
Fine arts	27,628	56.5	23.0	8.1	4.7	7.7
Humanities	60,781	68.7	15.8	6.7	4.7	4.1
Natural sciences	74,852	63.3	23.2	7.2	3.2	3.2
Social sciences	47,324	67.9	21.9	5.2	1.9	3.1
All other fields	29,042	53.5	31.2	9.0	3.4	3.0

Source: National Study of Postsecondary Faculty (NSOPF).

such as business, fine arts, and humanities reported that they spent more time on teaching than faculty in education. Education faculty ranked last in the time they spent on research activities, and first on their administrative duties. In 1987 faculty in education spent considerably more time on teaching (61.5%) and less time on research (11.2%) than they did in 1992.

Teaching and Research

Other than the fine arts, where the faculty had mean classroom contact hours of 11.9, education faculty ranked higher than any other field at 10.0 contact hours in 1992. Faculty contact hours had risen slightly from the 1987 average of 9.1.

TABLE 4.7

Time Allocation of Full-Time Instructional Faculty and Staff in Four-Year Institutions

1992	Full-time faculty and staff	Teaching activities (%)	Research activities (%)	Administ. activities (%)	Other activities (%)
All programs	405,783	50.8	21.1	13.2	14.7
Agriculture/ home econ	9,698	42.1	30.7	13.0	14.2
Business	28,885	54.1	17.9	12.1	15.7
Education	*30,127*	*53.8*	*13.1*	*16.5*	*16.2*
Engineering	20,381	48.5	28.1	11.2	12.0
Fine arts	26,874	56.5	15.4	12.3	15.6
Humanities	54,093	59.7	17.8	13.1	9.1
Natural sciences	79,633	50.0	29.1	11.1	9.7
Social sciences	48,030	50.5	23.6	13.4	12.2
All other fields	44,346	52.9	16.1	15.6	15.2
1987					
All programs	414,832	53.2	20.4	13.7	12.6
Agriculture/ home econ	10,104	50.4	27.6	13.4	8.7
Business	28,630	60.3	16.0	11.5	12.2
Education	*31,812*	*61.5*	*11.2*	*16.2*	*11.1*
Engineering	20,915	56.2	22.4	12.3	9.1
Fine arts	27,628	55.2	19.3	11.9	13.6
Humanities	60,781	62.2	16.9	14.5	6.5
Natural sciences	74,852	53.8	26.7	12.3	7.2
Social sciences	47,324	54.3	22.1	14.0	9.7
All other fields	29,042	59.8	14.1	14.2	11.9

Source: National Study of Postsecondary Faculty (NSOPF).

Again, other than the fine arts, education faculty published fewer refereed publications than any other field. Between 1987 and 1992 the publication rate for education faculty went down slightly from 1.5 to 1.3.

Part-Time Faculty

In 1987 there were 8,953 part-time faculty in education; in 1992 there were 20,733. Over two-thirds of part-timers in 1992 held the rank of instructor or lecturer, which was equivalent to 1987.

Less than 5 percent of them are on the tenure track. Sixty eight percent of part-time faculty did not hold a doctorate in 1992 as opposed to 77 percent of full time faculty who did. The average age of part-time faculty was fifty years old. Women accounted for 64 percent of the part-timers. Minority

TABLE 4.8
Classroom Hours and Student Contact of Full-Time Instructional Faculty and Staff

1992	*Full-time faculty and staff*	*Mean classroom hours*	*Mean student contact hours*
All programs	405,783	9.4	303.4
Agriculture/ home econ	9,698	8.5	229.2
Business	28,885	9.4	299.5
Education	*30,127*	*10.0*	*270.4*
Engineering	20,381	7.7	223.3
Fine arts	26,874	11.9	252.2
Humanities	54,093	9.6	257.7
Natural sciences	79,633	8.5	338.7
Social sciences	48,030	8.6	309.2
All other fields	44,346	9.7	281.5
1987			
All programs	414,832	8.5	272.3
Agriculture/ home econ	10,104	7.1	226.9
Business	28,630	9.0	300.6
Education	*31,812*	*9.1*	*227.5*
Engineering	20,915	7.8	249.5
Fine arts	27,628	11.1	245.1
Humanities	60,781	9.3	248.6
Natural sciences	74,852	7.9	311.9
Social sciences	47,324	8.0	301.1
All other fields	29,042	9.4	267

Source: National Study of Postsecondary Faculty (NSOPF).

representation was equivalent to what it was for full-time faculty. Two-thirds of part-timers efforts were spent on teaching, and 5.1% was spent on research. The remainder was split between administrative duties and "other activities."

Mean contact hours for part-time faculty was significantly less than for full-time faculty.

Recall that full-time faculty in education spent 10.0 contact hours in class, whereas part-timers reported they spent 5.9. Full-time faculty also were more likely to use essay exams than part-timers, and over 90 percent of full-time faculty had regularly scheduled office hours, whereas less than 60 percent of part-time faculty scheduled office hours (Benjamin, 1998). Finally, 88 percent of the part-time faculty reported that they were satisfied with their workload.

TABLE 4.9

Publications in Past Two Years by Full-Time Instructional Faculty and Staff in Four-Year Institutions (mean number)

1992	Full-time faculty and staff	Refereed/ juried publica-tions	Reviews non-refereed	Books/ book chapters	Mono-graphs/ tech-nical reports	Presen-tations/ exhibits	Patents/ copy-right/ software
All programs	405,783	2.4	1.6	0.6	1.1	5.1	0.2
Agriculture/ home econ	9,698	3.8	5.0	0.6	2.7	7.0	0.2
Business	28,885	1.9	1.3	0.5	1.3	2.9	0.2
Education	*30,127*	*1.3*	*1.7*	*0.5*	*1.2*	*5.8*	*0.1*
Engineering	20,381	3.7	1.9	0.5	2.8	5.3	0.4
Fine arts	26,874	0.9	1.5	0.3	0.3	18.3	0.2
Humanities	54,093	1.4	1.8	0.8	0.4	3.1	0.1
Natural sciences	79,633	3.7	1.1	0.5	1.1	3.5	0.2
Social sciences	48,030	1.9	1.8	0.9	1.2	4.1	0.1
All other fields	44,346	1.2	2.1	0.6	1.2	3.8	0.1
1987							
All programs	414,832	2.5	1.9	0.7	1.1	4.9	0.2
Agriculture/ home econ	10,104	3.1	3.1	0.5	1.6	4.7	0.3
Business	28,630	1.4	1.1	0.4	0.9	2.0	0.2
Education	*31,812*	*1.5*	*2.0*	*0.5*	*1.0*	*5.1*	*0.2*
Engineering	20,915	2.7	1.7	0.5	2.1	3.2	0.7
Fine arts	27,628	0.9	1.6	0.2	0.3	15.9	0.3
Humanities	60,781	1.6	2.7	0.8	0.3	3.2	0.1
Natural sciences	74,852	3.3	1.2	0.5	1.6	3.0	0.4
Social sciences	47,324	2.2	2.0	1.0	1.0	3.4	0.1
All other fields	29,042	1.2	3.1	0.4	1.4	4.0	0.1

Source: National Study of Postsecondary Faculty (NSOPF).

Discussion: Trends and Conjectures

As with any survey, NSOPF, however helpful, has gaps and shortcomings. One wonders, for example, what education faculty meant when they filled in "other activities" so that one discovers they spent more time doing that work than research. Similarly, what one group considers "teaching," another might consider "service." The NSOPF data is also self-reported so one is never entirely sure of the precision of the overall percentages.

I am also hesitant to accept at face value that 88 percent of part-time faculty are satisfied with their work. One interpretation, obviously, is that

TABLE 4.10
Academic Rank and Type of Part-Time Instructional Faculty and Staff in Four-Year Institutions

1992	Part-time faculty and staff	Full professor (%)	Associate professor (%)	Assistant professor (%)	Instructor/ lecturer (%)	Other (%)
All programs	199,046	12.2	9.1	9.9	59.0	9.8
Agriculture/ home econ	1,317		24.3		66.2	9.5
Business	16,970	13.8	6.3	8.0	62.9	9.1
Education	20,733	8.5	5.1	6.8	66.4	13.3
Engineering	6,394	19.6	6.8	11.2	49.2	13.2
Fine arts	20,707	12.4	4.8	8.5	63.0	11.3
Humanities	29,206	7.7	4.4	5.8	74.0	8.2
Natural sciences	22,332	12.5	7.0	8.0	59.1	13.4
Social sciences	20,504	11.1	8.4	11.4	60.7	8.6
All other fields	30,895	21.4	6.7	5.7	56.7	9.6
1987						
All programs	148,011	7.8	6.6	14.0	61.1	10.5
Agriculture/ home econ	1,919	11.0	16.4	2.1	57.6	13.0
Business	13,674	11.7	2.3	5.7	60.3	20.1
Education	8,953	5.9	6.4	8.4	66.2	13.2
Engineering	5,273	10.0	15.9	9.3	63.1	1.7
Fine arts	20,889	3.3	3.9	6.8	68.3	17.7
Humanities	21,091	4.3	3.8	7.1	74.0	10.8
Natural sciences	21,060	12.2	9.1	3.5	66.3	8.8
Social sciences	10,602	1.4	5.6	18.3	67.2	7.5
All other fields	16,999	12.9	2.2	11.4	68.2	5.3

Source: National Study of Postsecondary Faculty (NSOPF).

they are satisfied. An alternative interpretation is that individuals sought employment as full-time professors and were unsuccessful; they ended up as part-time faculty and lowered their expectations. They then compensated by saying that they were satisfied with their lot in life.

Further, in the institutions I visited I discovered what one might surmise about part-time faculty: any survey probably underreports the actual number. Accurate data on full-time tenure-line faculty is relatively easy to document and it has been done for at least a generation. Part-time faculty is another matter indeed. Some individuals admitted in interviews that they did not even keep accurate information about part-time faculty, but they were able to give "ball-park figures." How one counts a part-time faculty member also varies from institution to institution. Some institutions, for example, do not count

TABLE 4.11
Time Allocation of Part-Time Instructional Faculty and Staff in Four-Year Institutions

1992	Part-time faculty and staff	Teaching activities (%)	Research activities (%)	Administ. activities (%)	Other activities (%)
All programs	199,046	55.1	9.5	6.4	28.6
Agriculture/ home econ	1,317	54.5	3.4	8.8	33.3
Business	16,970	50.4	4.9	6.3	37.8
Education	*20,733*	*64.3*	*5.1*	*13.0*	*16.8*
Engineering	6,394	40.7	21.1	5.2	33.0
Fine arts	20,707	55.0	10.6	4.2	30.2
Humanities	29,206	69.9	9.3	4.0	16.6
Natural sciences	22,332	58.3	16.4	4.7	20.6
Social sciences	20,504	48.6	13.8	6.7	30.6
All other fields	30,895	45.2	7.5	6.8	39.6
1987					
All programs	148,011	51.1	7.8	4.4	36.7
Agriculture/ home econ	1,919	57.0	11.4	3.0	28.7
Business	13,674	45.3	1.3	3.4	50.0
Education	*8,953*	*70.5*	*3.5*	*6.6*	*19.4*
Engineering	5,273	54.7	7.4	3.8	34.0
Fine arts	20,889	45.2	14.5	2.4	37.9
Humanities	21,091	71.8	6.2	3.7	18.4
Natural sciences	21,060	58.8	10.8	7.2	23.3
Social sciences	10,602	46.6	7.7	4.4	41.3
All other fields	16,999	42.7	4.5	1.8	51.0

Source: National Study of Postsecondary Faculty (NSOPF).

graduate students who teach a class as a part-time faculty member and other institutions do. Other institutions count someone who teaches one course as a part-timer, and others count the number of courses taught by part-timers to get the number of part-time faculty. Obviously, valid and reliable generalizable data is hard to come by. Thus, the number of part-time faculty actually may be greater than what has been reported; at a minimum it certainly is not as accurate as that which exists for full-time faculty.

Nevertheless, even with gaps in the data, it is possible to offer one seemingly obvious, but significant, conclusion, that leads to a corollary point: the field of education is not in a period of growth if one defines growth as an increase in the number of full-time tenure line faculty, and there is no data that suggest that any turnaround is likely to occur. Indeed, the fastest growing

TABLE 4.12
Classroom Hours and Student Contact of Part-Time Instructional Faculty and Staff

1992	Part-time faculty and staff	Mean classroom hours	Mean student contact hours
All programs	199,046	6.5	167.1
Agriculture/ home econ	1,317	7.5	188.6
Business	16,970	7.0	164.0
Education	20,733	5.9	123.0
Engineering	6,394	6.5	197.9
Fine arts	20,707	6.4	123.3
Humanities	29,206	7.3	177.4
Natural sciences	22,332	5.9	160.9
Social sciences	20,504	5.7	172.7
All other fields	30,895	4.9	120.7
1987			
All programs	148,011	5.8	141.8
Agriculture/ home econ	1,919	4.5	112.2
Business	13,674	5.9	157.2
Education	8,953	5.5	99.9
Engineering	5,273	4.6	125.2
Fine arts	20,889	6.8	122.8
Humanities	21,091	5.6	139.5
Natural sciences	21,060	4.8	142.9
Social sciences	10,602	5.2	175.3
All other fields	16,999	5.1	129.1

Source: National Study of Postsecondary Faculty (NSOPF).

sectors of postsecondary education are in nontraditional institutions: for-profit and corporate universities where the idea of full-time faculty is anathema. Thus, how one defines "education faculty" in terms of characteristics, work, roles, and responsibilities, is likely to undergo as much, if not more, change in the next generation as has occurred during any time in the twentieth century. Such a conjecture, based on the data presented here, as well as larger contextual issues, such as the rapid rise of for-profit universities and governmental disinclination to invest in traditional educational training, suggests the following:

1. *Education faculty will diminish in private research universities.*

If current trends continue, except for a handful of AAU institutions (e.g., Stanford, Harvard) education as a school, college, or department is likely to disappear from private universities and colleges. As Kennedy

TABLE 4.13
**Satisfaction with Workload by Part-time Instructional Faculty and Staff
in Four-Year Institutions**

		Satisfaction with work load		
1992	*Part-time instructional faculty and staff*	*Dissatisfied (%)*	*Somewhat satisfied (%)*	*Very satisfied (%)*
All programs	199,046	15.2	37.3	47.5
Agriculture/ home econ	1,317	27.1	14.9	58.0
Business	16,970	10.3	37.6	52.1
Education	*20,733*	*12.0*	*22.7*	*65.3*
Engineering	6,394	3.4	48.2	48.4
Fine arts	20,707	25.9	36.1	38.0
Humanities	29,206	22.2	39.6	38.2
Natural sciences	22,332	12.5	45.6	41.9
Social sciences	20,504	13.4	36.9	49.7
All other fields	30,895	10.0	36.9	53.1
1987				
All programs	148,011	14.3	30.4	55.3
Agriculture/ home econ	1,919	12.5	48.8	38.8
Business	13,674	15.0	27.6	57.4
Education	*8,953*	*7.6*	*25.3*	*67.1*
Engineering	5,273	4.6	39.3	56.2
Fine arts	20,889	23.3	23.7	53.0
Humanities	21,091	17.6	27.6	54.7
Natural sciences	21,060	4.7	35.6	59.7
Social sciences	10,602	21.7	43.9	34.5
All other fields	16,999	16.9	25.0	58.1

Source: National Study of Postsecondary Faculty (NSOPF).

mentions in her chapter, the example of what happened at the University of Chicago is instructive (Bronner, 1997). The purpose of the study of education—intellectually and practically—at Chicago was unclear; the size of the faculty was minuscule, and its power was negligible. Of consequence, education as an area of inquiry was phased out.

One might expect similar occurrences at other similar institutions. Education has never been a high-status field, but there has always been a market for those who majored in education. If the broader market (e.g., proprietary institutions and for-profit institutions) offers cheaper alternatives, then one needs to question what an education faculty's purpose is at major research private universities.

The NSOPF data show that education faculty's research output is low. Further, graduate programs historically have been one way to gauge the prestige of an institution. But if the movement continues from full-time to part-time faculty for education professors, the need to train faculty obviously lessens. Further, such training will not be for faculty positions in similarly prestigious institutions, but instead for second- and third-tier colleges and universities and for on-line courses and majors. The result will be a filtering out of education programs and schools at private research universities until it reaches a level that the market can sustain.

2. *Education faculty will diminish in small and medium-size private institutions.*
During a time of downsizing, if not retrenchment, small programs and departments that historically have had low status will be the first areas to disappear. The graying of education faculty will enable a provost or dean to close an area as professors retire; hence, the pitched battles that often occur over program closure in a department where a majority of the faculty have a decided investment in the program will most likely not occur.

Where such debates about program closure take place, education faculty will be particularly vulnerable in high-status small and medium-size institutions. Again, faculty publish less than their peers so their intellectual importance to a college campus may be thought of as questionable. As the focus of teacher certification shifts to nonpostsecondary institutions, education's definition as a profession will be brought even further into question. Ironically, the increase in part-time faculty will lead to circular reasoning: few critics of tenure call for its abolition; however, when full-time tenure line faculty are replaced by part-time instructors at some point there is a dividing line that tips the balance so that a traditional department is no more than a conglomeration of part-time staff. As noted, part-time faculty have significantly fewer individuals in their ranks with doctorates, often a sine quo non of academic life in premier institutions. Education faculty, then, will see their raison d'être and utility further eroded. Programs will either be closed or transferred to units such as Continuing Education. Education will not be taught by education faculty, but by faculty trained in other disciplines and working in those departments and schools.

Such changes will not only take place in private AAU institutions, but also in small and medium-size elite institutions where education historically has been a minor program that had a handful of students. Again, the irony of part-time faculty's rise will lead to education's demise. In general, smaller institutions pride themselves on teaching excellence and faculty availability to the student body. As education shifts from full-time to more part-time faculty, if current conditions remain as outlined by NSOPF, education faculty will spend less time on issues that are currently defined as indicators of quality teaching—out of class interactions with students, in-class essays, office hours, and the like.

The result again will be the assertion that education serves no useful purpose. It does not add to the teaching stature of small- and medium-size institutions, and those individuals who desire such a degree will increasingly find more economical avenues to obtain such training—proprietary and for-profit institutions. As I have suggested throughout this chapter: context matters. Massive, on-line courses will affect different institutions in different ways. The ability to attract students through the Internet will affect education faculty who offer undergraduate training in a manner different from those who offer master's degrees. Thus, Internet-based courses may not affect private prestigious undergraduate institutions where the clientele will still desire a campus-based experience; however, master's degrees will be impacted where the clientele are often working adults.

3. *Education faculty will be redistributed within the public domain.*

Public institutions may experience dramatic shifts. Those AAU and/or research institutions where education has not played a significant role may well undergo the same scenario that I outlined for private institutions. Thus, universities such as Michigan State and UCLA might maintain their Schools and Colleges, while similar institutions in other states (e.g., Oregon) will not. Or at a minimum, what one currently means by "school of education" will be dramatically reconfigured. The University of Oregon's College of Education, for example, may become a College of Special Education where other traditional functions (teacher education, higher education) are eschewed (Kempner, 1998).

State universities are most likely to maintain a presence in the educational field, but their status will drop even further as research is eschewed entirely, and part-time faculty continue to increase at disproportionate rates. Although these institutions also will experience competition from the for-profit sector, the expected boom in college-age youth in some states will enable state universities to maintain enrollments, but not grow. Lowered costs will still prove desirable to students who want a degree from a four-year institution.

In many respects the most unresolved and interesting question will be the function of the community colleges. The role of education in a community college can not be divorced from larger systemic issues. If community colleges continue to be seen as self-enclosed institutions where someone either obtains a terminal associate degree or a vocational certificate, then the potential for education becoming a dominant force is unlikely. However, if community colleges not only continue to develop transfer agreements with four-year institutions, but also become seen as viable—if not central—options for the first two years of a bachelor's degree in the public realm, then education's focus may shift to the community college. Traditionally, community colleges also are those institutions with higher percentages of part-time faculty, and faculty without doctorates, which would be in keeping with the current trend of education faculty. In essence, education would become less of a profession akin to medicine and law, and more like an occupational trade.

Finally, the for-profit and proprietary sector is currently experiencing the largest rise in training teachers of any organizational type. One is hard pressed to suggest that their populations will diminish, but no one is certain from where they will take their students. It is certainly possible, as with any new organization, that the for-profits will create new markets from which to gain their constituencies. However, one of the assumptions of this paper is that traditional institutions also will be affected by increased competition from new markets.

4. *The rise of part-time faculty needs to be addressed.*

Certainly, one implication of the trends outlined here is the need for great forethought and action about the role, training, and nurturance of part-time faculty. If part-time faculty are to continue to increase, then clearly, educational programs, schools, and colleges need to provide enhanced opportunities for professional development. True, such faculty may not require opportunities to attend research conferences, but they will surely desire training about the parameters of how to improve their teaching. Further, institutions will not only need to train this new cadre of individuals, but resources will need to be provided that for the most part are currently missing. Simply stated, one can not expect part-time faculty to hold office hours if they do not have an office. One ought not expect part-time faculty to develop out-of-class relationships with students, if they are only paid for their time in-class.

Conclusion

Many have argued for one reason or another that "tenure is not the issue" in the recent discussions about the professorate (Breneman, 1997; Chait and Trower, 1997; Adamany, 1997; Byrne, 1997). And yet, the data that has been offered here suggests disturbing implications about tenure's viability for those who support tenure. Tenure, it appears, is a delicate structure dependent on a number of variables in order to maintain viability and strength. More important, one wonders not simply about tenure's health and well-being, but also about the future of the field of education. To call for alternative employment options in a field seems at face-value to be fine and good. However, facts and actions are rarely discrete and they do not occur in isolation. One action influences another, which in turn, influences another—and so on.

The field of education is not in a period of robust growth, but it is in a time of dynamic change. At present, when an institution hires more part-time faculty they are most likely hiring fewer full-timers. More part-time faculty means fewer tenured faculty as well. What I have suggested here is that such actions will inevitably influence where one finds the field of education, and who is found in education, a generation from now. Some will read the implications of what I have written with alarm; others will applaud the implications and see it as increased market segmentation and differentiation such as higher education is experiencing in general.

As with most changes in U.S. higher education, there is little overall coordination or planning about such transformations. Rather, they occur idiosyncratically on a campus-by-campus, even program by program, basis. However, whether one supports or decries such changes, one point that might be taken from the data and discussion presented here is that those who care about education's future might be more proactive about how the field should evolve as it enters the twenty-first century.

References

Adamany, D. (September 26–28, 1997). "A University President Reflects on the Role of Adjunct Faculty in the Contemporary Research University." *Conference on the Growing Use of Part-Time/Adjunct Faculty.* Washington, DC: American Political Science Association.

Benjamin, E. B. (1998). "Declining Faculty Availability to Students Is the Problem—But Tenure Is Not the Explanation." In W. G. Tierney (ed.), "Tenure Matters: Rethinking Faculty Roles and Rewards." *American Behavioral Scientist*, 41(5), 716–735.

Breneman, D. W. (1997). "Alternatives to Tenure for the Next Generation of Academics." *AAHE Forum on Faculty Roles and Rewards Working Paper Series.* Washington, DC: American Association for Higher Education.

Bronner, E. (September 1997). "End of Chicago's Education School Stirs Debate." The *New York Times*, p. A27.

Bullough, R. V., Jr. et al. (1997). "Long-Term PDS Development in Research Universities and the Clinicalization of Teacher Education." *Journal of Teacher Education*, 48(2), 85–95.

Byrne, J. P. (1997). "Academic Freedom without Tenure?" *AAHE Forum on Faculty Roles and Rewards Working Paper Series.* Washington, DC: American Association for Higher Education.

Carnegie Forum on Education and the Economy. (1986, May). *A Nation Prepared: Teachers for the Twenty-First Century: The Report of the Task Force on Teaching as a Profession.* Washington, DC: The Forum.

Chait, R. & Trower, C. A. (1997). "Where Tenure Does Not Reign: Colleges with Contract Systems." *AAHE Forum on Faculty Roles and Rewards Working Paper Series.* Washington, DC: American Association for Higher Education.

Clifford, G. J. & Guthrie, J. W. (1988). *A Brief for Professional Education: Ed School.* Chicago, IL: University of Chicago Press.

Conant, R. W. (1998, February). "The Decline and Fall of Schools of Education." *The Phelps-Stokes Fund Dialogue: An Essay of Opinion and Policy,* 7.

Cornbleth, C. & Ellsworth, J. (1994). "Teachers in Teacher Education: Clinical Faculty Roles and Relationships." *American Educational Research Journal,* 31(1), 49–70.

Glazer, N. (1974). "The Schools of the Minor Professions." *Minerva,* 12(3), 346–364.

Goodlad, J. I., Soder, R., & Sirotnik, K. A. (eds.). (1990). *Places Where Teachers Are Taught.* San Francisco, CA: Jossey-Bass.

Judge, H. (1982). *American Graduate Schools of Education: A View from Abroad.* New York, NY: Ford Foundation.

Kempner, K. (1998). Oregon's College of Education. Personal correspondence.

Koerner, J. D. (1963). *The Miseducation of America's Teachers.* Boston: Houghton Mifflin.

National Education Association (NEA) Higher Education Research Center. (1997). Full-time "Non-tenure-track Faculty: Gender Differences." *Update,* 3(5).

———. (1996 September). "Full-Time Non-Tenure-Track Faculty." *Update,* 2(5).

———. (1995 September). "Tenure." *Update,* 1(3).

Tierney, W. G. (ed.). (1998). *The Responsive University: Restructuring for High Performance.* Baltimore, MD: The Johns Hopkins University Press.

Timpane, P. M. & White L. S. (eds.). (1998). *Higher Education and School Reform.* San Francisco, CA: Jossey-Bass.

CHAPTER 5

The Evolving Production Functions of Schools of Education

SARAH E. TURNER

Faculty roles and rewards in schools of education[1] are inextricably linked to the "outputs" of schools of education. In essence, what do schools of education do? Across all institutions, the answer would most certainly include training teachers for elementary and secondary schools, providing continuing education for these professionals, training administrative and support personnel for schools, educating professionals in higher education administration, conducting research on educational practice and finance, and providing direct support to local schools. While this set of activities is by no means exhaustive, colleges and universities differ appreciably in their relative levels of concentration in each of these activities. Overall, there have been marked fluctuations in the relative emphasis given to these activities over time.

Schools of education represent one of the most dynamic components of colleges and universities over the last three decades: their enrollments expanded at a rate greater than that of a burgeoning higher-education industry in the late 1960s and early 1970s. Then the twin forces of contracting undergraduate enrollments and shifts in student interest away from the field of education, particularly on the part of women, produced a period of retrenchment that lasted through the late 1980s. Yet, changes over the last three decades run much deeper than fluctuations in enrollment. The shifting market environment for educational professionals led schools of education to make substantial and continuing adjustments in the mix of training they provide. Degree and course offerings have changed dramatically and, within colleges and universities, alternative combinations of faculty inputs have been employed in a range of areas.

An increasing number of postsecondary institutions are competing to provide training for prospective teachers and educational professionals. New entrants and institutions expanding their offerings often use different combinations of inputs, such as a lower fraction of tenure faculty or increased emphasis on site-based delivery. At the same time, many schools of education have altered their curricular offerings to adapt to increasingly specialized needs of the educational marketplace.

The purpose of this chapter is both to identify the major transformations among schools of education over the last three decades and to provide a behavioral explanation for these adjustments. The first objective is descriptive and involves measuring the changes in the outputs of schools of education over time. The main output observable to the researcher is the number of degrees awarded at various levels and across fields. To be sure, such measures leave something to be desired as they lack both a qualitative dimension and fail to capture other unrecorded services and training activities. Three trends stand out in the empirical evidence. First, there has been an overall shift away from undergraduate training toward postbaccalaureate programs. Second, the major providers of master's-level training are increasingly private colleges and universities without substantial research infrastructure. The large number of "new entrants" in this area indicates that the market has become much more competitive over the last decade. Finally, there is modest evidence suggesting that research universities are increasingly concentrating on specialized programs outside the sphere of traditional teacher training.

The second objective, explaining why these changes have occurred, relies on an economic model of how schools of education decide which activities to pursue and what combination of faculty and other resources to employ to meet their objectives. At least at a conceptual level, there exists a production function defining the relationship between "inputs" such as faculty, student time, and capital resources and the "outputs" of a school of education. Because colleges and universities differ appreciably in their cost structures and missions, schools of education may offer very different combinations of outputs or may use varying combinations of resources to produce a common output like a certified teacher. Changes in relative input costs, the demand for educational services, or institutional objectives all affect the combination of outputs that a school of education will offer. The price and quantity of outputs from schools of education must be expected to respond to markets outside schools of education.

A key hypothesis of this chapter is that schools of education vary markedly in their production functions and associated cost functions and, as a result, there will be wide variation in institutional responses to the changing educational marketplace. After sketching a theory of the factors affecting the behavior of schools of education, the next section outlines the determinants of student demand, focusing particularly on the question of how the expected earnings function affects the decision to invest in postbaccalaureate training in education. The final section discusses the policy implications of the considerable—and increasing—heterogeneity in the outputs of schools of education. One of the main themes of this chapter is that schools of education live in a faster changing environment than many imagine: dramatic changes in market structure have occurred over the last three decades, and the transformations are likely to continue well into the future.

The commonsense observation that many people may choose to teach or to invest in programs offered by schools of education for a wide range of reasons beyond compensation or cost is not a sufficient reason to reject the implications of an economic model of schools of education. Changes in market variables, such as the wages paid to teachers relative to other professions, certainly affect the willingness of some individuals—those at the margin—to enter teaching. A key question, largely beyond the scope of this analysis, is how those potential teachers at the margin compare in aptitude to those whose decisions would be unaffected by a wage change or a change in the cost of teacher training.

While the goal of this chapter is to assess the market structure and outputs of schools of education, there are many important issues concerning both the place of schools of education in the university and the relationship between schools of education and their constituencies that remain unaddressed. Foremost among these is the question of how (or whether) schools of education improve the effectiveness of teachers in the classroom. Teacher training remains the bread and butter activity of schools of education, yet evidence concerning how differences in the resources and curricula of schools of education affect the performance of education professionals is sparse.

Outputs and Market Structure

Perhaps the most widely cited and easily quantifiable measure of the "output" of a school of education is the number of teachers and administrative and support personnel that it trains. As is well known, total graduates at the B.A. level and above in education programs have fluctuated considerably with a peak of 311,279 degrees conferred in 1973, a decline to 174,257 in 1987, and then a rebound to 226,276 in 1995. These shifts reflect both changes in the size of the population of undergraduates and fluctuations in the attractiveness of teacher training relative to other career paths. The decline in the share of B.A. degrees awarded in education from slightly more than 18 percent of all B.A.s in 1975 to less than 10 percent in 1995 reflects the waning interest among undergraduates in teaching careers. After a temporary spurt of growth from the three decade low of 90,782 in 1987, the number of B.A.s awarded in education have held at a plateau of about 114,000 through the early 1990s. (See Figure 5.1). A related phenomenon is that undergraduates are increasingly receiving professional training for teaching through five-year programs that award the B.A. in a concentration within the arts and sciences.

Figure 5.1. Changes in degrees awarded in education, by level, 1966–1995

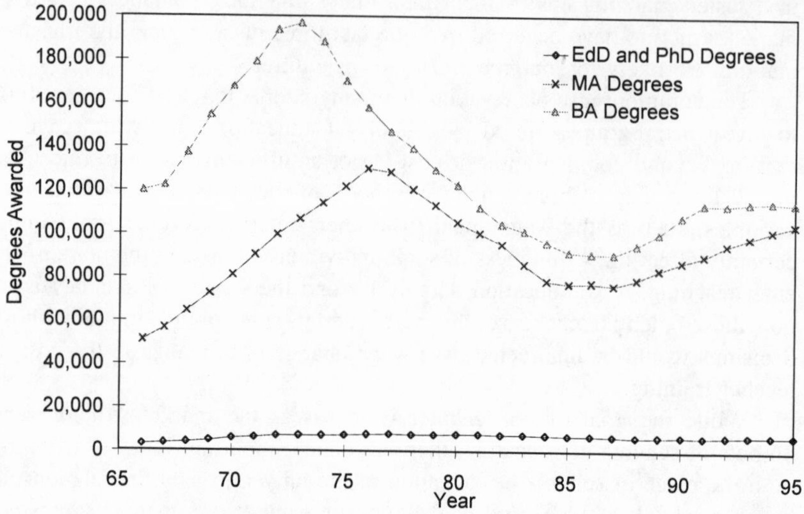

Source: Author's calculations from the annual institutional "Earned Degrees Conferred" survey conducted by the National Center for Education Statistics of the U.S. Department of Education. These data were part of the Higher Education General Information Survey (HEGIS) before 1987 and were captured in the Integrated Postsecondary Education Data System (IPEDS) in subsequent years.

For this reason, the drop off in the total share of college graduates preparing to teach may be smaller than the decline in B.A. degrees.

While the total number of postbaccalaureate degrees in education also declined from the mid-1970s to the mid-1980s, the fall-off was not nearly as severe as within baccalaureate programs. As a result, the composition of degrees awarded by schools of education has changed appreciably over the last three decades, with an overall shift away from undergraduate training. While nearly two-thirds of degrees awarded in 1970 were at the B.A. level, B.A.s account for only about one-half of the degrees awarded by schools of education today. Overall, the bulk of this shift in emphasis occurred between 1970 and 1975; the proportion of M.A. and Ph.D./Ed.D. degrees in education appears relatively constant over the twenty years between 1975 and 1996 (Figure 5.2).

Aggregate trends in degrees awarded under the broad rubric of "Education" over the last two decades belie decisive changes among providers—schools, programs and departments of education—in the type of training provided. Figures 5.3A, 5.3B, and 5.3C present the distribution of degrees

Figure 5.2. Changes in the distribution of degrees awarded in education, by level, 1966–1995

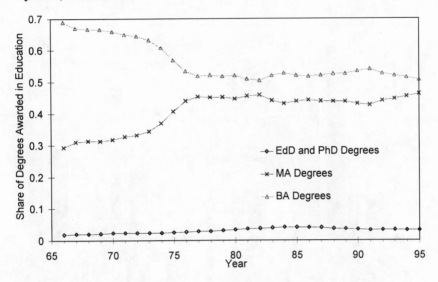

Source: Author's calculations from the annual institutional "Earned Degrees Conferred" survey conducted by the National Center for Education Statistics of the U.S. Department of Education. These data were part of the Higher Education General Information Survey (HEGIS) before 1987 and were captured in the Integrated Postsecondary Education Data System (IPEDS) in subsequent years.

awarded at the B.A., M.A., and doctorate levels by Carnegie classification. While Carnegie classifications do not provide "definitive" characterizations of institutional mission, they do provide a useful taxonomy in that they classify colleges and universities by their relative investments in research and graduate teaching.[2] The smallest change in the distribution of degrees by type of institution has occurred at the B.A. level (Figure 5.3A): large public, comprehensive universities have provided between 35 and 40 percent of the newly minted B.A.s in education in each year since 1966. Doctorate institutions (Doctorate 1 and Doctorate 2 in the Carnegie taxonomy) also continue to provide between 10 and 15 percent of the new B.A.s in education. To the extent that there has been a sizable change in this arena, it has been away from public research universities and toward the "Private Baccalaureate II" schools.

The bigger changes in the source of training in the field of education have occurred at the postbaccalaureate level. There is a decided and continuing shift away from research universities as leaders in the production of advanced degrees. At the M.A. level, the shifts across sectors of postsecondary institutions

Figure 5.3A. Distribution of B.A. degrees awarded in education by institution type and year

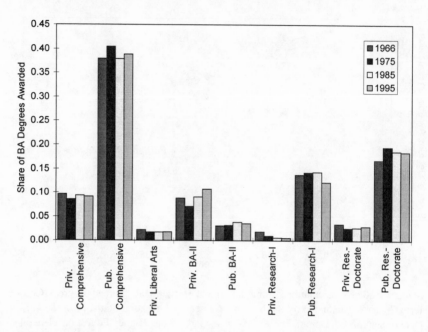

Source: Author's calculations from the annual institutional "Earned Degrees Conferred" survey conducted by the National Center for Education Statistics of the U.S. Department of Education. These data were part of the Higher Education General Information Survey (HEGIS) before 1987 and were captured in the Integrated Postsecondary Education Data System (IPEDS) in subsequent years.

occurred in two waves. In the first wave, between the late 1960s and early 1970s, there was a dramatic decrease in the share of M.A. degrees granted at research universities (both public and private) as schools of education expanded markedly in the other sectors. The share of degrees awarded by private research universities fell from 8 percent to 4 percent and the share awarded by public research universities fell from 24 percent to 16 percent. Since this was a period of overall growth, this was an instance of a greater rate of expansion in masters programs among the public comprehensive and general doctorate programs. A second wave of change has occurred in the more recent decade as private comprehensive institutions became major sources of output (with more than one-fifth of the M.A. degrees awarded). To give this trend some resonance, consider the range of institutions with large changes in the number of M.A.s awarded. Among the schools with

Figure 5.3B. Distribution of M.A. degrees awarded in education by institution type and year

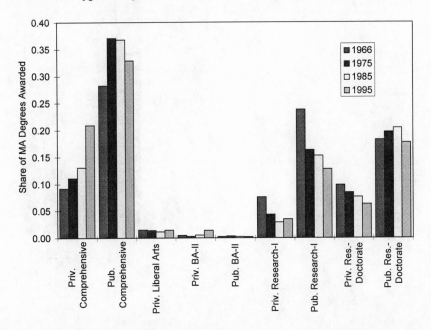

Source: Author's calculations from the annual institutional "Earned Degrees Conferred" survey conducted by the National Center for Education Statistics of the U.S. Department of Education. These data were part of the Higher Education General Information Survey (HEGIS) before 1987 and were captured in the Integrated Postsecondary Education Data System (IPEDS) in subsequent years.

increases of more than 200 in the annual number of M.A. degrees awarded in education between 1985 and 1995 are: Gonzaga University in Washington State, Chapman University in California, and Dowling University in New York.

A different dynamic dominates the distribution of degrees awarded at the doctoral level. In 1966, a little more than one half of all Ph.D./Ed.D. degrees in education were awarded by public, research I universities, and nearly a fifth were awarded by private, research I universities; by 1995, the public share had slipped to 43 percent and the private share had dropped to 10 percent. The exodus of the private institutions occurred between 1966 and 1975, while the public research institutions have decreased their relative output more gradually over the interval (Figure 3C). To be sure, many of the trends in the distribution of doctorate degrees in education are mirrored by trends in

Figure 5.3C. Distribution of Ph.D./Ed.D. degrees awarded in education by institution type and year

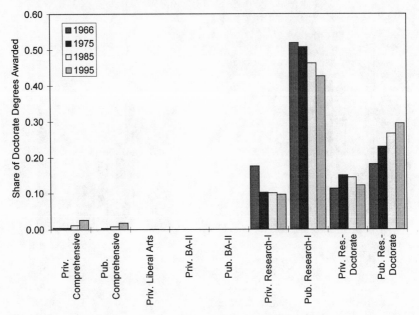

Source: Author's calculations from the annual institutional "Earned Degrees Conferred" survey conducted by the National Center for Education Statistics of the U.S. Department of Education. These data were part of the Higher Education General Information Survey (HEGIS) before 1987 and were captured in the Integrated Postsecondary Education Data System (IPEDS) in subsequent years.

Note: Underlying data for figures 5.3A–C are the NSF-Caspar compilation of data from the HEGIS/IPEDS institutional surveys of degrees conferred.

specific disciplines within the arts and sciences (see, e.g., the discussion in chapter 4 of Bowen and Rudenstine [1992]).

Focusing more narrowly on the "top 25" graduate programs in education, their loss of market share at the graduate level has been dramatic. While the inclusion or exclusion of institutions from the *U.S. News and World Report* ranking may be arbitrary at the level of the individual school, in the aggregate, these rankings are a reasonable way of identifying the most well-regarded schools of education. Among the 2,241 schools awarding advanced degrees in education over this interval of nearly three decades, the top 25 (as ranked in 1997) awarded more than 37 percent of all Ph.D./Ed.D. degrees and more than 13 percent of M.A. degree in 1966. By 1995, these shares had

Figure 5.4. Distribution of institutions awarding the M.A. in education

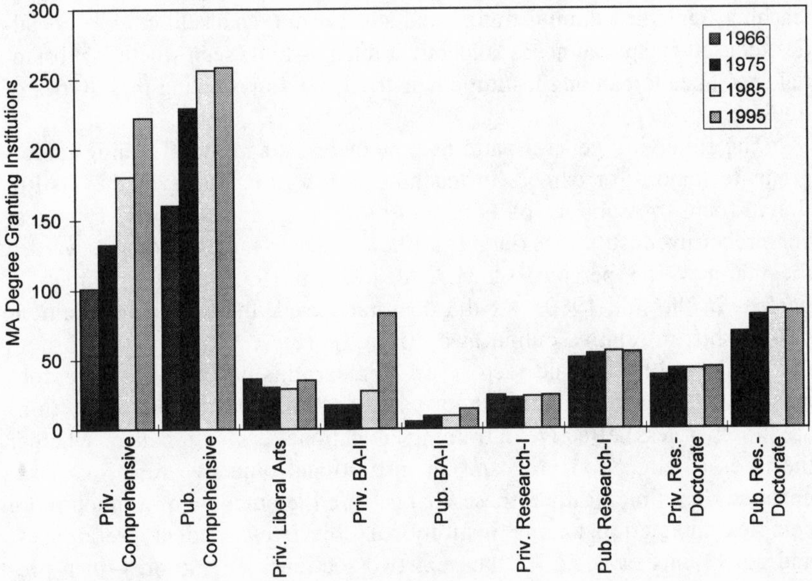

Source: Author's calculations from the annual institutional "Earned Degrees Conferred" survey conducted by the National Center for Education Statistics of the U.S. Department of Education. These data were part of the Higher Education General Information Survey (HEGIS) before 1987 and were captured in the Integrated Postsecondary Education Data System (IPEDS) in subsequent years.

shrunk to about 21 percent of Ph.D./Ed.D. degrees and a little less than 6 percent of all M.A. degrees. As discussed later, differences in cost structures across institutional types and differences in student demand have been key forces driving this pattern.

The changes in the institutional representation of postbaccalaureate degree awards is not simply a case of the relative expansion of some programs and the relative contraction of others. Rather, many institutions that did not previously award master's degrees in the field of education have entered this market. As shown in Figure 5.4, 120 institutions began awarding M.A. degrees in education between 1985 and 1995, with nearly all of this increase concentrated in the private, nonresearch sectors.

Further research will yield a more nuanced picture of the changes that have occurred in the offerings of postsecondary institutions in the training of professionals in the field of education. In particular, one question to consider is the extent to which there are sizable differences among institutions in the content focus of degree programs. Many institutions have programs to train a range of educational professionals in occupations other than classroom teaching, including administration and supervision, counseling, and specialties focused on special needs students. It remains to be seen whether substantial specialization among institutions is occurring in providing these types of training.

The following general patterns nonetheless stand out. Training undergraduate majors for careers in teaching is a waning share of the institutional focus of schools of education. At the graduate level, four-year comprehensive institutions (largely without research infrastructures) awarded the majority (53 percent) of M.A. degrees in 1995, up from about 37 percent in the mid-1960s. At the doctorate level, there is also a demonstrable shift in relative output away from the research universities in both the public and the private sectors. To be clear, this pattern of change does not provide any information about whether different types of institutions are more (or less) effective in training educational professionals or whether the roles of education programs in institutional objective functions have changed over time. Rather, these changes are the outcome of a much more complex interaction among institutional objectives, student preferences, and constraints or costs. In the next two sections, we explore—in a preliminary way—the roles of student demand and institutional costs in determining these outcomes.

While the number of "degrees conferred" by schools of education is the most easily quantified output of schools of education, it is hardly the only measure. Sponsored research is a major—and perhaps expanding—product of schools of education. Perhaps the largest targeted source of research funds available to programs in education is through the Department of Education's Office of Educational Research and Improvement that makes awards for specific research initiatives as well as large institutional grants. These large awards or "center" grants provide multi-million-dollar support over a period of several years for research in topics such as early childhood development and learning, assessments of student learning and achievement, second language learning, and postsecondary improvement. While these major grants often involve collaboration among several postsecondary institutions, the primary recipients are concentrated among nationally prominent research institutions. In 1997 alone, center grants accounted for more the $27 million in research awards to just ten institutions.[3] Institutions surely weigh the relative costs of expanding research initiatives relative to degree programs at the margin, and increased competitiveness in the market for providing broadly based teacher training may well have provided a strong incentive for some institutions to shift their portfolios toward research.

Cost Structures and Varying Responses to Student Demands

Providers of training in educational disciplines adapt to the incentives created by student demand, but how depends considerably on their cost structures, institutional strengths or objectives, and the structure and competitiveness of the overall market. In explaining what has transpired, it is useful to step back and examine the varying cost structures and areas of comparative advantage of schools of education across the postsecondary spectrum. Each activity of a school of education can—at least in theory—be described in terms of a production function that relates how inputs can be combined to produce a level of "output," where "output" in this case refers to the skills implicit in any degree level. Some institutions such as research institutions may benefit from economies of scope, whereby their overall size provides an advantage in competing in a range of markets.[4] Different institutions may well use different combinations of "inputs" to produce a given level of output, depending on the costs of these factors. "Inputs" include faculty and other staff, the times and locations of course offerings, and capital resources such as computers.

In equilibrium, there is no incentive for a school of education to enter or exit program areas or to change their tuition prices. However, each time demand forces shift or there is a change in the possible combination of faculty inputs that could be used, the school must reconsider its choices. Demand shifts for a school of education may be induced by changes in the offerings of programs that are close substitutes or changes in the wages or employment prospects of education professionals. For example, if school districts moved to raise the wages of teachers with master's-level training, more teachers would seek this credential and the demand for master's-level programs in schools of education would increase. Such a shift would lead schools of education to consider expanding their existing programs, creating new programs, and potentially raising their charges. The next section provides some evidence on the relationship between the market incentives offered to education professionals and the demand-side effects for schools of education.

The determinants of supply in each program area include the applicable production function and the prices of inputs such as faculty salaries, classroom space, and so on. Since schools of education are linked to colleges and universities administratively, institutional guidelines on compensation structure and tenure policy may lead to substantial differences in costs and production possibilities. For example, institutions with long-standing commitments to a tenure structure may be reluctant to support the substitution of potentially less-expensive adjunct faculty for tenured faculty in degree programs.

At the heart of such potential substitutions is the question of whether the nature of the product—or the return to the investment in obtaining the degree—changes with the alternative faculty structure. If qualitative differences result then the issue is product differentiation. If not, the school has just altered the combination of inputs, leaving output unchanged. If there is no difference in the employment opportunities for students with the same "degree" produced using different inputs, we would be inclined to reject the importance of product differentiation.

How schools of education respond to changes in market forces depends on the definition of the market area for their degree programs. At one extreme, the market might be framed in terms of a model of institutional monopoly with a single university as the sole provider of training in a limited geographic area; in this case, the school of education would face a downward-sloping demand curve in each degree market. At the other extreme, the market for educational training might be viewed as very competitive—either at a national or local level—with many institutions offering the same degree programs. At the undergraduate level, Hoxby (1997) has argued that the market for undergraduate education has been transformed in the postwar era from local autarkies to a very competitive national market, with a greater degree of concentration of the most able students at institutions with the highest level of subsidy. In Hoxby's model, much of the competition among schools has occurred along the quality dimension.

Transformations in schools of education suggest a much different market structure, owing to the rigidity in the economic rewards and the emphasis placed on combining employment with advanced study. For the M.A. degrees in particular, competition is keen, but the determining variable seems to be cost and the relevant market is local. In this case, "cost" reflects both direct out-of-pocket expenses incurred by the student plus the implicit time-costs associated with convenience of schedule, location, and so forth.

The ease of market entry among private colleges and universities in recent years supports the hypothesis that cost competition has increased. There is some anecdotal evidence to suggest that schools of education and, particularly their teacher certification programs, have served as "cash cows" for colleges and universities, providing revenues that could be used to subsidize other institutional objectives. As such, tuition revenues exceeded program costs and such implicit profits would suggest opportunities for entry by other providers, unless universities could sustain barriers to entry. Major universities appear to have lost market power in their local areas as a range of new providers exploit nontraditional delivery methods to provide postbaccalaureate degree training.[5]

To be sure, not all degree programs in education fit the model of localized competition. Programs emphasizing specialized training, those with a high research component, and those that are capital intensive are unlikely to fit this model. Such programs are not easily replicated outside the environment of a research university. Examples include interdisciplinary Ph.D. training and capital intensive laboratory work.

At two extremes, research universities tend to employ tenure-track faculty with both research and teaching responsibilities while comprehensive schools tend to rely more heavily on teaching faculty.[6] Schools of education within these institutions often represent microcosms of their parent institutions with a sizable library, generous classroom space, and a considerable administrative and support infrastructure. The "research" in research universities requires considerable input of faculty time, graduate student involvement, and other financial support. Research productivity is emphasized in the tenure process, as well.

Providers of training in education may face a choice: competing directly on a cost basis in local markets or differentiating their products in terms of quality or specialization. In the model suggested here, institutions with the highest "fixed" and "variable" costs may choose not to participate in the highly competitive local markets. Schools of education at research universities are likely to face particularly high costs within their traditional institutional structures owing to factors such as sizable commitments to physical plants, to tenure and doctorate level faculty, and to research productivity.[7] Unless it can be demonstrated that the teaching labor market rewards presumed differences in degree "quality" rather than degree level, high cost institutions will be unable to compete for students in markets where there are a large number of alternative providers. Instead, such schools will focus on degrees related to their areas of specialization.

This discussion is largely consistent with the empirical evidence as research universities have been most likely to abandon or reduce their emphases on the most competitive areas such as teacher training. At the extreme, one prestigious private research university (the University of Chicago) closed its program in education studies altogether. If, given their cost structures, schools of education at private research universities must find a viable market niche in sponsored research and doctorate instruction, it may be that only a handful of these programs will survive into the next decade (Tierney, 1998).

With cost structures closely mirroring those of their private research counterparts, state-supported research universities may face the toughest decisions in considering whether to provide degrees similar to those offered by institutions with much lower personnel costs and low-fixed costs. Yet, flagship public institutions face a (perceived) public responsibility to participate in a range of training functions that may serve to improve the quality of the primary and secondary education in the state. In her essay in this volume, Jeannie Oakes argues eloquently that these institutions have a public responsibility to foster stronger connections with public schools and to initiate innovative programs for the training of teacher professionals. There are in fact a growing number of "model" initiatives sponsored by flagship universities including the widely acclaimed project at UCLA called "Center X—Where Research and Practice Intersect for Urban School Professionals." Such programs certainly signal the end of the era in that public institutions perceived to be in a position of industry leadership might use teacher training programs of modest quality as revenue-generating activities. However, the new models emerging at flagship universities are small in their direct contribution to the teaching pool and the continuation of high subsidy levels for these programs relies on the persistence of education as a focal issue in the political process.

Measurement of Demand Side Changes

Demand for places in schools of education among potential new teachers probably has less to do with the any particular dimension of teacher preparation training or cost than with the compensation awarded to teachers in the labor market. Real declines in the earnings for women in the teaching force vis-à-vis other employment opportunities for college graduates certainly explain much of the migration from teaching. These trends are shown clearly in Figure 5.5, which illustrates the trend in real earnings for women who teach and the ratio of the earnings of teachers to those in other occupations. The shift from a 1973 earnings premium of about 15 percent for teachers to a penalty of about 5 percent in 1995 no doubt explains much of the slide in demand. In this regard, the most powerful lever affecting enrollment in education schools is held by the external forces controlling compensation in the education sector and in other sectors.

While real earnings have risen for teachers over the last decade, as indicated by the upward slope of the curve in Figure 5.5 after 1981, it is earnings relative to the best offer that an individual might receive in a nonteaching occupation that is the relevant economic variable for predicting the demand for teacher training. Relative earnings are measured as the ratio of the earnings of teachers to the earnings of nonteachers among women with a college education.[8] As a host of other professional careers such as law and medicine opened for women in the early 1970s, many women who would have entered teaching in an earlier era chose disciplines in the social sciences, business, and the biological sciences (Turner and Bowen, 1990). In this respect, the decline in the relative wage premia shown in Figure 5.5 provides a strong explanation for the precipitous drop in B.A. degree concentration in education shown in Figure 5.1.

A high degree of structure and rigidity characterizes the overall wage structure in the teaching force: in many districts, earnings increase according to a formulaic wage structure based on years of experience and level of education.[9] The premia for additional credentials beyond the B.A. such as an

Figure 5.5. Mean annual wage and salary income, 1994 dollars, women only

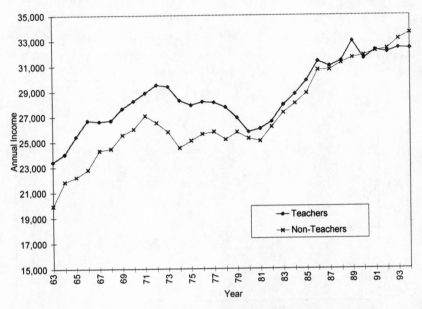

Sources: Data in Figure 5.5 is from the March CPS. Susanna Loeb graciously provided these data and they are from her research "Examining the Link between Wages and Quality in the Teacher Workforce: The Role of Alternative Labor Market Opportunities and Non-Pecuniary Variance" (with Marianne Page).

M.A. or Ed.D. are sizable. The determination of demand for postbaccalaureate programs in education is a function of how individuals respond to questions such as: What are the benefits to additional training? Does it matter where I receive my training? Should I attend part-time or full-time? Demand for postbaccalaureate degrees such as the M.A. and Ed.D. among those already in the teaching force is heavily influenced by local pay scales that have explicit links between educational attainment and earnings.

Increasing the premium for advanced degrees in a state or district should lead to corresponding increases in participation in advanced degree programs. Empirically, we suspect that either the premium associated with an advanced degree in education has risen over time or the costs of earning such a degree have declined appreciably. Using data from the CPS shown in Figure 5.6, we see the strong increase in the proportion of women in the teaching force with advanced degrees, with this share rising from less than 20 percent in 1974 to nearly 45 percent in 1994.

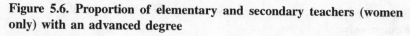

Figure 5.6. Proportion of elementary and secondary teachers (women only) with an advanced degree

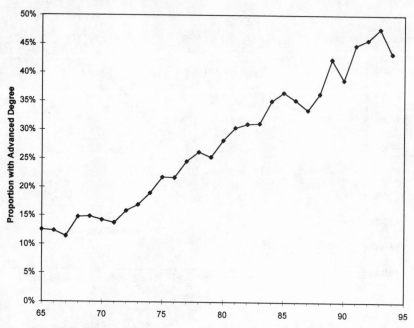

Source: Data in Figure 5.6 is based on calculations from the annual March CPS surveys using women with at least a college education. The primary-secondary teaching labor force is restricted based on the occupational designations of primary-secondary teacher and the appropriation educational industry designation.

   A sizable majority of individuals pursuing M.A. programs in education (and to some extent Ph.D. programs) do so part time. Notably, a far smaller proportion of students in other professional programs (particularly law and medicine) choose to pursue their studies part time, leading us to ask how the postbaccalaureate market differs in education. Thinking about the basic economics of the choice between attending full-time and part-time, students compare the stream of payments to: (1) working, taking classes over a much longer time horizon, and then receiving the earnings premium versus (2) attending school full-time, and then receiving the earnings premium somewhat sooner. In the most basic case, the choice reflects the value of the delayed earnings premium relative to the value of foregone earnings while attending school full-time.[10] Thus, it is not surprising that professional students in fields such as law, business, and medicine at the most prestigious schools are likely to attend full-time—the earnings premiums justify getting done fast.[11]

Another dimension of the decision to pursue graduate study in education is the question of *which school* a student will elect to attend.[12] An individual's desired program area will have a substantial effect on the range of institutions drawn into consideration. While some programs such as broadly based M.A. degrees in elementary teaching may be offered at several institutions in a local area, others may only be offered on-campus at a major university.

A student will be likely to travel further or to select a graduate institution based on the quality of its academic program if the labor market distinguishes among schools in the level of economic rewards it provides.[13] Outside of education, for example, M.B.A. recipients from nationally recognized programs can expect to receive a considerable earnings premium over individuals receiving M.B.A.s through an extension program of a comprehensive university. To be sure, considerable debate might well follow about the extent to which this premium reflected "skills" or the "credential," but the key point is that the labor market does perceive a difference. One need not look far to find strong indicators of the link between institutional choice and labor market rewards in such programs. Even among ranked programs, there are sizable differences in average salaries: the median starting salary among M.B.A. recipients from Stanford University, the top-ranked school according to *U.S. News and World Report* in 1996, was $82,000; moving down to just the twenty-fifth ranked school (the University of Maryland at College Park) leads to a drop in the expected starting salary of nearly $30,000 to $53,000 (*U.S. News and World Report*, 1997).

There appears to be little direct, monetary premium for degree quality in the education marketplace. In most districts, the salary increment associated with a postbaccalaureate degree is independent of the quality or the rigor of program awarding the degree. However, there are at least two kinds of "rewards" that have not been considered. First, nonmonetary benefits of training in education certainly resonate with individuals and program selection is likely to reflect such aspects. Second, it may well be true that the education labor market rewards quality through both greater job mobility within districts and greater transferability across districts.

Thus, the nature of the demand among postbaccalaureate students for programs in education reflects two joint decisions: whether to attend full-time or part-time and which school to attend. Such choices are often regarded as simultaneous, as variables affecting one decision will affect the other as well. The problem is modestly complicated by the issue of *location*. If students attend full-time, they can—at least in theory—choose among options at the national level. If students attend part-time, their choice set is dramatically constrained by distance and, to a lesser extent, the availability of various mechanisms for distance learning. This question of how far students will drive (and how frequently) is by no means well-resolved empirically. Nevertheless, the sign of the relationship is unambiguous: as distance (or commuting time) increases, the probability of a student choosing to attend a given school decreases. It is not surprising that institutions involved in postbaccalaureate training in education (as well as their counterparts in other types of postsecondary education serving part-time students) increasingly sound the mantra of realtors: "Location, Location, and Location."

Concluding Comments

The "price" that institutions are able to charge is sharply constrained by what people are able to pay and the extent to which the training they receive will be rewarded in the labor market. While there are certainly real rewards to individuals for obtaining postbaccalaureate training in terms of higher pay grades, such increments are certainly capped and financial rewards rarely vary with the quality of training. In other words, a degree is a degree in many fields. This is notably different from other professional fields in which rewards vary appreciably with the "quality" of the degree.

Institutions certainly take their cues from the labor market, and the policies used to determine both the level and variation in earnings at the district level will shape the offerings of schools of education in the decade to come. Local markets will continue to dominate the provision of broadly based postbaccalaureate degrees, while institutions with a research focus will become ever-more specialized in the types of training they provide. From a policy perspective, a key question is whether the current market provides the best incentives for the preparation of teachers and other education personnel and whether there are also sufficient incentives to encourage exploration of research innovations in teaching and learning.

One complaint often voiced in policy circles is that schools and colleges of education are "unresponsive" to the needs of the public schools and other constituents concerned with improving the delivery of educational services (Lincoln, 1998). Yet, consideration of the rapidly changing dynamics of the market for teacher training, particularly at the M.A. level, provides strong evidence that schools of education do respond to the labor market incentives that affect the decisions of their prospective students. At issue from a policy perspective is whether there is a mismatch between the reward structure for advanced-degree attainment and the type of training for teachers and other educational professionals that will lead to sustained improvement in elementary and secondary education. If so, the appropriate pressure point for public policy is not intervention in schools of education, but a radical restructuring of the incentives in the labor market to reward skill acquisition rather than credentials.

Notes

1. This chapter uses the term *Schools of Education* to refer generally to the academic units in colleges or universities providing training in education related areas and includes colleges of education and departments of education. Tierney (1998) provides a thorough discussion of the range of institutional settings and unit configurations housing faculty of education.

2. A few of the definitions from the Carnegie classification (1994) help to frame this discussion:

Research Universities I: These institutions offer a full range of baccalaureate programs, are committed to graduate education through doctorate, and give high priority to research. They award fifty or more doctoral degrees each year. In addition, they receive annually $40 million or more in federal support. (Research II institutions have lower levels of federal support and are included with doctoral in this analysis.)

Doctoral Universities (I and II): These institutions offer a full range of baccalaureate programs and are committed to graduate education through the doctorate. Doctoral I institutions award at least forty doctoral degrees annually in five or more disciplines [20 or more in II].

Master's (Comprehensive) Universities and Colleges I and II: These institutions offer a full range of baccalaureate programs and are committed to graduate education through the master's degree. They award forty or more master's degrees annually in three or more disciplines [Masters II award 20 or more M.A.s]

Baccalaureate (Liberal Arts) Colleges I: These institutions are primarily undergraduate colleges with major emphasis on baccalaureate degree programs. They award 40 percent or more of their baccalaureate degrees in liberal arts fields and are selective in admissions.

Baccalaureate Colleges II: These institutions are primarily undergraduate colleges with major emphasis on baccalaureate degree programs. They award less than 40 percent of their baccalaureate degrees in liberal arts fields or are less selective in admissions.

3. These institutions are UCLA ($3,042,183), Harvard University ($2,750,000), Stanford University (National Center for Postsecondary Improvement, $2,900,000), University of Washington ($1,499,570), University of Pennsylvania ($3,250,000), University of North Carolina ($2,941,125), University of California, Santa Cruz ($4,086,611), University of Michigan ($2,464,108), SUNY-Albany ($2,500,000), and University of Wisconsin-Madison ($2,500,000). These amounts are based on a review of the U.S. Department of Education's "Grant Awards Action" database (http://web99.ed.gov/grant/grtawd97.nsf/) for fiscal year 1997.

4. Goldin and Katz (1998) discuss the expansion in scope of research universities in the early twentieth century, arguing that the modern research

university is largely defined by substantial complementarities across disciplinary areas and between teaching and research.

5. For-profit or proprietary institutions are among the most aggressive new entrants in this market, with the M.A.-level training offered by the University of Phoenix throughout the southwest serving as a widely cited example.

6. To illustrate, consider the comparison between the University of Virginia and Mary Baldwin College, which aggressively promotes its M.A. offering in teaching in the Charlottesville area. While the Curry School at the University of Virginia has nearly one hundred tenure-track faculty, Mary Baldwin College has only four tenure-track faculty and fills its additional staffing needs through the employment of sixteen individuals classified as teaching faculty.

7. An alternative strategy for such institutions is to replicate the cost structures of their low-cost competitors, effectively segregating these "nontraditional" programs from those relying on the more traditional institutional norms.

8. Of course, the teaching force is not exclusively comprised of women, though we initially focus on this segment of the labor market because women continue to comprise the majority of the labor force of teachers.

9. Ballou and Podgursky (1997) define public school salaries as generally reflecting a grid that is based on experience and education. Only about 12 percent of these districts have provisions for merit pay, with the amounts at stake rarely exceeding 2 percent of base pay.

10. To frame the economic tradeoffs, think of a somewhat (over)simplified example in which an individual in a field like education faces a choice between attending school part-time toward an M.A. over four years while also receiving a salary of $20,000 per year, or attending full-time for two years. After completing the degree, the individual receives a wage premium of $5,000 until retirement at age sixty-five. A comparison case is that of an M.B.A. student who is promised a wage premium of $25,000 on receiving the degree. In the first case, the net present value of the decision to attend part-time (not considering the foregone cost of leisure) will be greater than the net present value of attending full-time. In the case of the M.B.A., the net present value of attending full-time will likely exceed the value of attending part-time because the "cost" of waiting the extra two years to receive the earnings premium is greater than the value of the foregone earnings stream while attending school.

11. Within these fields, there seems to be a positive correlation between the magnitude of the earnings premium and attending full-time. It is not altogether clear whether this is a selection effect or an indication that full-time students are likely to "learn more" through undivided study time and greater peer interaction.

12. In nearly all studies of the association between the degree attainment of teachers and student outcomes, there is no significant effect of teacher education on student performance (Hanushek, 1996). Still, a range of research studies including Ehrenberg and Brewer (1994) find that indirect measures of teacher characteristics such as quality of undergraduate institution and test scores are related to student outcomes.

13. For example, Ehrenberg (1989) finds that an increase in the rank of a graduate school approximately equal to a quintile among graduate schools leads to a predicted increase in starting salaries of about 6 percent after controlling for individual characteristics such as LSAT scores.

References

Ballou, D. & Podgursky, M. (1997). *Teacher Pay and Teacher Quality.* W. E. Upjohn Institute for Employment Research.

Bowen, W. G. & Rudenstine, N. (1992). *In Pursuit of the PhD.* Princeton: Princeton University Press.

Carnegie Foundation for the Advancement of Teaching. (1994). "A Classification of Institutions of Higher Education: A Technical Report." Princeton, NJ.

Ehrenberg, R. (1989). "An Economic Analysis of the Market for Law School Students." *Journal of Legal Education,* 39(5).

———. & Brewer, D. (1994). "Do School and Teacher Characteristics Matter? Evidence from "High School and Beyond." *Economics of Education Review,* 13(1), 1–17.

Goldin, C. & Katz, L. (1999). "The Shaping of Higher Education: The Formative Years in the United States, 1890–1940." *Journal of Economic Perspectives,* 13(1), 37–62.

Hanushek, E. (1996). "School Resources and Student Performance." In G. Burtless (ed.), *Does Money Matter?* Brookings.

Hoxby, C. (1997). "How the Changing Market Structure of U.S. Higher Education Explains College Tuition." *Mimeo.*

Lincoln, Y. (in press). "Resisting Reform: Tenure, Productivity and the Public School Crisis." In W. G. Tierney (ed.), *Faculty Work in Schools of Higher Education.* State University of New York Press.

Loeb, S. & Page, M. (1997). "Examining The Link between Wages and Quality in the Teacher Workforce: The Role of Alternative Labor Market Opportunities and Non-Pecuniary Variance." *Mimeo.*

Tierney, W. G. (in press). "Faculty of Education in a Period of Systematic Reform." In W. G. Tierney (ed.), *Faculty Work in Schools of Higher Education.* State University of New York Press.

Turner, S. E. & Bowen, W. G. (1990). "The Flight from the Arts and Sciences: Trends in Degrees Conferred." *Science*, 250.

U.S. Department of Education, National Center for Education Statistics. Various years. Higher Education General Information Survey (HEGIS), Degrees and Other Formal Awards Conferred surveys.

U.S. News & World Report. (1997). "Ranking of Graduate Programs in Education." <http://www4.usnews.com/usnews/edu/beyond/gdmbat1.htm>.

CHAPTER 6

Clinical Faculty in Schools of Education

Using Staff Differentiation to Address Disparate Goals

JAMES C. HEARN AND MELISSA S. ANDERSON

Schools of education have been buffeted in recent years by a variety of forces from within and outside their institutions. Budgetary pressures have tightened funding for traditional tenure-track faculty lines, even in the face of increasing faculty retirement rates. Legislators, business leaders, and other external observers have questioned the accountability of higher education to the larger public and, more bluntly, the utility of what is studied and taught in colleges and universities. Lampooned as out of touch with the nation's educational needs, education schools have been asked to accommodate to state initiatives favoring alternative teacher and administrator certification paths downplaying the role of courses and degrees in education. Violence, slumping test scores, and attrition in the nation's schools have created public pressures for solving pressing educational problems quickly. Inside universities, education schools have rarely fared well in campuswide strategic planning efforts, frequently finding themselves among the prime candidates for downsizing or closure.[1] Finally, although the traditional tenure system continues to serve many critical purposes, many institutional leaders associate it with substantial constraints on the flexible management of human resources.

Together, these forces have led schools of education in a variety of directions: toward more ambitious internal strategic planning, renewed engagement with external constituencies, expanded fund-raising efforts, aggressive retrenchment of programs and personnel, contracts with retired faculty for instruction and advising, and the implementation of early retirement plans, the "mortgaging" of faculty positions to aid timely recruiting of needed faculty, more hires of part-time faculty,[2] and the initiation of new employment categories for faculty.

It is this last trend that compels our attention in this paper. Across all disciplines, there has been remarkable growth in the hiring of faculty who are not on the traditional tenure track. U.S. Department of Education data (cited in Benjamin, 1998) suggest that 28 percent of all full-time postsecondary faculty in 1993 were not eligible for tenure, either because their institutions did not grant it or because they were on nontenurable appointments. This percentage was appreciably higher than that for the mid-1970s, and there is evidence that growth rates for this kind of position have increased in the 1990s (also see Baldwin et al., 1993; Gappa, 1996).[3] The trend is especially pronounced in professional fields, and recent research on faculty hiring patterns reveals that schools of education are among the leaders on campus in the hiring of faculty not on the traditional tenure track (Gappa, 1996).

Staff differentiation is an increasingly noteworthy response to demands that contemporary education schools address disparate goals with limited resources. Although staff differentiation can take many forms, we are especially interested here in education schools' use of clinical faculty positions.

What precisely do we mean by "clinical"? Among university faculty in counseling, business, law, social work, and the health professions, the term "clinical" commonly connotes a discipline's relevant domain of practice outside the university's walls (Warner, Houston, & Cooper, 1977; Gappa, 1996). The most prominent example is in university medical schools. There, "clinical faculty" are physicians who regularly see patients through university-affiliated facilities. They are thus easily distinguishable from research-oriented faculty with no active medical practice. In general, clinical faculty positions in research universities may be contrasted directly with traditional professorships in that they are more oriented to practice than to research.[4]

This linking of the term *clinical* and the larger field of practice holds in education, as well. Although the term has been used in a variety of ways in schools of education in universities, clinical faculty typically have experience as teachers or administrators in schools and school systems, are asked to draw on that practical experience in their teaching of university students, and are expected to nurture ties between schools of education and their external constituencies. In education as in other fields, clinical faculty are usually not expected to produce scholarly research on their own and are not on a tenure track.

There is one notable difference between clinical faculty in education and those in some other fields. In health-related fields, in particular, clinical faculty often receive significant financial rewards from the patient care that defines their clinical status, with salaries that surpass what they would earn as nonclinical faculty. In education, by contrast, a clinical faculty member at a university is likely to be relatively disadvantaged financially, given the critical importance of research as a criterion for pay and other rewards. This consistent salary disadvantage makes the clinical title in education less than perfectly analogous to the same title in other fields.

It is in the research universities that clinical faculty positions in education are most noteworthy, because it is in such settings that norms among other education faculty tend to deviate most starkly from a clinical orientation. That is, clinical education faculty in such settings form a distinctive group within schools where most faculty are asked to pursue scholarly research as well as teaching and service. Outside of the research universities, and especially in less selective colleges with sizable enrollments in education, education faculty have always been "clinical" in many respects.[5] That is, in such institutions an emphasis on teaching and collaboration with local and regional school systems lessens the likelihood that faculty will do significant amounts of research. Instead, they use their familiarity and relationships with school systems to enhance their teaching and to contribute to ongoing projects in the schools.

The notion of clinical faculty positions in university schools of education is by no means new, but debate over this approach has become more animated in recent years, and acceptance, formalization, and institutionalization of the idea may be growing. With that in mind, we undertook to examine the clinical initiative for this essay. As relative newcomers to this arena, we sought to buttress our understanding of the issues in two ways: systematically reviewing the literature on clinical faculty and interviewing individuals having experience with clinical faculty appointments and/or scholarly expertise regarding the topic.

We found the literature on clinical faculty strikingly thin overall and far more hortatory than scholarly on the whole. In this respect, we agree with the conclusions of Cornbleth and Ellsworth, who noted (1994, p. 67) that the literature:

> tends to be of two types. First, there are brief "bulletin-board" type program summaries in such publications as *The Holmes Group Forum*. Second, there have been a few more comprehensive reports published in teacher-education journals and/or available in ERIC microfiche. In general, these reports tend to be celebratory in tone and limited in details regarding the actual (as opposed to intended) activities, roles, and relationships of clinical faculty.

Lacking an empirically rich literature base, we found the comments and insights of our interview subjects especially helpful, particularly as we developed the inferences and recommendations that appear at the end of this paper. Our approach was determined by the limited time and other resources available to us. We identified three research universities with experience in developing clinical professorships in education, then interviewed five clinical faculty members at those institutions. Also, following leads from our literature review and suggestions by early interviewees, we interviewed nine people with leadership experience or scholarly expertise on clinical education faculty. This pool included nonclinical faculty members in education at four research universities, deans or associate deans at two research universities, and an officer of a prominent national professional association involved in clinical-faculty issues.

In this essay, we first investigate the history and rationale for clinical positions, then consider their present status, their varied forms, and the limited available evidence regarding their effectiveness. The essay concludes with recommendations for policy makers, administrators, and faculty interested in initiating or improving clinical positions.

Historical Background

Clinical initiatives in university schools of education stem from two general sources: parallel efforts in other professional schools and the writings of educational theorists.

Emergence of the Clinical Idea in Professional Schools

Early professors in law, medical, and education schools tended to be veterans of practice and latecomers to academic life. There was an uproar in 1873 at Harvard law school when a recent graduate with no legal experience was appointed to the faculty (Auerbach, 1971). The appointment was unprecedented. Nevertheless, as the notion of the academic career grew in professional schools and the research ethos overtook the U.S. university, professorships became a viable choice for new and talented professional-school graduates. Expectations that professors should first spend lengthy periods working in the field declined. Reward systems tilted toward scholarship and away from "the wisdom of practice" that had energized early faculty (Veysey, 1965).

With this trend as background, university medical schools began to see reasons to authorize clinical faculty positions that were formally separated from more research-oriented positions. After all, the economic viability and educational effectiveness of university hospitals often depended as much on clinical services as on research funding, if not more, and such services constituted a competitive and professional arena vastly different from that of research activity. Over time, notable differences in values, attitudes, and teaching practices have arisen between medical-school faculty in the basic sciences and those in clinical lines. Notably, "Medically qualified professors identify less with the academic profession (with university professors in the basic sciences, for example), looking instead to other physicians in the community as a preferred local reference group" (Clifford & Guthrie, 1988, p. 96).

Interestingly, the medical example has been of limited immediate applicability to schools of education. For one thing, in contrast to the pattern in education schools, clinical faculty in medical schools are generally better paid than other faculty. More fundamentally, while medical schools have been allowed by their host institutions to structure different faculty roles and institutionalize those roles, education schools in universities historically have been unable even to gain approval of a separate clinical track, much less develop firm alternative value and reward systems (Clifford & Guthrie, 1988, p. 256). Education faculties have historically been less differentiated than faculties of medical schools, even on the same campus.

Such an undifferentiated faculty configuration would seem to imply vulnerability for a professional school in a research-oriented institution, but university law schools provide an instructive example to the contrary. Clinical positions are rather rare in those schools, so one would expect research norms to be prominent there. Yet it appears that many such schools have successfully established an alternative to formally structuring clinical positions: endorsing clinical norms within traditionally structured faculty positions. For example, very few law faculty publish at the rates expected of faculty in other university units (Swygert & Gozansky, 1985), but law faculty appear to pay no price for their apostasy from the research norm. Despite their lower scholarly productivity, many are at the full professor level, and they are accorded appreciably more status and power than education faculty with comparable records (Clifford & Guthrie, 1988). As Clifford and Guthrie note (1988, p. 222) in regard to the situation as of the mid-1980s, "The rules clearly were different according to who was playing the game." Law schools have apparently been able to embrace clinical norms without establishing formal clinical tracks.

The medical and law examples suggest that education faculty in research universities often work within the worst possible context for serving clinical needs: an absence of alternative faculty lines (as in medical schools) and an absence of a professional environment welcoming of clinical orientations within traditional faculty lines (as in law schools). Many tenured and tenure-track faculty in schools of education have eschewed research and continued to pursue interests in teaching and service to the field, of course, but have done so at some risk to their careers, advancement, and salary increments. With all faculty positions in university schools of education similarly structured, and with no underlying acceptance of clinical norms by senior peers and administrators, there is little incentive for individual faculty to attend to alternative, less scholarly goals. To do so may have career-stalling, or even career-threatening, implications.

The Clinical Theme in Education

Around the turn of the century, many school systems, the National Education Association, John Dewey (1904), and others advocated the laboratory-school concept for university schools of education, that is, the establishment of institutionally affiliated elementary and secondary schools. The rationales for such schools inevitably centered on the need to connect teacher preparation to practice, but the logic of the advocates varied significantly. Dewey argued that "Only the scientific aim . . . can furnish a reason for the maintenance by a university of an elementary school. It is not a normal school or a department for the training of teachers. It is not a model school. It is not intended to demonstrate any one special idea or doctrine."[6] Thus Dewey did not see a direct service or didactic role for such schools. Other advocates disagreed, arguing that requiring education majors to work in such settings would serve as a necessary supplement to the theories and ideas being taught in their university courses.

Resistance to the lab-school concept was often strong in research universities, mainly because lab schools were viewed as unrepresentative of the research ideal on those campuses. To the extent that they were viewed as practice-oriented rather than experimental and scientific, their survival was threatened. In the longer-term, their fate on such campuses depended upon their integration into the broader scholarly goals of their host institutions (Clifford & Guthrie, 1988). Few met that challenge, and virtually none survive today.

In the 1950s, the impulse to link practice and teacher education emerged in other forms. There were numerous recommendations for involving classroom teachers more directly in teacher education on university campuses (Cornbleth & Ellsworth, 1994). Interestingly, the term "clinical professor" was first used in education in 1962 by Professor Robert Bush of Stanford to describe a "highly skilled classroom teacher with whom a group of trainees would be placed and who, in addition, would be accorded the status of clinical professor by the teacher preparation institution" (cited in Kazlov, 1976, p. 340). Around the same time, James Conant (1963) defined the clinical professor in somewhat broader fashion than Bush: "a special type of college or university-level teacher educator, a professorial position with qualifications which included in-depth knowledge and skill both in subject matter and pedagogy."[7] Conant, a former Harvard president and a science and education adviser to several U.S. Presidents, was a very visible national figure at the time, so his argument for instituting clinical professorships in education helped bring the issue to the fore. In the ensuing years, debate continued around both definitions and policy.[8] With attention to the clinical concept growing, the Carnegie Corporation of New York funded a conference at Northwestern University in 1966 on the topic (see Hazard, 1967).

In the 1970s, there was still little consensus on the need for or value of clinical appointments, beyond a broad agreement that clinical faculty could provide a useful link between university instruction and teaching practice in elementary and secondary schools (Warner, Houston, & Cooper 1977). Ten years after the publication of Conant's call for clinical faculty, the first national survey concerned with implementation of the clinical professor concept found that "there was little agreement on the role of the clinical professor and that many of the 879 institutions surveyed were in doubt as to whether they qualified for the survey" (Kazlov, 1976, p. 340). Many institutions used the term as a title for any college faculty member responsible for supervising student teachers, while others used the term for "a practicing teacher whose services are purchased by the institution on a part-time basis" (Warner, Houston, & Cooper, 1977, p. 16).

The ambiguities and stagnation persisted into the early 1980s. In a review of the field as of that time, Cornbleth and Ellsworth (1994) found little evidence of implementation of Conant's formal clinical-faculty concept. They attribute that pattern to declining enrollments in K–12 education, declining numbers of students in teacher-education programs, budget cuts in schools and universities, and faculty retrenchment on campus.

In the later 1980s, however, attention to clinical issues reemerged. A significant impetus for the development of clinical faculty positions came from the Holmes Group (1986, 1990, 1995), a consortium of reform-minded deans of major schools of education. Holmes members proposed the formation of university-school partnerships and expanded roles for classroom teachers in teacher education (Cornbleth & Ellsworth, 1994). In keeping with those recommendations, schools of education in the 1980s increasingly experimented with "Professional Development Schools," entities designed to improve (1) preservice education of teachers, (2) professional development of experienced teachers, and (3) research collaboration between K–12 teachers and university faculty (Bullough et al., 1997). As initially conceived years earlier, "PDS" efforts provided university appointments for schoolteachers.[9] The PDS concept came to be defined and implemented in the 1980s in a wider variety of ways, ranging from schools where future teachers honed their skills in the final stages of their preparation to centers where experienced teachers come together for in-service education (Dittmer & Fischetti, 1996).[10]

The Holmes Group and other reformers of the 1980s envisioned that PDS efforts would require the use of clinical faculty. As a result, there arose a close association between such efforts and clinical professorships in education. Because the very visible Holmes recommendations encouraged the hiring of clinical faculty in the service of the PDS concept, many contemporary education-school faculty associate the concept of clinical faculty with the PDS movement. It should be noted, however, that the Holmes reports generally used a rather narrow notion of the clinical concept: teacher-education programs' appointments of tenured schoolteachers as university faculty.

Clinical Faculty in the Contemporary Era

There exist virtually no data on the recent prevalence or growth of clinical faculty positions in U.S. schools of education. Abdal-Haqq (1995) provides a useful institution-by-institution summary of initiatives and some summary data, but his coverage is limited to PDS efforts and largely ignores clinical initiatives outside of teacher-education programs. To our knowledge, no individual or organization has attempted to survey the domain on a systematic or regular basis.[11] Sadly, there is also little hard evidence on the benefits, risks, effectiveness, costs, and efficiency of contemporary clinical initiatives in education. This appears to be an arena abundant in opinion but sorely lacking in solid research findings. There are, however, three noteworthy themes apparent in the available empirical literature.

First, the PDS movement has been a prime contributor to new staffing patterns on campus, including the use of clinical faculty. Such was the case at the University of Utah. That institution was among the first to implement the clinical faculty concept in teacher education in concert with the PDS movement. In 1986, only one of thirty-four full-time faculty members in the Department of Educational Studies was on a non-tenure-track clinical appointment, but by 1996 twelve of thirty-five full-time faculty were in clinical positions (Bullough et al., 1997).

Second, clinical faculty are becoming increasingly important in education programs beyond teacher education. As noted earlier, the PDS movement has focused on the preservice education of teachers, and the clinical faculty movement in education has also generally focused on that aspect of schools of education. There are other venues for clinical positions, however. Once again, the University of Utah was a pioneer, developing in this case clinical-faculty efforts for administrator preparation. In 1991, a symposium at the annual meeting of the University Council on Educational Administration focused on the university's new initiative in this arena (Pounder et al., 1991). Primary among the purposes of this initiative at Utah was a desire to link theory and practice more effectively. Also important in the new efforts were a desire to separate the Ed.D. and Ph.D. degrees at Utah and a desire to help meet demands of students and prospective employers. A similar rationale lay behind efforts along the same lines at the University of Minnesota in the early 1990s.

Third, there is extraordinary variation among clinical faculty nationwide. The following list presents dimensions along which our review of the literature and our interviews indicated substantial differences in clinical appointments at research universities:

1. *Workload:* Is the position full-time or part-time?[12]
2. *Tenure status:* Is the position on the tenure track? Although most clinical positions are non-tenure-track, the development of differentiated tenure tracks is feasible and has been discussed.
3. *Rank:* Is there a rank gradation among clinical faculty positions (e.g., assistant, associate, full)?
4. *Geographic location:* Is the position based in a particular site away from the university campus, such as another postsecondary campus or a building owned by a school system?
5. *Contractual terms:* Is the position on a fixed-term contract or are arrangements more open-ended?
6. *Evaluation system:* Is there a standardized evaluation system in place for clinical faculty, or are evaluations conducted on an informal, case-by-case basis?
7. *Salary schedule:* Is the salary system standardized across clinical faculty (e.g., uniform yearly increments, perhaps moderated by seniority) or are faculty evaluated individually as to merit in salary awards?
8. *Governance role:* Are clinical faculty granted a role in unit governance by tenure-track, traditional faculty?
9. *Level of instruction and advising:* Are clinical faculty involved with undergraduate students, graduate students, or both?
10. *Role responsibilities:* Are clinical faculty responsible only for teaching, or do they also play leadership roles in their units (e.g., administering a graduate-level cohort program)?
11. *Curricular focus:* Do clinical faculty teach "technical" courses (e.g., school budgeting), or are they also active in generalist courses (e.g., politics of education, educational evaluation)?
12. *Practical experience as a hiring criterion:* Is accumulated practical expertise a primary hiring criterion?
13. *Attention to integration of theory and practice:* Is systematic integration of theory and practice a significant aspect of the responsibilities of the clinical faculty member?
14. *Advising responsibilities:* Is the clinical faculty member allowed to advise master's and doctoral students through the thesis stage?
15. *Community relations:* Do clinical faculty have formal responsibilities for improving the relationships between the university and the larger community?
16. *Joint responsibilities:* Do clinical faculty have formal working responsibilities in other organizations beyond the university, such as schools, school systems, and postsecondary institutions?
17. *Targeted student clientele:* Is the clinical initiative targeted on students interested in K–12 schools alone (e.g., preservice teachers or school administrators) or on students with other interests such as postsecondary and nontraditional settings?

Inferences and Recommendations

Our interviews and literature review suggest three general inferences about clinical faculty positions. First, the potential effects of expanding the use of these positions are numerous. Our respondents and our literature review provided us a long list of possible effects, and we hypothesized some more ourselves. Mortimer et al. (1985) argue that the use of full-time non-tenure-track positions has several advantages: political feasibility (e.g., no removal of the tenure system), absence of potential grounds for AAUP censure, enrichment of academic curriculum, additional flexibility via the absence of future financial and programmatic commitments, attention to activities institutional leaders deem of questionable centrality, and clarity and certainty for all parties regarding the future. In addition, expanded use of clinical faculty may help schools of education serve disparate goals simultaneously; reduce their dependence on transient part-time faculty with no real identification with the institution; focus attention on particular responsibilities in teaching, service, or research; escape the constraints of a tenure-centered staffing system; increase their community responsiveness; expand their reach; promote diversity; improve their program delivery; and reduce their costs of instruction. Adding such positions may also help institutions buffer their tenure-line faculty from external pressures and preserve their autonomy and other professional perquisites.[13] The use of such positions may even help schools more fully serve their stated missions.

The use of such positions may also, however, alienate those in traditional faculty lines, put at risk the considerable benefits of established tenure systems, distract units from core focuses, diminish attention to research and theory,[14] create hierarchical "two-tier" systems among faculty that disturb the sense of unity and community in units, lessen the exposure of students to tenured faculty, complicate administration, decrease the quality of student advising and support,[15] bring into units people with only marginal commitments to ongoing institutional goals, and make units more vulnerable to institutional retrenchments. The addition of such faculty may also provide those tenured faculty who are so inclined an implicit invitation to ignore or downplay issues of practice in their own teaching and research.

Second, the nature of the specific effects of clinical appointments depends in good part on the context in which clinical positions are introduced. There is substantial variation in the implementations of this approach to faculty staffing and in the setting in which it is introduced. Its ultimate effects are probably, therefore, quite situation-specific.

Third, despite the long list of hypothetical effects, too little is known empirically about the implementation, influences, and implications of clinical approaches in education. Because of limited resources and time, our own examination of the use of clinical positions could be neither comprehensive nor rigorous enough to warrant firm conclusions about ultimate benefits and costs, at either the macro or institutional level. Is the investment in such positions a way for schools of education to adapt more effectively, preserving the old virtues while addressing new realities? Or is it one more step in the corruption of a valued and functional staffing system? To put it simply, clinical positions have unclear implications for both quality and efficiency.

Having acknowledged that the clinical orientation can bring both potential gains and potential risks, that in this domain context is all, and that far too little is known about the entire matter, what can we possibly suggest for policy makers, administrators, and faculty interested in initiating or improving clinical-faculty positions? We face two less-than-optimal choices here. We could simply end with the familiar, anticlimactic call for more research. Or we could make recommendations that, because of the absence of that research, may seem banal and obvious. The problem seems important, and our analysis of the issues has given us some initial opinions on what needs to be done. So, whether foolishly or boldly, we proceed here with the latter course:

1. *Learn about the experiences and ideas of others involved in clinical initiatives.* One of the striking findings of our review and interviews is that many institutions move ahead with clinical initiatives without having studied either what has happened before or how others have conceptualized optimal clinical efforts. There is a literature on clinical faculty in education, albeit not a literature built from extensive empirical research, and there are deans and faculty around the country willing to share their insights on the topic. Outside the field of education lies a more developed literature on clinical faculty, and that literature from medicine, law, and other fields provides further insights worth the attention of leaders in education. Education leaders who ignore these sources may increase the risks facing their initiatives.

2. *Formally and rigorously define the terms of clinical-faculty positions in schools of education.* At a minimum, leaders should address appointment length, salary, evaluation, governance role, and supervisory arrangements. Non-tenure-track faculty in general (clinical faculty in education being one of many groups in this category) confront numerous problems. As many as one half of all faculty on U.S. campuses, and over one-fourth of those working full-time, are in untenurable positions, and the employment status of these faculty has become a primary policy concern in the 1990s.[16] Surveys by the American Association of University Professors have revealed a number of problems in the ways these faculty are treated on campus (1993). In response, the AAUP has recommended that institutions provide such faculty formally specified appointment terms, regular

written evaluations, and opportunities to participate in faculty governance (ibid.). More recently, a number of authors have called for the development of differentiated staffing plans to accommodate the emerging differentiation in the roles of university faculty (Chait, 1997).

The clinical faculty appointment, as we have described it here, is still a relatively new phenomenon in schools of education—"a rare bird indeed," in the words of one of our interviewees. Clinical faculty in education are beginning to benefit from the nation's new attention to non-tenure-track faculty, however. At the University of Minnesota, growth in the ranks of clinical faculty in education was a primary impetus for the development of new formal guidelines for various kinds of academic appointments (University of Minnesota College of Education and Human Development, 1997; Associate Dean Carol Boyer, personal communication, December 18, 1997).

Such institutions are realizing that, although clinical and other faculty are alike in many ways, it is critical to make distinctions separating them in terms of responsibilities and expectations. Clinical faculty usually do not vote on promotion and tenure of faculty, often they do not have full graduate-faculty status, and they typically are not responsible for producing research. College and departmental administrators need to address such differences in an open, timely and deliberate way, both with the clinical faculty and with the regular faculty, so that everyone involved will come to something of a common understanding of clinical faculty members' roles. Doing so reduces the ambiguity of clinical positions, a potential source of considerable anxiety and stress.

It is important to stress that institutions may have several kinds of clinical faculty appointments. Clinical faculty may focus on teaching, networking with K–12 schools, administrative responsibilities, action research, or other things. Schools of education should consider a wide range of types of clinical appointments and deliberately configure each one to address the needs of students, programs, faculty, and other constituents. Clinical faculty should not automatically be expected to assume every responsibility that might possibly accompany a clinical appointment; neither should colleges have such a limited conception of the clinical role that they miss the opportunity to configure a clinical appointment in an innovative and productive way.

In view of the different contributions and responsibilities of clinical faculty, it is important for schools of education to develop appropriate standards and processes by which clinical faculty can be evaluated and rewarded. So complicated could this issue become that it might be a primary reason why few institutions have institutionalized the clinical professorship. Our interviewees recommended models that give clinical faculty parallel ranks (e.g., "clinical assistant professor," "clinical associate professor") and parallel promotion crit∍ria (e.g., replacing research with "writing" or "publication" in the expectation that such writing could involve publication for practitioners, or raising expectations for teaching and service loads while lowering requirements for obtaining external funding).

3. *Conduct ongoing analyses of clinical efforts.* A group-level corollary to the preceding item is that schools of education need to acknowledge the capacity of their clinical faculty as a group and monitor their performance as a group. It is not enough simply to define responsibilities and evaluate performance at the individual level. For example, if clinical faculty do not receive full graduate-faculty status, they will be limited in their contributions to advising students and chairing graduate-student committees. Should a department's faculty have too many clinical faculty, it may find itself taking on too many students and too much instruction, without due consideration of the attendant advising and committee-service loads. Similar concerns may be raised about opportunity costs from the potential loss of research funding accompanying investment in clinical rather than traditional faculty lines. Schools of education need to balance the productivity that clinical faculty might make possible against the responsibilities that regular faculty alone can assume.

4. *Structure clinical faculty positions to foster productivity.* Like regular faculty, clinical faculty are likely to have responsibilities in many different arenas of the university. They seem, however, especially susceptible to a dispersion of responsibility and effort because of the ties they are likely to have with many external constituents. Also, in addition to their teaching and service loads, clinical faculty may have significant administrative loads, such as helping direct a cohort of graduate students or coordinating a cooperative venture between the university and school districts. Leaders of the University of Utah's efforts in teacher education have increasingly found that the clinical role is so demanding that people in those positions have great difficulties maintaining their teaching connections in K–12 schools while also playing active roles in their university departments (Bullough et al., 1997). The varied aspects of clinical faculty's responsibilities suggest the importance of clarity in structuring positions.[17] One factor inhibiting productivity is vagueness in appointments, for example, a clinical professor having a joint appointment between two or more university units. Joint appointments involve greater ambiguity of roles, responsibilities, expectations, and evaluative criteria for clinical than for regular faculty. While clinical appointments will often necessarily involve working across units, having a single academic home in one department or unit within the university unquestionably will simplify the difficulties of these appointments.

5. *Structure clinical faculty positions to foster successful recruitment to the role as well as satisfaction in the position.* Those hiring clinical faculty should recognize the nonmonetary factors influencing decisions to take such a position. Nonmonetary factors such as a desire to influence the preparation of educational leaders, the opportunity for change and stimulation, and the opportunity for professional recognition can help attract experienced administrators to clinical positions (Pounder, 1994). Some clinical faculty come to their positions near retirement, after previous careers in teaching or administration. They may view the clinical position as a capstone experience. Others come to the university as midcareer professionals who see clinical positions as part of an evolving accumulation of expertise and experience. Schools of education will be more likely to attract excellent clinical faculty if they are attentive to the career paths of such professionals and support them in ways that will serve them well upon completion of the clinical professorship.

6. *Act to integrate the clinical and scholarly impulses in schools of education.* Specifically, leaders should seek to integrate clinical faculty into university life and to encourage nonclinical faculty to become more involved in issues of practice. According to Bullough et al. (1997), the Utah experience with clinical faculty in teacher education has produced some positive and some negative outcomes. Faculty there generally agree that preservice teacher education is being well served but some clinical faculty perceive themselves as second-class citizens in their department and suggest that their arrival has coincided with a withdrawal of tenure-track faculty from involvement in schools, from the world of practice, and from teacher education.

   While nonclinical faculty have to come to an understanding and appreciation of clinical faculty work, clinical faculty have to be introduced to the world of tenured or tenure-track faculty. Clinical faculty can get caught up in the demand side of graduate programs, perhaps overidentifying with the needs and wants of their student or practitioner clientele without considering the unavoidable limits of the (university's) supply side. Clinical faculty might come to look on regular faculty with resentment, if they see their own teaching loads as heavier, their own work involving more in-office hours, and their rewards lagging behind those of their nonclinical colleagues. Some may come to think that they do the "real work" of educating administrators and teachers. Departments or education schools that make a deliberate effort to introduce clinical faculty to the full range of regular-faculty work experiences, expectations, and responsibilities, while affirming the irreplaceable contributions of clinical faculty, may be able to avoid, or at least ameliorate, such outcomes.

In much of their work, clinical faculty are directly involved with practitioners. One potential problem is that regular faculty will, in a sense, hand off their own responsibility for significant interactions with practitioners to their clinical colleagues. They might do so for what appear to be sensible, appropriate reasons: the clinical faculty are more comfortable working in both worlds (university and schools) and can "do a much better job of it." The result could be practitioners' more limited access to regular faculty, as well as a disjuncture in expectations and *modus operandi* between regular faculty and the students/clinical faculty group. To guard against this possibility, we recommend that schools of education emphasize the linkages between clinical and regular faculty in their interactions with students and other practitioners. They may have different roles, but their roles should be intertwined and complementary.[18]

7. *Acknowledge the professional and political concerns of tenure-track faculty when clinical positions are initiated.* According to Bullough et al. (1997), tenure-track faculty may express reservations about the conceptual knowledge of clinical faculty members and may also express regret over the transformation of faculty lines from tenure-track to clinical. Some of those interviewed for the present essay noted very similar concerns. It is critical that clinical initiatives be fully explained and defended to nonclinical faculty, because without support from that group, and without acknowledgment of their legitimate concerns, effectiveness is sure to be compromised.

8. *Acknowledge the potential benefits of clinical positions.* The community ties and special linkage-building capabilities of clinical faculty are among the primary resources they bring to universities. Such faculty have a capacity to improve programs internally and externally by bridging the university/community divide. Our interviewees noted again and again the valuable contributions that clinical faculty can make, focusing particularly on the fact that clinical faculty's *recent* administrative or teaching experience brings "real credibility" and "the reality of the practitioner world" to programs in education. The advantage of clinical faculty over adjunct faculty in providing a point of contact between the university and practitioner worlds is their relative permanence and their ongoing commitment to both spheres. Programs that adopt the clinical-professorship model could use it to attract students into their programs.

In fact, some of our interviewees noted the critical role that clinical faculty can play in admissions of graduate students. As they become well-known in the schools and other educational organizations as ambassadors for the university, they become an important link for prospective students and the university faculty. Students may even decide to enter a particular graduate program because they know or have worked with a particular clinical faculty member. Further, clinical faculty members can play an important role on admissions committees by using their familiarity with the extra-university community to interpret candidates' personal statements and lists of experiences. As one interviewee put it, they have "instinct for how candidates would fit into graduate work."

Clinical faculty can also help in a broader way by connecting students' work to "real-world" concerns. At the University of Utah, one effect of the initiative in hiring clinical faculty in educational administration was the production of student theses that directly affected school or system policies in the state (Pounder, 1995). To the extent student theses relate effectively to pressing policy and practice concerns, they can affect policy and practice. Surely, that is a benefit to be pursued.

9. *Be sensitive to compositional disparities.* There may be potential for clinical faculty ranks to become more diverse in racial/ethnic and gender composition than the ranks of traditional faculty (see Gappa, 1996). Certainly, across the United States, the pool of those who have valuable experience in schools and school systems is increasingly diverse. Of course, diversity among university faculty is to be praised. However, achieving diversity in clinical positions may deflect institutions from feeling a need to hire diverse faculty in nonclinical lines. Several observers commented to us that they worried about that possibility, and about the prospect of clinical faculties becoming the main or only home for minority and female voices in some units.

10. *Consider clinical initiatives in strategic terms.*[19] The hiring and continuation of clinical faculty must be considered part of the larger strategic posture of a school of education. Clinical faculty are often asked to serve roles that are critical to the financial and educational fates of departments and schools. In pure enrollment and tuition terms, they may be central to units' success, especially when research funding is not robust. Yet, clinical faculty are sometimes viewed by tenured faculty as peripheral actors in achieving an education school's mission, and some tenured faculty see clinical faculty as occupying lower rungs in their schools' stratification systems. In such a context, facing facts about the role of clinical faculty is not only a needed step toward greater fairness but also a sensible step toward more effective strategic planning.

As a school or department addresses the role of its clinical initiatives, it inevitably must examine in concert the cumulative strategic risks of clinical faculty hiring over time. Often, clinical hires are made incrementally. That is, such hires may take place as a need arises, and sometimes as leaders recognize the unlikelihood of obtaining a regular faculty line in a given area. Over time, a department or college may find itself with a sizable cadre of clinical faculty, without ever having planned such a development, or considered its ramifications. Notably, the existence of large numbers of clinical faculty may make units especially vulnerable to the actions of a cost-cutting provost. Thus, the hiring of clinical faculty on a case-by-case basis may make infinitely good sense, but in the larger, "macro" sense such hires may cumulatively represent a regrettable error by a college or department.

11. *Build the literature.* There is a pressing need for more publicly available work on the clinical initiative in schools of education, especially for work that goes beyond the hortatory into actual empirical analyses of effectiveness. Likely to be of special use are examinations of (1) the effects of clinical faculty appointments on other aspects of education schools, such as curriculum, emphasis on research, the careers of other faculty, reward systems, contractual arrangements, and so forth; and (2) the benefits and costs of full-time appointments for clinical faculty. Some schools around the country have had to plunge into clinical initiatives without the benefit of learning of the experiences of others. After all, uncertainty can stall worthwhile efforts needlessly. It would be inappropriate, though, if those who innovate in this area did not produce a knowledge base available to all. For the most part, universities do not compete with each other across state lines for students in teacher education and educational administration. There is no reason for information on successes and failures in this domain to remain private and unpublished. If all involved treat the clinical initiative as something of a national experiment with results to be shared communally, the benefits would far outweigh the costs.

Conclusion

Responding to the clinical impulse in university schools of education is in some respects an act of courage. Education schools in research-oriented institutions often seek to weaken their connections to practice and become more "academic" in their research and teaching. In doing so, they tend to emulate faculty in other, more established behavioral and social-science fields, especially psychology. The result is configurations and activities often derivative of those other fields, with the consequence that education schools continue to suffer from relegation to second-tier status on campus.

Suggesting that this pattern is linked to an ongoing syndrome of intellectual ambivalence, weak technology, and muddled mission, Clifford and Guthrie (1988) argue that education schools' traditional strategies of appeasement and accommodation should be abandoned. Schools should seek instead:

to identify a . . . professional purpose which will strengthen American education, then align education school activities in a manner consistent with that
course of action. Continual attempts to compensate, supplicate, and accommodate higher status opinion on university campuses waste time and siphon en-
ergy from the more important task of preparing teachers and other professional
educators in the most effective and professionally enhancing fashion possible.
(p. 341)

Clifford and Guthrie argue that schools of education should begin "taking the profession of education, not academia, as their main point of reference" (p. 349). Among the tactics stressed by those authors for achieving that
goal are improving external relations; aligning internally to prevent parochi-
alism, insularity, and self-regard; and promoting interaction among colleagues.
Although clinical faculty are not among the major concerns of Clifford and
Guthrie, each of these themes is in keeping with the results of our analysis.
The nurturing of close contacts with external communities is a core element
in the rationale for clinical positions, and the mixing of faculty in various
roles with each other seems to require careful attention in light of the difficulties
encountered in departments with many clinical faculty.

The risk in so fully embracing the professional-school model, and in the
attendant use of clinical faculty, is that the results may be seen as simply
confirming the initial doubts of others about the necessity and appropriate-
ness of schools of education in research universities. Given the less-than-
optimal outcomes of earlier years' efforts in this direction by education schools,
it is not unlikely that schools may orient themselves more aggressively to the
world of school practice but fail in their efforts to address the real needs of
schools. The possibilities of failure may be just as great for those who choose
the practice orientation as for those who choose an orientation to traditional
scholarship in the social sciences.

The consequences of either choice can be dire. On the one hand, education programs at numerous research universities (e.g., Duke, Michigan) were
closed or substantially retrenched in the 1970s and 1980s because of a perceived orientation to questions of practice at the expense of research funding
and scholarly productivity. On the other hand, research-oriented education
programs have also been hit hard in recent years. Most recently, events at the
University of Chicago attest to the difficulties faced by education schools that
are heavily oriented to research. It was there that John Dewey sought so
famously to meld theory and practice in the laboratory school he founded.
After the university closed its education department in 1997, "insiders and
outsiders [contended] that the decline started in the late 70's when Chicago's
education department stopped its day-to-day involvement with teacher training and schools, devoting itself more purely to theory" (Bronner, 1997, p.
A21).

Thus, the clinical impulse itself may be risky, but so are the alternatives. It appears that the very existence of education schools on research-university campuses is an iffy thing, and appropriate strategies for survival and success are surely debatable. Our conclusion from this review is that, if schools are to pursue a clinical orientation in their faculty appointments and their activities, they should do so only after focused deliberation and attentive planning.

Such a conclusion could be justifiably dismissed as obvious and superficial were it not for the fact that the analytic approach has not been typical in this arena. Entering this exploration, we expected to find a robust literature and active debates about clinical faculty. Instead we found that many institutions have moved ahead on these positions without substantial attention to literature and have implemented and evaluated their efforts without sharing their conclusions in published form. Perhaps these developments are a function of the current fiscal environment, or of the heavy demands on those involved, or of the nature of the reward systems under which faculty and administrators traditionally operate. Whatever the reason, there can be little question that there is a need now for systematic attention to the topic. We have a rich legacy of abstract and hypothetical rumination about clinical faculty positions, but no great legacy of empirical work on them. Admittedly, clinical positions assume enough distinct forms to challenge any researcher. Still, the need for "cartographers" and "classifiers" of the domain is great, as is the need for reporters and experimentalists. We hope this paper might prompt at least a start along those lines.

Acknowledgments

The authors gratefully acknowledge the diligent research assistance of Sharon Hodge and Janet M. Holdsworth, the very helpful comments of those we interviewed for this project, a very useful critical review by Betty Malen, and the insightful observations of colleagues involved in Bill Tierney's April 1998 invitational seminar in San Diego.

Notes

1. In a recent, highly visible case, the University of Chicago's department of education, founded by John Dewey, was selected for closure (Bronner, 1997).

2. According to the U.S. Department of Education, between 1987 and 1995 the proportion of part-time faculty rose from 34 to 41 percent (*Chronicle of Higher Education*, 1998). Gappa (1996) suggests schools of education are among the leaders in hiring part-timers.

3. Interestingly, there appear to be differences by institutional type and gender in rates of nontenurable appointments (Benjamin, 1998; Baldwin et al., 1993; Gappa, 1996): private institutions seem to be home to much of the growth in nontenurable positions, and women are far more likely than men to be found in those positions.

4. In Gappa's (1996) across-discipline typology of nontenurable faculty, clinical faculty would tend to fall under the domains of "teaching appointments" and appointments as "professors of practice."

5. A further word about this essay's scope: we do not consider here what are typically called "adjunct" university faculty or other affiliated faculty who have no regular teaching, advising, or community responsibilities. In most cases, our scope also would not include those who have responsibilities limited to teaching alone (i.e., staff most often termed "instructors," "instructional faculty," or "lecturers").

6. Cited in Clifford and Guthrie, 1988, p. 275.

7. Cited in Warner and Houston, 1977, p. 16.

8. Some faculty published stinging indictments of the clinicalization in schools of education, often along the line that the wholesale adoption of a clinical orientation in schools of education would kill any pretense to scholarship in such units as well as any hope that they could foster real educational improvement (see Walton, 1971).

9. See Bolster (1967) for some early thoughts on such efforts. Also see the comments of John Goodlad cited in Maidment (1967).

10. This differentiation in the interpretation of a key reform concept is reminiscent of the controversies surrounding the old laboratory schools, discussed earlier.

11. Of course, the extreme differentiation in the use of the term "clinical" imperils from the start the usefulness of any survey of that kind.

12. Although this paper and most other sources assume full-time status for clinical faculty, that approach is not universal.

13. This perspective fits into Meyer and Rowan's (1978) observation that educational institutions often act to protect their technical cores (especially the teaching and learning activities of their permanent faculty) from external authorities seeking oversight and accountability. Whether the potential for clinical faculty to help preserve the autonomy of tenured faculty is a good or bad thing may be a matter for debate.

14. See Labaree (1995).

15. See Benjamin (1998) for a more elaborate discussion of this risk.

16. American Association of University Professors (1993).

17. See Baldwin et al. (1993) for a perceptive discussion of some of the special stresses of nontenurable appointments.

18. This may be overly optimistic, some of our colleagues suggest. The particulars of such efforts clearly deserve more thought.

19. We are indebted to David Breneman, Yvonna Lincoln, and Sarah E. Turner for insightful comments on this aspect of our essay.

References

Abdal-Haqq, I. (1995). *Professional Development Schools: A Directory of Projects in the United States*, 2nd ed. Washington, DC: American Association of Colleges for Teacher Education.

———. (1996). "An Information Provider's Perspective on the Professional Development School Movement." *Contemporary Education*, 67, 237–240.

American Association of University Professors [AAUP]. (July–August 1993). Report: "The Status of Non-Tenure-Track Faculty." *Academe*, 79(4), 39–46.

Auerbach, J. S. (1971). "Enmity and Amity: Law Teachers and Practitioners, 1900–1922." *Perspectives in American History*, 5, 551–601.

Baldwin, R. G. et al. (1993). "Destination Unknown: An Exploratory Study of Full-Time Faculty off the Tenure Track." *Research in Higher Education*, 34(6), 747–761.

Benjamin, E. (1998). "Declining Faculty Availability Is the Problem—But Tenure Is Not the Explanation." *American Behavioral Scientist*, 41(5), 716–735.

Bolster, A. S. (1967). "The Clinical Professorship: An Institutional View." In W. R. Hazard (ed.), *The Clinical Professorship in Teacher Education: Report of a Conference at Northwestern University in Cooperation with the Carnegie Corporation of New York*. (ERIC Document Reproduction No. ED 026 291.)

Bronner, E. (1997 September). "End of Chicago's Education School Stirs Debate." *New York Times*, A21.

Bullough, R. V. et al. (1997). "Long-Term PDS Development in Research Universities and the Clinicalization of Teacher Education." *Journal of Teacher Education*, 48(2), 85–95.

Buttery, T. J., Henson, K. T., Ingram, T. E., & Smith, C. (1986). "The Teacher in Residence Partnership Program." *Action in Teacher Education*, 7(4), 63–66.

Case, C. W., Norlander, K. A., & Reagan, T. G. (1993). "Cultural Transformation in an Urban Professional Development Center: Policy Implications for School-University Collaboration." *Education Policy*, 7(1), 40–60.

Chait, R. (1997). "Thawing the Cold War over Tenure: Why Academe Needs More Employment Options." *Chronicle of Higher Education*, February 7, pp. B4–B5.

Chronicle of Higher Education. (August 28, 1998). *Chronicle Almanac Issue*, 45(1), 29.

146   JAMES C. HEARN AND MELISSA S. ANDERSON

Clark, R. W. (1996). "Professional Development Schools." *Contemporary Education*, 67, 244–248.

Clifford, G. J. & Guthrie, J. W. (1988). *Ed School: A Brief for Professional Education*. Chicago: University of Chicago Press.

Collier, R. E. & Collins, J. F. (1967). "Plans for Joint Appointees: Montgomery County and the University Of Maryland." In W. R. Hazard (ed.), *The Clinical Professorship in Teacher Education: Report of a Conference at Northwestern University in Cooperation with the Carnegie Corporation of New York*. (ERIC Document Reproduction No. ED 026 291.)

Conant, J. B. (1963). *The Education of American Teachers*. New York: McGraw-Hill.

———. (1967). "Joint Appointees as Supervisors of Practice Teaching: A Summary." In W. R. Hazard (ed.), *The Clinical Professorship in Teacher Education: Report of a Conference at Northwestern University in Cooperation with the Carnegie Corporation of New York*. (ERIC Document Reproduction No. ED 026 291.)

Cornbleth, C. & Ellsworth, J. (1994). "Teachers in Teacher Education: Clinical Faculty Roles and Relationships." *American Educational Research Journal*, 31(1), 49–70.

Darling-Hammond, L. (1994). *Professional Development Schools: Schools for Developing a Profession*. New York: Teachers College, Columbia University.

Dewey, J. (1904). "The Relation of Theory to Practice in Education." Reprinted in M. L. Borrowman (ed.) (1965). *Teacher Education in America: A Documentary History*. New York: Teachers College Press.

Dittmer, A. & Fischetti, J. (1996). "A 'No Recipe' Approach to PDS." *Contemporary Education*, 67, 221–225.

Fullan, M. G. (1995). "The Limits and the Potential of Professional Development." In T. R. Guskey and M. Huberman (eds.), *Professional Development in Education: New Paradigms and Practices*. New York: Teacher College Press.

Gappa, J. M. (1996). "Off the Tenure Track: Six Models for Full-Time, Nontenurable Appointments." *Working Paper Series on Faculty Roles and Rewards, Inquiry #10*, American Association for Higher Education. Washington, DC: American Association for Higher Education.

Goodlad, J. (1990). *Teachers for Our Nation's Schools*. San Francisco: Jossey-Bass.

Granito, J. A. (1967). "A State-Wide View of the Clinical Professorship." In W. R. Hazard (ed.), *The Clinical Professorship in Teacher Education: Report of a Conference at Northwestern University in Cooperation with the Carnegie Corporation of New York*. (ERIC Document Reproduction No. ED 026 291.)

Hazard, W. R. (1967). "The Tutorial and Clinical Program of Teacher Education at Northwestern University: An Outline of Cooperative Planning and Development." In W. R. Hazard (ed.), *The Clinical Professorship in Teacher Education: Report of a Conference at Northwestern University in Cooperation with the Carnegie Corporation of New York.* (ERIC Document Reproduction No. ED 026 291.)

———— (ed.). (1967). *The Clinical Professorship in Teacher Education: Report of a Conference at Northwestern University in Cooperation with the Carnegie Corporation of New York.* (ERIC Document Reproduction No. 026 291.)

———— & Chandler, B. J. (1972). "The Clinical Professor in Teacher Education." *Phi Delta Kappan*, 53, 370–371.

Holmes Group, The. (1986). *Tomorrow's Teachers: A Report of the Holmes Groups.* East Lansing, MI: Author.

————. (1990). *Tomorrow's Schools: Principles for the Design of Professional Development Schools.* East Lansing, MI: Author.

————. (1995). *Tomorrow's Schools of Education.* East Lansing, MI: Author.

Howey, K. R. (1996). "Revisiting the Purposes of Professional Development Schools." *Contemporary Education*, 67, 180–186.

Kazlov, G. (1976). "Whatever Happened to the Clinical Professor?" *Journal of Teacher Education*, 27, 340–341.

Labaree, D. F. (1995). "A Disabling Vision: Rhetoric and Reality in "Tomorrow's Schools of Education." *Teachers College Record*, 97(2), 166–205.

Levine, M. & Trachtman, R. (1997). *Making Professional Development Schools Work: Politics, Practice, and Policy.* New York: Teachers College, Columbia University.

Love, F. E. et al. (1996). "Evolution of Professional Development Schools." *Contemporary Education*, 67(2), 10–212.

Maidment, R. (1967). "A Prototype of the Clinical Professor in Education." In W. R. Hazard (ed.), *The Clinical Professorship in Teacher Education: Report of a Conference at Northwestern University in Cooperation with the Carnegie Corporation of New York.* (ERIC Document Reproduction No. ED 026 291.)

Maxwell, S. A. (1996). "The Pattern Quilt Metaphor: Revisiting the PDS concept." *Contemporary Education*, 67, 196–199.

Meyer, J. & Rowan, B. (1978). "The Structure of Educational Organizations." In M. W. Meyer and Associates (eds.), *Environments and Organizations.* San Francisco: Jossey-Bass.

Michael, L. S. (1967). "Responsibilities of School Systems for Clinical Experiences." In W. R. Hazard (ed.), *The Clinical Professorship in Teacher Education: Report of a Conference at Northwestern University in*

Cooperation with the Carnegie Corporation of New York. (ERIC Document Reproduction No. ED 026 291.)

Mortimer, K. P., Bagshaw, M., & Masland, A. T. (1985). *Flexibility in Academic Staffing: Effective Policies and Practices.* ASHE-ERIC Higher Education Reports, 1985, Report No. 1. Washington, DC: Association for the Study of Higher Education.

Murray, F. B. (1993). " 'All or None' Criteria for Professional Development Schools." *Educational Policy,* 7(1), 61–73.

Nelson, R. H. (1967). "Administrative Arrangements for the Clinical Professorship." In W. R. Hazard (ed.), *The Clinical Professorship in Teacher Education: Report of a Conference at Northwestern University in Cooperation with the Carnegie Corporation of New York.* (ERIC Document Reproduction No. ED 026 291.)

Nutting, W. C. (1982). "Professional Development Centers: The Utah Experiment." *Phi Delta Kappan,* 63, 394–395.

Petrie, H. G. (ed.). (1995). *Professionalization, Partnership, and Power.* New York: State University of New York Press.

Pounder, D. G. (1994). "Work Incentives to Attract Clinical Faculty." *People and Education,* 2(1), 14–36.

———. (1995). "Theory to Practice in Administrator Preparation: An Evaluation Study." *Journal of School Leadership,* 5, 151–162.

———. et al. (1991). *The University of Utah's Field-Based Doctoral Program: A Multi-Dimensional Approach to Advanced Administrative Preparation.* Proceedings of a symposium of the University Council for Educational Administration. (ERIC Document Reproduction Service ED 341 134.)

Ross, J. (1995). "Professional Development Schools: Prospects for Institutionalization." *Teaching and Teacher Education,* 11, 195–201.

Scannell, D. P. (1996). "Evaluating Professional Development Schools: The Challenge of an Imperative." *Contemporary Education,* 67, 241–243.

Shulman, L. S. (1986). "Those Who Understand: Knowledge Growth in Teaching." *Educational Researcher,* 15(2), 4–14.

Sirotnik, K. A. & Goodlad, J. I. (eds.). (1988). *School-University Partnerships in Action: Concepts, Cases, and Concerns.* New York: Teachers College, Columbia University.

Smith, J. (1995). "Teachers' Work and the Labor Process of Teaching: Central Problematics in Professional Development." In T. R. Guskey & M. Huberman (eds.), *Professional Development in Education: New Paradigms and Practices.* New York: Teachers College Press.

Smith, W. E. (1996). "When PDS Stakeholder Work Together: Reflections on Collaboration and Serendipitous Discoveries in a Preservice Field Experience." *Contemporary Education,* 67, 230–232.

Steffel, N., Breault, R., Weisenback, R., & Pellico, G. (1996). "Reflections on Our Journey: Creating a Community of Learners." *Contemporary Education*, 67, 226–229.

Stevenson, R. B. (1993). "Critically Reflective Inquiry and Administrator Preparation: Problems and Possibilities." *Educational Policy*, 7(1), 96–113.

Stiles, L. (1967). "The Clinical Professor as a Member of the Interdisciplinary Team." In W. R. Hazard (ed.), *The Clinical Professorship in Teacher Education: Report of a Conference at Northwestern University in Cooperation with the Carnegie Corporation of New York*. (ERIC Document Reproduction No. ED 026 291.)

Stoddart, T. (1993). "The Professional Development School: Building Bridges between Cultures." *Educational Policy*, 7(1), 5–23.

Swygert, M. I. & Gozansky, N. E. (1985). "Senior Law Faculty Publication Study: Comparisons of Law School Productivity." *Journal of Legal Education*, 35, 373–394.

Teitel, L. (1993). "The State Role in Jump-Starting School/University Collaboration: A Case Study." *Educational Policy*, 7(1), 74–95.

———. (1996). "Getting Down to Cases." *Contemporary Education*, 67, 200–205.

University of Arizona Cooperating Teacher Project, The. (1988). *The University of Arizona Cooperating Teacher Project*. Tucson: College of Education. (ERIC Document Reproduction Service No. ED 308 155.)

University of Minnesota College of Education and Human Development, The. (1997). "A Differentiated Staffing Model for Academic Appointments." Unpublished policy document. Minneapolis: Author.

Veysey, L. (1965). *The Emergence of the American University*. Chicago: University of Chicago Press.

Walton, J. (1971). "Clichés and Metaphors in the Study of Education." *School Review*, 80(1), 76–85.

Warner, A. R., Houston, W. R., & Cooper, J. M. (1977). "Rethinking the Clinical Concept in Teacher Education." *Journal of Teacher Education*, 28(1), 15–18.

Williams, R. O. (1996). "Professional Development Schools: Facing the Challenge of Institutionalization." *Contemporary Education*, 67, 171–179.

Wolfe, D. M., Schewel, R., & Bickham, E. P. (1989). "A Gateway to Collaboration: Clinical Faculty Programs." *Action in Teacher Education*, 11(2), 66–69.

CHAPTER 7

Professors of Education and Academic Freedom

Uncharted Waters

PHILO HUTCHESON

Professors engage in a variety of tasks in their daily work; in general, these tasks fall under the headings of research, teaching, and service. In both research and teaching, and at times in service, inquiry is a central part of what professors do. In research, professors must examine traditional and new ideas, using any number of methods, and draw conclusions; in teaching, professors share information and knowledge with students, raising questions and at times offering answers about issues. And, in service, professors bring their expertise to a problem, using inquiry to aid in the solution. These fundamental activities give rise to a complex and challenging notion, academic freedom, and tenure. Simply stated, to what extent does society at large as well as institutions of higher education accept inquiry? Are professors to engage in inquiry only to the point of reaffirming an established order, or are we willing as citizens and academics to allow professors to inquire even if troubling questions and answers arise about our individual and social behavior? This chapter argues that the protection of academic freedom and tenure has been important for education professors, and is likely to become even more important.

Education professors engage in research, teaching, and service, and occupy a central role in the ongoing development of the country. They educate the future teachers in the nation's schools, the future administrators, and through continuing education and graduate education, they further educate (perhaps even reeducate) teachers and administrators. Questions of both method, especially in the areas of pedagogy and management, as well as content in both teaching specialities and social and cultural foundations, form the basis of their inquiry. Their role in research, teaching, and service has been highlighted in recent decades by such reports as *A Nation at Risk* and

151

Goals 2000. This chapter seeks to raise questions about the role of academic freedom and tenure for education professors, examining what challenges to education professors' academic freedom and tenure have typically occurred and what contemporary problems in education may mean for education professors.

In view of the challenges to society and institutions that occur as a result of inquiry in the academy, there are disparate views regarding academic freedom, and there is even a tendency to individual interpretation.[1] The American Association of University Professors (AAUP) has been examining challenges to academic freedom and tenure since 1915, and is thus the oldest continuous source of information about such challenges. Furthermore, in 1915, 1925, and 1940, the AAUP developed national policy statements on academic freedom, and the 1940 Statement on Principles of Academic Freedom and Tenure has been endorsed by a wide range of organizations, whose membership ranges from mostly professors to mostly administrators. This chapter offers an analysis of academic freedom and tenure cases as reported by the American Association of University Professors, and thus that organization's definition serves as the point of departure. The 1940 Statement of Principles on Academic Freedom and Tenure states:

(a) The teacher is entitled to full freedom in research and in the publication of the results, subject to the adequate performance of his other academic duties; but research for pecuniary return should be based upon an understanding with the authorities of the institution.

(b) The teacher is entitled to freedom in the classroom in discussing his subject, but he should be careful not to introduce into his teaching controversial matter which has no relation to his subject. Limitations of academic freedom because of religious or other aims of the institution should be clearly stated in writing at the time of the appointment.[2]

The AAUP proposes that institutions assure such freedom through the device of academic tenure and the 1940 Statement outlines specific procedures in regard to the award and removal of tenure. The Statement indicates that "teachers or investigators should have permanent or continuous tenure, and their service should be terminated only for adequate cause, except in the retirement for age, or under extraordinary circumstances because of financial exigencies" and that moral turpitude may be cause for dismissal. The Statement also indicates that professors should exercise restraint in their public utterances in view of their special positions as experts.[3] Tenure is the device that protects, to some degree, professors' academic freedom.[4]

Some scholars have argued that professors may not need tenure. For example, in one form of this argument, several scholars working with the American Association for Higher Education have presented various models for alternatives to tenure.[5] Tenure is seen as costly, as inflexible, and as politically unfeasible. While the debate over the costs of tenure is unresolved, even advocates of tenure acknowledge that it is a lifetime economic contract between the institution and the professor.[6]

Thus academic freedom is the freedom to inquire and to communicate the results of that inquiry in the classroom, and tenure offers protection for the exercise of that inquiry. Yet the AAUP definition has important exceptions to such freedom, first for institutions with religious aims (although a 1970 interpretation eschewed that exception, indicating that church-related institutions no longer needed to depart from the principle of academic freedom). Second, and more important, as a highly experienced AAUP leader has noted, the restrictions on public utterances (which in reinterpretation even allow for institutional consideration of dismissal) are in fact restrictions on freedom of speech as constructed in the First Amendment of the United States Constitution.[7] Both of these restrictions have consequences for education professors facing academic freedom and tenure issues, as evidenced in the following analysis.

Education Professors and Issues of Academic Freedom and Tenure

Even given the limitations on freedom of speech inherent in the 1940 Statement, the issue of academic freedom among professors of education raises substantial questions because of their service to the nation. In a public view, education professors are responsible for the education of, among others, schoolteachers and school administrators, people intrinsically involved in the development of the children of our nation. At times, the interest in teachers and their effect on students, especially in terms of how they teach students to view their social, political, and economic relations, has been high.[8] At least since the development of normal schools in the mid-nineteenth century, when the Whig view of educating immigrants to their "appropriate station in life," the polity and some education policy makers have assumed that teacher educators ought to educate for society as it existed on their terms.[9] This suggests an instrumentalist view of education, as society expects teachers (and in their preparation by education professors) to teach students for the aims of society, especially as it is viewed by dominant groups. In contrast, challenges to the status quo—such as those offered by John Dewey—have suggested that teacher educators ought to educate for the critique and subsequent development of society. Thus in a professional view, what constitutes the boundaries of appropriate education in pedagogy and administration is an important question. What then of academic freedom cases involving education professors? What have been the issues in AAUP cases, and have they changed over time?

Academic freedom and tenure cases published in the journal of the American Association of University Professors (named the *AAUP Bulletin* and then changed to *Academe* in 1978) represent cases that the organization has not been able to resolve in private negotiation with the professors and institutions involved, and thus are cases that highlight problems of academic freedom and tenure. In the spring of 1956 the Association of American University Professors issued a report on several cases it had not investigated during the McCarthyism period; following that report it resumed its standard procedures for the investigation of academic freedom and tenure cases.[10] Hence the reports from 1956 (following the spring report) through 1997 offer a comprehensive and relatively consistent view of academic freedom and tenure issues. A review of the reports on cases as reported in the *AAUP Bulletin* and *Academe* from the mid-1950s to the present indicates that a minority of the cases involved education professors, and issues ostensibly focused on technical concerns such as due process rather than substantive questions about the freedom of inquiry.

From 1956 to 1997 the AAUP published reports on 171 different institutions involving 1,643 professors in which the Association's investigating committee identified professors' disciplines or fields of study. (The large number of professors is primarily due to actions at two institutions, the City University of New York in the mid-1970s in a dismissal of 1,000 faculty members and San Diego State University's dismissal of 111 professors in the early 1990s. Most AAUP investigations addressed academic freedom and tenure problems of 1, 2, or 3 professors.) Of the 171 cases, 11 involved education professors, about 6 percent of the total number of cases. There were 33 education professors in those ten cases; in one instance an institution dismissed 16 education professors, so for the most part, as with the overall situation regarding AAUP investigations, most of the reports review the dismissal of one or two professors.[11]

As Table 7.1 indicates, most of the cases with education professors focus on tenure and procedure issues. That is, administrations chose to dismiss faculty members, some of whom had tenure, without appropriate due process, and an education professor was one of those dismissed. Often administrations chose to use financial problems (not necessarily financial exigency) as the reason for professors' termination, and the institutional definitions of financial problems originated with the administration and not the faculty.

Administration choices about whom to dismiss under the guise of financial difficulties beg the question about procedures versus personalities or the exercise of academic freedom. In a broad sense, the case at Southern Nazarene University reveals the problem, as the president claimed first financial problems, then "individual reasons" for the dismissals, and finally insisted that two of the seven dismissed were for reasons of moral turpitude. Yet throughout the process of dismissals and the subsequent AAUP investigation, the

TABLE 7.1
Academic Freedom and Tenure Cases Involving Education Professors:
Reasons for Dismissal

Institution	Conflict with Administration	Financial Problems	Program Quality	Professor's Political Activity	Moral Turpitude
Catawba	X				
Eastern Washington	X				
Texas Tech		X	X		
Columbia College (MO)				X	
Yeshiva		X			
Eastern Oregon		X			
Temple		X			
Jackson State		X			
Southern Nazarene		X			(X)*
Claflin	X				
North Greenville	X	X			

*According to the president of Southern Nazarene University, reasons for dismissing two of the seven professors (one of whom was an education professor) included moral turpitude, but there were no specific conditions of such behavior nor were the two professors identified.

president refused to identify the individual reasons or the instances of moral turpitude. As the AAUP report states:

> President Gilliland has asserted that he withheld the "individual reasons" for dismissing these professors out of a concern "to protect them and their reputations." Whatever may have motivated him, the investigating committee finds that his unsubstantiated indictments of this group of professors—in which everyone and no one stood accused of highly severe offenses and deficiencies—served to besmirch the reputations of the entire group while denying all of them the elementary safeguards of due process they needed to defend themselves.[12]

While the AAUP was able to pass judgment on the institution based on the issue of procedural safeguards, personality and academic freedom issues remained obscure although disheartening (see Table 7.1).

In other instances, it is not clear to what degree an education professor's expertise was part of the issue. In the case of Claflin College professor Alma Stegall, her dismissal resulted from her challenges to the administration. Colleagues described her as "willing to speak on controversial issues, as an effective speaker, and has having a good deal to say."[13] Most of her challenges appear, however, to be on the topic of the education of Claflin College students, and in one instance she opposed an initiative to focus on teaching the underprepared student using student outcomes, as measured on standardized examinations. Although not calling on the education literature per se, her responses speak to the literature:

> She opposed a requirement that mid-term and final examinations at the college include multiple-choice questions. She opposed the introduction of an exit examination. She stated on several occasions that a teacher cannot teach a student who does not attend class, who does not do homework, and who does not study. She argued that students must be challenged to work hard and to do their best.[14]

Professor Stegall began college teaching in 1947 as a professor of education, and held that position at different institutions continuously since then. The AAUP report does not present direct evidence that academic freedom issues relating to professors' expertise were part of the problem but focuses instead on her repeated opposition to the administration as the academic freedom issue. Nor did Professor Stegall argue that she spoke from the perspective of an education professor in her opposition to the administration.

Thus this case represents another ambiguity. At what point does an education professor qua expert on educational matters, exercise academic freedom based on freedom of speech principles rather than scholarly principles? One problematic characteristic of the 1940 Statement is the apparent difference between the authority of the academic expert, clearly falling under the purview of academic freedom as defined by the AAUP, and the Constitutional freedom to speak. Stegall's opposition to the administration illuminates this problem, as it is not clear whether she is speaking as an expert or as a citizen.

In general, academic freedom cases as such are uncommon, at least in the reports of the AAUP. The majority of reports from the late 1950s to the late 1990s focus on procedural issues or financial reasons; only a handful of cases address the freedom of inquiry.[15] In the late 1950s, cases still arose in which supposed Communist affiliation was a central issue, and in the 1960s, there were some academic freedom and tenure cases that involved professors' views on such issues as civil rights and the Vietnam War. As examples of issues about the freedom of inquiry, the special report of 1956 highlights cases regarding Communism. By the early 1970s, cases were much more likely to focus on procedural questions: whether the institution had tenure policies and practices, and whether the institution followed acceptable (according to the AAUP) tenure policies and practices. Thus academic freedom cases—rather than tenure cases—tended to be notable exceptions. For example, in 1979 the Association reported on the refusal of the University of Maryland to appoint Bertell Ollman as a professor, in great part because of his Marxist views, and in 1988 the AAUP reported on the dismissal of the Rev. Charles Curran by The Catholic University of America, largely because his inquiry raised issues contrary to the stated principle of the Roman Catholic Church.[16] The only academic freedom and tenure case involving an education professor that directly engaged issues of academic freedom occurred at Columbia College (Missouri) in which the dismissal resulted from the professor's work in antiwar activities.[17] Thus the cases that involved education professors are not especially different from those involving professors from other fields. They are, however, overall apparently less likely to be subjects of dismissals than professors in other fields.

The overall percentage of education professors varies over time, and given the large number of professors dismissed in two cases, offering a national comparative picture is difficult. Nevertheless, in general, it appears that the percentage of education professors involved in AAUP academic freedom cases (6% of the cases analyzed) is only slightly smaller than their national representation. Federal data do not coincide with the years of this analysis, but as examples, in 1963 almost 8 percent of all full-time faculty were in education, in 1968 approximately 10 percent of all full-time professors were in education, and in 1996 about 7 percent were in education.[18] Yet empirical research about the professoriate since the 1950s offers some specific findings that suggest that education professors would be far less likely to encounter attacks on their academic freedom.

Challenging Authority, The Context for Education Professors

In order to place this study of education professors in an appropriate context, the professional viewpoints and the political and social views of professors require discussion. Clearly academic freedom, with its opportunities for expressions of potentially troubling issues, entails consideration of how professors think about the world. How education professors think about the world apparently has a considerable impact on the nature of their encounters with academic freedom issues.

Empirical investigations of the political and social views of professors are intermittent in the post–World War II period. The earliest of the surveys, and to date still the most powerful, is the study of social science professors during McCarthyism conducted by Paul Lazarsfeld and Wagner Thielens. More recent studies include *The Divided Academy* by Everett Ladd and Seymour Lipset, and Richard Hamilton and Lowell Hargens's, "The Politics of the Professors: Self-Identifications, 1969–1984." Each of these works reveals a consistent characteristic of education professors, their tendency to be much more middle-of-the-road or even conservative than most other professors grouped by discipline or field of study.

Lazarsfeld and Thielens collected data from 2,451 social science professors, and added insights gleaned from interviews with selected members of their survey sample. Their findings regarding professors at teachers colleges (reflecting the nature of teacher education in the mid-1950s, when much of that preparation occurred at specialized institutions) are highly indicative about possible sources of academic freedom conflicts. For example, Lazarsfeld and Thielens report that 40 percent of the professors at teachers colleges judged faculty-administration relations as unusually good, the highest proportion of any cohort in the study. Lazarsfeld and Thielens argue that this sentiment exists at teachers colleges because "their central task is not to carry out research along the frontiers of knowledge, but instead to train their students to transmit the cultural heritage."[19]

Pressures to avoid controversy are a direct way of suppressing academic freedom, and teachers college professors were less likely to report increases in such pressures than professors at private or public institutions, although they were as likely as professors at Protestant colleges and much more likely than Catholic college professors.[20] Lazarsfeld and Thielens complemented the examination of external pressures with one regarding professors' views on controversy. They established an estimate of professors' willingness to accept inquiry into "controversial issues," a permissiveness scale, which in the context of the McCarthy era was best illustrated by Communism. While professors at teachers colleges ranked in the middle of the scale, only 27 percent were permissive, indicating that a large proportion did not think that their institutions should permit the expression of controversial issues on their campuses.[21] And, in general, the interviews with professors at teachers colleges confirmed their stance on controversial issues. The discussion of interviews highlights one example of a professor at a teachers college who, in responding to a request to list membership in "political groups or organizations interested in public affairs," offered the Home School Group and the Red Cross. The discussion also documents administrative resistance to the research project at teachers colleges, in some cases to the degree that researchers were unable to collect anything but the most circumspect responses.[22]

In *The Divided Academy*, Ladd and Lipset examined professors' political, social, and economic views, illustrating academics' perspectives in comparison to themselves and to the public. They used data from the 1969 Carnegie Commission Survey of Student and Faculty Opinion, a national survey of 60,000 professors. In one case, Ladd and Lipset grouped five questions on political and social issues and created a "Liberalism-Conservatism Scale." Of twelve groups by disciplinary divisions or fields of study (such as social sciences or business), education professors ranked eighth (the most liberal, ranked first, were social science professors, the most conservative, ranked twelfth, were agriculture professors).[23]

Ladd and Lipset attempt to locate the distribution of professors' political, social, and economic perspectives in a historical sense, arguing, "A field of study becomes highly ideological when, under a given set of circumstances, it offers a fulcrum for the rejection of established social arrangements."[24] In this sense, then, the position of education professors becomes clear; by and large, as noted by Lazarsfeld and Thielens, these professors engaged in the reproduction of the social order. Calls for change were typically no more radical than the liberal yet instrumental definitions of John Dewey. Another perspective on this argument obtains in consideration of the responsibilities of education professors, how they spent their time across the generalized occupational requirements of research, teaching, and service in the late 1960s. Of twenty-four disciplines and fields of study, education professors ranked twenty-second (tied with English, with business as the lowest ranking) in the percentage primarily committed to research rather than teaching.[25]

A more recent investigation of professors' political views, using Carnegie survey data from 1969 and 1984, indicates that education professors continue to hold centrist views. Hamilton and Hargens found that in general there was a slight shift away from left and liberal political identification among all disciplines and fields; education professors reflected that shift. In 1969 41.5 percent of the education professors surveyed indicated a left or liberal identification, while in 1984 38.5 percent indicated those political interests. There was, however, an increase in the percentage of education professors who identified themselves as left wing, from 2.7 percent to 4.3 percent from 1969 to 1984; those identifying themselves as liberal evidenced a decline. Hamilton and Hargens also reported that professors who publish are much more likely to be left or liberal, while conservative faculty are much less likely to publish.[26] These findings indicate little change in political identification or relationships between inquiry and political identity among education professors from the 1950s to the 1980s.

In sum, then, it would appear that in general, education professors would not be particularly likely to encounter problems in the area of academic freedom, primarily for two reasons. First, as they practice their profession, they are most concerned with the education of teachers; that is to say, teaching rather than inquiry is their primary occupational activity. Second, as they construct their practice, they are more interested in ensuring the transmission of culture than the critical questioning of whose culture, how it is transmitted, and what the consequences are. Nevertheless, the review of AAUP cases indicates that they appear to be generally as likely to encounter academic freedom and tenure challenges as their colleagues.

One reason for the level of dismissals may be in an area that scholars are just beginning to explore fully—the complex relationships between gender and institutional decisions in higher education. As Sheila Slaughter argued, there was a gendered nature of academic freedom and tenure issues in the

1980s; institutions often removed women professors before considering the removal of other faculty members. Slaughter indicated that women occupy an especially vulnerable place in the academy.[27] This problem is evident in the education professoriate. In the cases from 1980 to the present, nine of the dismissed education professors were women, and only two were men.[28] Education professors nationally of course represent no such gender distribution although they form a cohort within the professoriate with far greater representation of women than overall. According to federal data, approximately 51 percent of the full-time education professors in 1992 were women, while only 33 percent of all full-time professors are women.[29]

Recent developments in teacher education—in social foundations and curriculum, pedagogical methods, and research—suggest, however, that academic freedom may become more of a conundrum for colleges of education than it has been in the past. Since the late 1960s and early 1970s, as increasing numbers of groups have achieved some level of public cultural identity and self-consciousness, their uneasiness with the social order—including the conduct of schooling in America—has translated into inquiry into teacher education. This inquiry has not celebrated the traditional ways of transmitting traditional comprehensions of culture.

These interpretations have manifested themselves in a broad spectrum of themes and theories. As examples, Maxine Greene argued in 1986 that educators should engage students in substantial ways: "We might try to make audible again the recurrent calls for justice and equality. We might reactivate the resistance to materialism and conformity."[30] Another author critiqued pedagogical methods:

> The critical issue is the degree to which we hold the moral conviction that we must humanize the educational experience of students from subordinated populations by eliminating the hostility that often confronts these students. This process would require that we cease to be overly dependent on methods as technical instruments and adopt a pedagogy that seeks forge a cultural democracy where all students are treated with respect and dignity.[31]

And in research, in their groundbreaking work, *Naturalistic Inquiry*, Yvonna Lincoln and Egon Guba argued, "Research in the conventional sense usually exploits people, . . . for knowledge is power that can be used against the people from whom the knowledge was generated." They suggested that naturalistic inquiry avoided that problem by engaging respondents in inquiry and knowledge formation.[32] In this sense, then, Ladd and Lipset's assessment of a field's likelihood of becoming ideological when "it offers a fulcrum for the rejection of established social arrangements" seems to have more potential application to education professors in the 1990s and beyond than it would have in earlier decades.

Any apprehensions about academic freedom (which Lazarsfeld and Thielens documented as a key issue of academic freedom) necessarily entail external pressures. And here, potential external sources of pressure seem to be offering increasing attention to the arguments that are finding their way into colleges of education.[33] Teacher education has become an important political issue, and a number of educational issues have attracted substantial political ire. Not the least of these issues would be the whole language and phonics debate, one that is highly charged in the political realm as entire states (e.g., California) declare first one and then the other as the method for reading instruction. The Oakland school board decision to institute, and then its decision to rescind, Eubonics instruction, highlights the political storms increasingly surrounding education. Nor are only large states or large urban areas the ones that have faced questions about educational methods and content. In the small town of Presque Isle, Maine, a school has wrestled with the question of single-sex education in mathematics, even though such provisions violate federal law.[34] Finally, as schools of education become more involved in outreach activities such as professional development schools, they will receive even more attention from external constituencies. And the public political temperament in regard to many educational issues does not coincide with that of professors, although neither group is monolithic in its outlook. Nevertheless, as the McCarthyism era shows, when the public and the polity decide that professors are not sufficiently American, professors suffer.

A Caveat, and Another Caveat

First, the historical trends evidenced in AAUP cases involving education professors indicate that they too need the protections afforded by academic freedom and tenure. In roughly the same proportion as their colleagues overall, education professors have faced dismissals for a variety of reasons, including disagreement with their administrations, financial pressures on institutions, and in one case, for political viewpoints. Furthermore, the gendered nature of the education professoriate suggests that it may be especially vulnerable to administrative decisions to remove professors. In all of these cases, the professors' performance as teachers or scholars was not an issue: academic freedom and tenure must stand in order to protect education professors from egregious assaults on their work.

Second, the issue of teacher education has begun to receive increasing attention from governing boards and state legislatures, both of which have also in the past twenty years been more and more interested in the daily affairs of the institutions for which they are legally responsible. As that attention to the daily affairs of education professors encompasses the developing professorial interest in such areas as critical pedagogy or postmodernism or naturalistic inquiry, or in such politically charged fields as bilingual education or reading instruction, academic freedom and tenure will likely become even more problematic for education professors. While the waters of academic freedom and tenure have been murky for education professors thus far, the course ahead is even less clear.

Notes

1. For a thorough treatment of wide-ranging interpretations of the meaning of academic freedom during McCarthyism, see Ellen Schrecker, *No Ivory Tower: McCarthyism and the Universities* (New York: Oxford University Press, 1986). This work documents the varying perspectives on academic freedom within the professoriate as well among college and university administrators and trustees and such public groups as state and federal government officials, businesspeople, and journalists. See also Commission on Academic Tenure in Higher Education, *Faculty Tenure* (San Francisco: Jossey-Bass Publishers, 1973), Edmund L. Pincoffs, *The Concept of Academic Freedom* (Austin, Texas: University of Texas Press, 1972), and Louis Menand, ed., *The Future of Academic Freedom* (Chicago: University of Chicago Press, 1996). The Pincoffs and Menand volumes each offer a variety of interpretations of academic freedom.

2. "1940 Statement of Principles and Interpretive Comments," *Policy Documents Reports 1984 Edition*, 6th ed. (Washington DC: American Association of University Professors, 1989), 3. For a list of the endorsers, see 7–9. On the development of the various statements on academic freedom, see Richard Hofstader and Walter P. Metzger, *The Development of Academic Freedom in the United States* (New York: Columbia University Press, 1955), 480–490.

3. Ibid., 4 on tenure, 3–4 on public utterances.

4. On tenure's limited protection of academic freedom, see Rolf Sartorius, "Tenure and Academic Freedom," in *The Concept of Academic Freedom*, ed. by Edmund L. Pincoffs (Austin: University of Texas Press, 1975), 133–158.

5. See Cathy A. Trower, "Tenure Snapshot," *New Pathways: Faculty Careers and Employment for the Twenty-First Century*, Working Paper #2 (Washington, DC: American Association for Higher Education, March 1996); Richard Chait and Cathy A. Trower, "Where Tenure Does Not Reign: Colleges with Contract Systems," *New Pathways: Faculty Careers and Employment for the Twenty-First Century*, Working Paper #3 (Washington, DC: American Association for Higher Education, March 1997); David W. Breneman, "Alternatives to Tenure for the Next Generation of Academics," *New Pathways: Faculty Careers and Employment for the Twenty-First Cen-*

tury, Working Paper #14 (Washington, DC: American Association for Higher Education, April 1997).

6. Richard Chait, "Ideas in Incubation: Three Possible Modifications to Traditional Tenure Policies," *New Pathways: Faculty Careers and Employment for the Twenty-First Century*, Working Paper #9 (Washington, DC: American Association for Higher Education, August 1998) on costs, inflexibility, and political consequences. On the debate over the costs of tenure, see Robert W. McGee and Walter E. Block, "Academic Tenure: An Economic Critique," in *Academic Freedom and Tenure: Ethical Issues*, Richard T. De George, ed., (Lanham, Maryland: Rowman & Littlefield Publishers, 1997), 156–175, who argue against the economic benefits of tenure, and Michael S. McPherson, and Gordon C. Winston, "The Economics of Academic Tenure: A Relational Perspective," in *Academic Labor Markets and Careers*, David W. Breneman and Ted I. K. Youn, eds. (New York: The Falmer Press, 1988), 174–199, who argue that tenure is a cost-effective measure. On the economic contract, see Howard R. Bowen and Jack H. Schuster, *American Professors: A National Resource Imperiled* (New York: Oxford University Press), 235.

7. On the 1970 interpretation, see "1970 Interpretive Comments," *Policy Documents and Reports 1984 Edition*, 5 and on the reinterpretation of public statements, see "1940 Interpretations," *Policy Documents and Reports 1984 Edition*, 4–5. On the restrictions on the First Amendment, see William Van Alstyne, "The Specific Theory of Academic Freedom and the General Issues of Civil Liberties," in *The Concept of Academic Freedom*, Edmund L. Pincoffs, ed. (Austin: University of Texas Press, 1975), 81–82.

8. See, for example, Robert E. Summers, ed., *Freedom and Loyalty in Our Colleges* (New York: H. W. Wilson Company, 1954), 66, on teacher education and its relationship to un-American activity in the McCarthy era.

9. Jurgen Herbst, *And Sadly Teach: Teacher Education and Professionalization in American Culture* (Madison: University of Wisconsin Press, 1989), 13–24.

10. This examination excludes the report of the Special Committee on Academic Freedom and Tenure in the Quest for National Security for two reasons. First, that report removed a backlog of academic freedom and tenure cases for the AAUP, and as such was not part of the standard investigative procedures for the Association. Second, the report often gave only brief reviews of cases, and in several cases there is no indication of professors' disciplines or fields of study. See "Academic Freedom and Tenure in the Quest for National Security," *AAUP Bulletin*, 42 (Spring 1956), 49–107. There are, however, subsequent investigations of institutions that were initially reviewed in the 1956 report; these more extensive reports are included in the analysis.

11. The author wishes to thank Bruce Kreutzer from Atlanta, Georgia, for his assistance in locating the academic freedom and tenure cases involving

education professors from 1975 to 1997 and providing summaries of their characteristics. The cases from 1956 to 1997 are: "Catawba College," *AAUP Bulletin*, 43 (Spring 1957), 196–224; "Eastern Washington College of Education," *AAUP Bulletin*, 43 (Spring 1957), 225–241; "Texas Technological College," *AAUP Bulletin*, 44 (March 1958), 170–187; "Academic Freedom and Tenure: Columbia College (Missouri)," *AAUP Bulletin*, 57 (December 1971), 513–517; "Academic Freedom and Tenure: Yeshiva University," *Academe*, 67 (August 1981), 186–195; "Academic Freedom and Tenure: Eastern Oregon State College," *Academe*, 68 (May–June 1982), 1a–8a; "Academic Freedom and Tenure: Temple University," *Academe*, 71 (May–June 1985), 16–27; "Academic Freedom and Tenure: Jackson State University (Mississippi)," *Academe*, 72 (May–June 1986), 1a–5a; "Academic Freedom and Tenure: Southern Nazarene University (Oklahoma)," *Academe*, 72 (November–December 1986), 7a–11a; "Academic Freedom and Tenure: Claflin College (South Carolina)," *Academe*, 74 (May–June 1988), 41–48; "Academic Freedom and Tenure: North Greenville College (South Carolina)," *Academe*, 79 (May–June 1993), 54–64.

12. "Academic Freedom and Tenure: Southern Nazarene University (Oklahoma)," 10a–11a.

13. "Claflin College (South Carolina)," 41.

14. Ibid., 42.

15. For examinations of the AAUP focus on procedures in the 1970s and 1980s, see Sheila Slaughter (1981). "Political Action, Faculty Autonomy and Retrenchment: A Decade of Academic Freedom, 1970–1980," in *Higher Education in American Society*, 1st ed., Philip G. Altbach and Robert O. Berdahl (Buffalo: Prometheus Books, 1981), 73–100; Sheila Slaughter, "Academic Freedom in the Modern University," in *Higher Education in American Society*, Philip G. Altbach and Robert O. Berdahl, eds. (Buffalo: Prometheus Books, 1987), 77–105; and Sheila Slaughter, "Academic Freedom at the End of the Century: Professional Labor, Gender, and Professionalism," in *Higher Education in American Society*, 3rd ed., Philip G. Altbach, Robert O. Berdahl, and Patricia J. Gumport, eds. (Buffalo: Prometheus Books, 1994), 73–100.

16. "Academic Freedom and Tenure: University of Maryland," *Academe*, 65 (May 1979), 213–227; "Academic Freedom and Tenure: The Catholic University of America," *Academe*, 36 (October 1989), 27–40.

17. "Academic Freedom and Tenure: Columbia College (Missouri)," 513–517.

18. *The Education Professions: A Report on the People Who Serve Our Schools and Colleges—1968* (Washington, DC: United States Government Printing Office, 1969), Table 52, 332; *Digest of Educational Statistics 1973* (Washington, DC: United States Government Printing Office, 1974), Table 102, 85; *Digest of Educational Statistics 1996* (Washington, DC: United States Government Printing Office, 1996) Table 227, 240.

19. Paul L. Lazarsfeld and Wagner Thielens, Jr., *The Academic Mind: Social Scientists in a Time of Crisis* (Glencoe, IL: The Free Press, 1958), 3 on sample size, Figures 1–13; 26 on faculty-administration relations. The other cohorts and and respective responses were private (29%), public (21%), Protestant (35%), and Catholic (36%). See p. 27 for discussion of purpose of teachers' colleges.

20. Ibid., Figure 2–2a, 40.

21. Ibid., 113 on controversial issues, Figures 5–6; 128 on scale.

22. Ibid., 338 on political group memberships, 338–340 on administrative resistance.

23. Everett Carll Ladd, Jr., and Seymour Martin Lipset, *The Divided Academy: Professors and Politics* (New York: McGraw-Hill Book Company, 1975), Table 10, p. 60.

24. Ibid., 73.

25. Ibid., Appendix C, 349.

26. Richard F. Hamilton and Lowell L. Hargens, "The Politics of Professors: Self-Identification, 1969–1984," *Social Forces,* 71(30), 1993: 603–627.

27. Sheila Slaughter, "Academic Freedom at the End of the Century: Professional Labor, Gender, and Professionalism," 96.

28. Academic Freedom and Tenure: Yeshiva University," 186–195, two women; "Academic Freedom and Tenure: Eastern Oregon State College," 1a–8a, one woman; "Academic Freedom and Tenure: Temple University," 16–27, one woman, two men; "Academic Freedom and Tenure: Jackson State University (Mississippi)," 1a–5a, one woman; "Academic Freedom and Tenure: Southern Nazarene University (Oklahoma)," 7a–11a, two women; "Academic Freedom and Tenure: Claflin College (South Carolina)," 41–48, one woman; "Academic Freedom and Tenure: North Greenville College (South Carolina)," 54–62, one woman.

29. *Digest of Educational Statistics 1996* Tables 222 and 232, on all professors and Tables 227 and 240 on education professors.

30. Maxine Greene, "In Search of a Critical Pedagogy," *Harvard Education Review*, 56 (November 1986), 440.

31. Lilia I. Bartolomé, "Beyond the Methods Fetish: Toward a Humanizing Pedagogy," *Harvard Education Review*, 64 (Summer 1994), 190.

32. Yvonna S. Lincoln and Egon G. Guba, *Naturalistic Inquiry* (Beverly Hills: Sage Publications, 1985), 31.

33. The author would like to thank Professor Sheila Slaughter, of the University of Arizona, for sharing her acute assessment of these issues and their relationship to academic freedom and tenure for education professors.

34. Richard A. Durost, "Single Sex Math Classes: What and for Whom? One School's Experiences," *NASSP Bulletin*, 80 (February 1996), 27–31.

References

"Academic Freedom and Tenure: The Catholic University of America," *Academe*, 36 (October 1989): 27–40.

"Academic Freedom and Tenure: Claflin College (South Carolina)," *Academe*, 74 (May–June 1988): 41–48.

"Academic Freedom and Tenure: Columbia College (Missouri)," *AAUP Bulletin*, 57 (December 1971): 513–517.

"Academic Freedom and Tenure: Eastern Oregon State College," *Academe*, 68 (May–June 1982): 1a–8a.

"Academic Freedom and Tenure in the Quest for National Security," *AAUP Bulletin*, 42 (Spring 1956): 49–107.

"Academic Freedom and Tenure: Jackson State University (Mississippi)," *Academe*, 72 (May–June 1986): 1a–5a.

"Academic Freedom and Tenure: North Greenville College (South Carolina)," *Academe*, 79 (May–June 1993): 54–62.

"Academic Freedom and Tenure: Southern Nazarene University (Oklahoma)," *Academe*, 72 (November–December 1986): 7a–11a.

"Academic Freedom and Tenure: Temple University," *Academe*, 71 (May–June 1985): 16–27.

"Academic Freedom and Tenure: University of Maryland," *Academe*, 65 (May 1979): 213–227.

"Academic Freedom and Tenure: Yeshiva University," *Academe*, 67 (August 1981): 186–195.

"Academic Freedom and Tenure, 1940 Statement of Principles and 1970 Interpretive Comments," AAUP Policy Documents & Reports (Washington, DC: American Association of University Professors, 1984), pp. 3–9.

Bartolomé, L. I. (1994). "Beyond the Methods Fetish: Toward a Humanizing Pedagogy," *Harvard Education Review*, 64, 173–194.

Bowen, H. R. & Schuster, J. H. (1986). *American Professors: A National Resource Imperiled.* New York: Oxford University Press.

Breneman, D. W. (1997). "Alternatives to Tenure for the Next Generation of Academics," *New Pathways: Faculty Careers and Employment for the Twenty-First Century*, Working Paper #14. Washington, DC: American Association for Higher Education.

"Catawba College," *AAUP Bulletin*, 43 (Spring 1957): 196–224.

Chait, R. (1998). "Ideas in Incubation: Three Possible Modifications to Traditional Tenure Policies," *New Pathways: Faculty Careers and Employment for the Twenty-First Century*, Working Paper #9. Washington, DC: American Association for Higher Education.

———. & Trower, C. A. (1997). "Where Tenure Does Not Reign: Colleges with Contract Systems," *New Pathways: Faculty Careers and Employ-*

ment for the Twenty-First Century, Working Paper #3. Washington, DC: American Association for Higher Education.

Commission on Academic Tenure in Higher Education, *Faculty Tenure*. San Francisco: Jossey-Bass Publishers, 1973.

Digest of Educational Statistics 1996. Washington, DC: United States Government Printing Office, 1996.

Digest of Educational Statistics 1973. Washington, DC: United States Government Printing Office, 1974.

Durost, R. A. (1996). "Single Sex Math Classes: What and for Whom? One School's Experiences," *NASSP Bulletin*, 80, 27–31.

"Eastern Washington College of Education," *AAUP Bulletin*, 43 (Spring 1957): 225–241.

The Education Professions: A Report on the People Who Serve Our Schools and Colleges—1968. Washington, DC: United States Government Printing Office, 1969.

Greene, M. (1986). "In Search of a Critical Pedagogy." *Harvard Education Review*, 56, 427–441.

Hamilton, R. F. & Hargens, L. L. (1993). "The Politics of Professors: Self-Identification, 1969–1984," *Social Forces*, 71(30), 603–627.

Herbst, J. (1989). *And Sadly Teach: Teacher Education and Professionalization in American Culture*. Madison: University of Wisconsin Press.

Hofstader, R. & Metzger, W. P. (1955). *The Development of Academic Freedom in the United States*. New York: Columbia University Press.

Ladd, E. C., Jr., & Lipset, S. M. (1975). *The Divided Academy: Professors and Politics*. New York: McGraw-Hill Book Company.

Lazarsfeld, P. L., & Thielens, W., Jr. (1958). *The Academic Mind: Social Scientists in a Time of Crisis*. Glencoe, IL: The Free Press.

Lincoln, Y. S. & Guba, E. G. (1985). *Naturalistic Inquiry*. Beverly Hills: Sage Publications.

McGee, R. W. & Block, W. E. (1997). "Academic Tenure: An Economic Critique." In R. T. De George (ed.), *Academic Freedom and Tenure: Ethical Issues* (pp. 156–175). Lanham, MD: Rowman & Littlefield Publishers.

McPherson, M. S. & Winston, G. C. (1988). "The Economics of Academic Tenure: A Relational Perspective." In D. W. Breneman & T. I. K. Youn (eds.), *Academic Labor Markets and Careers* (pp. 174–199). New York: The Falmer Press.

Menand, L. (ed.). (1996). *The Future of Academic Freedom*. Chicago: University of Chicago Press.

Pincoffs, E. L. (ed.). (1972). *The Concept of Academic Freedom*. Austin: University of Texas Press.

Policy Documents and Reports 1984 Edition, 6th ed. Washington, DC: American Association of University Professors, 1989.

PHILO HUTCHESON

Schrecker, E. (1986). *No Ivory Tower: McCarthyism and the Universities.* New York: Oxford University Press.

Slaughter, S. (1981). "Political Action, Faculty Autonomy and Retrenchment: A Decade of Academic Freedom, 1970–1980." In P. G. Altbach & R. O. Berdahl (eds.), *Higher Education in American Society* (pp. 73–100). Buffalo: Prometheus Books.

———. (1987). "Academic Freedom in the Modern University." In P. G. Altbach & R. O. Berdahl (eds.), *Higher Education in American Society*, 3rd ed. (pp. 77–105). Buffalo: Prometheus Books.

———. (1994). "Academic Freedom at the End of the Century: Professional Labor, Gender, and Professionalism." In P. G. Altbach, R. O. Berdahl, & P. J. Gumport (eds.), *Higher Education in American Society*, 3rd ed. (pp. 73–100). Buffalo: Prometheus Books.

Summers, R. E. (ed.). (1954). *Freedom and Loyalty in Our Colleges.* New York: H. W. Wilson Company.

"Texas Technological College," *AAUP Bulletin*, 44 (March 1958): 170–187.

Trower, C. A. (1996). "Tenure Snapshot," *New Pathways: Faculty Careers and Employment for the Twenty-First Century*," Working Paper #2. Washington, D.C.: American Association for Higher Education.

Van Alstyne, W. (1975). "The Specific Theory of Academic Freedom and the General Issues of Civil Liberties." In E. L. Pincoffs (ed.), *The Concept of Academic Freedom* (pp. 59–85). Austin: University of Texas Press.

CHAPTER 8

The Fragmented Paradigm

Women, Tenure, and Schools of Education

JUDITH GLAZER-RAYMO

Faculty tenure is being scrutinized by state policy makers, boards of trustees, and university presidents as scholars and practitioners weigh a number of proposals to redefine the criteria for evaluating and rewarding faculty work. Early warning signals of the erosion of tenure have been sounded by unions, professional associations, and learned societies. These signals are implicit in the introduction and enforcement of systemwide productivity and workload mandates. No longer a temporary "blip" on the academic labor market screen, the traditional faculty reward system is undergoing paradigmatic change. It is ironic but not irrelevant that this trend coincides with women's increased participation in higher education as recipients of undergraduate and graduate degrees and as members of the professoriate.

In this chapter, I utilize a feminist perspective to analyze critically the impact of changing employment policies on women faculty and to demonstrate how power and privilege operate in tenure policy making. My research is informed by a recognition of "the gendered consequences of neutral practices [and policies] through which academic culture is created and recreated" (Bensimon & Marshall, 1997). Since the academic culture of schools, colleges, and departments of education (hereafter referred to as SCDEs) is dominated by the preparation of teachers for our nation's schools, I focus specifically on the role and status of women education faculty. Throughout this research, I am particularly cognizant of what Glassick, Huber, & Maeroff (1997) refer to as "the fragmented paradigm," the dichotomy between research, teaching, and service through which academic institutions have historically allocated differential rewards for each aspect of faculty work:

169

Most college and university guidebooks implicitly suggest that different types
of standards apply to different kinds of faculty work, leaving the impression
that standards for research and creative work come from various disciplines;
standards for teaching are institutionally defined; and standards for professional
service vary so greatly by project and profession that hardly any guidance can
be offered. This fragmented paradigm reflects the differential respect accorded
research, teaching, and applied scholarship at most institutions. It also, we
believe, helps perpetuate the hierarchy that places greatest importance on research. (p. 22, 23)

The Professional School of Education

SCDEs are much maligned and misunderstood. Originating in the
midnineteenth century as two-year normal schools for the preparation of
predominantly female teachers, the feminization of the teaching profession
has been one of the most widely critiqued aspects of educational practice.
Early male domination of the American Federation of Teachers (AFT), the
National Education Association (NEA), and state boards of education, based
on an ideology of a united profession with no official distinctions between
teachers and administrators, men and women, reinforced women's low professional status: "The belief system that undergirded this official ideology of
professionalism was meritocratic and universalistic; if males were running
things, it was because they were more committed and competent professionals" (Tyack and Hansot, 1982, p. 193). As Clifford and Guthrie also point out
in their history of SCDEs, "gender has been recognized only sotto voce in the
low relative status of schools of education in academe" (1988, p. 153). Indicative of its lower status in the hierarchy of professions, education as well
as social work and nursing—in fact, the feminized occupations—are sometimes referred to as minor or semiprofessions, differentiated from "a few
well-established, prestigious, and strongly credentialed, exclusive occupations
such as medicine, law, and certified public accounting" (Freidson, 1994, p.
153). This viewpoint has been reinforced by a number of critical reports
emanating from task forces, commissions, and state governing boards. Critiques of these reports acknowledge women's absence in proposals for elevat-
ing the status of SCDEs. In discussing the report recommendations, Weis
accurately observes that gender is "the missing component" in their emphasis
on credentialing and certification of teachers and students and their complete
disregard for issues of gender inequality (1997, p. 75). By ignoring the importance of these issues, she suggests that these task forces and commissions
condone their existence and marginalize those who pursue equity objectives.
They also accentuate the gender-neutral environment in which these schools
operate, preparing teachers for a historically feminized profession but giving
little recognition to the impact of gender on existing policies.

The preparation of teaching professionals, the main task of most SCDEs, is carried out in an array of public and private research and doctoral-granting universities, comprehensive institutions, and liberal arts colleges. Their programs are regulated by state governing boards that collaborate in the certifying and credentialing process of school of education graduates. Of the 1,300 SCDEs operating in all 50 states, the National Council for Accreditation of Teacher Education (NCATE) currently accredits only 500. In contrast, there are 182 accredited law schools and 127 accredited medical schools, operating almost entirely under the aegis of their national associations (Association of American Law Schools and Association of American Medical Colleges), adhering to the standards of universally recognized accrediting boards (American Bar Association and American Medical Association), and awarding universally accepted degrees to their graduates (Juris Doctor and Doctor of Medicine).

Women's Status in SCDEs

Enrollments and Degrees

Education produces more women graduates than any other professional field. In 1994, of the 214,446 education degrees conferred, women earned 76 percent: 75.8 percent of all bachelor's and 76.5 percent of all master's degrees.[1] Women's higher academic attainment in education is evident in the doctoral statistic alone: in 1970, they earned only 21 percent of all Ph.D./Ed.D. degrees: by 1980, this proportion more than doubled to 47.2 percent, and by 1994–1995 it tripled to 62 percent. The proliferation of education degrees is evident in the taxonomy employed by the National Center for Educational Statistics (NCES). By 1997, it collected data on thirty-five subfields in which students obtain undergraduate and graduate degrees in education (Snyder, Hoffman, & Geddes, 1997). These encompass nineteen teaching fields ranging from agricultural to trade education and sixteen other education fields ranging from curriculum and instruction to adult, higher, and continuing education. Many of these subfields now have their own professional associations that also serve accrediting and licensing functions, making it more difficult to define the mission of SCDEs and further fragmenting the roles and status of their faculty. Nevertheless, teacher education remains the primary focus of national efforts to redefine the work of faculty in SCDEs.

Women's prominence in the academic pipeline is evident in the fact that by 1994 they obtained the majority of doctorates in fifteen of the sixteen education subfields and fourteen of the nineteen teaching fields with their largest increases in educational leadership/school administration. The complexity of the education profession is evident in the NCATE standards, developed by representatives of SCDEs and twenty-eight professional associations including the National Council of Teachers of English, the National Council of Teachers of Mathematics, the National Science Teachers Association, and the National Council for the Social Studies (NCATE, 1994). From an histori- cal perspective, "the professionalization of education through the route of academic specialization in university-oriented SCDEs both fragmented the field and loosened the bonds between professional practice and professional education. In the process, school administration and educational research [became] self-conscious professions; teaching [did] not" (Clifford & Guthrie, 1988, p. 117, 118).

Women Faculty

In 1970, there were 2,525 institutions and 450,000 instructional faculty, 23 percent of whom were women (Snyder & Hoffman, 1996, p. 175). By 1993, the establishment of more than 1,000 new colleges and universities raised the total to 3,632. In this twenty-three-year period, instructional and noninstructional faculty more than doubled to 933,373, 38.7 percent women and 61.3 percent men, 59.6 percent full-time and 40.4 percent part-time, 71 percent in public and 29 percent in private institutions, 69.4 percent in four- year and 31.6 percent in two-year colleges. Of the 554,903 full-time instruc- tional faculty, 33.5 percent were women compared to 24.3 percent in 1975. An AAUP survey found that 52 percent of full-time faculty held tenure in 1995, the same proportion as in 1975. More alarming is their observation that, between 1975 and 1995, the proportion of full-time faculty in non- tenure-track positions increased from 19 to 28 percent whereas the proportion of tenure-track faculty declined from 29 to 20 percent (Wilson, 1998, p. A12). Earlier, it reported that women's tenure rate is only 48 percent of tenured faculty, no more than a 2 percent improvement in twenty years, and much lower than for men who enjoy a 72 percent tenure rate (AAUP, 1996). The NCES determined that women hold more full-time than part-time positions only in private four-year institutions (45.6%) and are in the majority com- pared to men only in private two-year colleges (52%) (Snyder & Hoffman, 1996, p. 229).

Women comprise 51 percent of full-time SCDE faculty. Nevertheless, the National Survey of Postsecondary Faculty (NSOPF) data show the persis- tence of the gender queue in SCDEs:[2] in the five years between 1987 and 1992, the percentage of full-time women education faculty in four-year insti- tutions declined from 78 to 59 percent and the percentage of women part-time faculty doubled from 22 to 41 percent (Kirshstein, Matheson, & Jing, 1997, p. 15). By 1993, NCES data also show that women comprised 67 percent of all part-time faculty in SCDEs versus 47 percent of full-time faculty (Snyder, Hoffman, & Geddes, 1997): 38.5 percent in master's-level institutions, 40 percent in doctoral universities, and 45 percent in liberal arts colleges. By race and ethnicity, white women faculty in SCDEs were more likely to be teaching part-time (58.8%) than full-time (41.9%), while women faculty of color divided almost equally between full-time (9.3%) and part-time (8.5%). An AACTE survey of 1,700 member institutions noted that women were only 15.8 percent of education deans and 27.8 percent of department chairs (AACTE, 1994). Women faculty in educational leadership programs increased from 12 to 29 percent between 1986 and 1994, reflecting their growing numbers in the academic pipeline (McCarthy & Kuh, 1997). Although women full professors in educational leadership increased from 4 to 19 percent in six years, they were more likely to be hired at lower ranks than men, less likely to come from the ranks of school district administrators, and less likely to be tenured (ibid.). In contrast to higher education, women teachers predominate in American schools. They account for nearly three-fourths (73%) of the 2.6 million public school teachers: 87 percent at the elementary level and 53 percent at the secondary level and three-fourths of the 380,000 private school teachers: 92 percent at the elementary level and 63 percent at the secondary level (Henke, Choi, & Geis, 1996).

Gender, Tenure, and Teacher Education Reform

In assessing changing perceptions of tenure, a feminist critical analysis of its origins and development reveals a serious disjuncture between women's presence in the academic pipeline and their status in the university. In SCDE's, this gap has been exacerbated by growing criticism of teacher education faculty and students. Although the majority of those in SCDEs are women, the inattentiveness to both gender and race in both conservative and liberal critiques of teacher education, reinforces the status quo in which tenure and promotion are both illusory targets for many qualified women, including women of color.

Origins of Tenure

Incremental changes in professional school tenure policies under the rubric of renewable contracts are occurring at a time when women are becoming the majority of doctorate recipients as well as entry-level faculty. The concept of tenure originated at a time when the professoriate was predominantly male, white, and firmly rooted in the arts and sciences. By 1940, concern about the erosion of academic freedom led the American Association of University Professors (AAUP) and the Association of American Colleges (AAC&U) to issue a joint Statement of Principles on Academic Freedom and Tenure. In gender-neutral language (equated at the time with fairness and objectivity), the statement called for a maximum period of probation not to exceed seven years for all faculty, with service beyond that period constituting continuous appointment or tenure. Throughout the ensuing decades, it became the prototype for subsequent policy statements with a salutary impact on faculty governance and the protection of faculty rights in dealing with recalcitrant boards of trustees and autocratic presidents. Between 1941 and 1976, one hundred professional associations and learned societies endorsed the 1940 Statement of Principles. These included the American Association for Higher Education, the Association of American Colleges of Teacher Education, the American Educational Research Association, the American Federation of Teachers and the National Education Association (AAUP, 1976).

Gender Equity and Tenure

By the 1960s, academic freedom and tenure had become institutionalized as the optimum employment standard in a burgeoning higher education system. Its guidelines did not distinguish between the experiences of men and women faculty in the tenure evaluation process until 1972, when Title VII of the Civil Rights Act of 1964 was extended to higher education and Title IX of the Education Amendments was enacted. Encouraged by federal support for equity, women faculty designed strategies to end employment discrimination. Mounting evidence of gender inequities in hiring, tenure, and promotion policies and practices led to the establishment of commissions on the status of women (Glazer, 1997) and to class action lawsuits challenging inequities in salaries, benefits, and working conditions for women (LaNoue & Lee, 1987). Between 1968 and 1973, a period of great upheaval in higher education, professional associations, learned societies, and academic institutions revisited their personnel policies to assure their compliance with federal guidelines. In 1973, the AAUP-AAC Commission on Academic Tenure reiterated its support for faculty tenure as "a major bulwark of both the academic freedom and the economic security of faculty members in higher education," a means of attracting men and women of ability into the teaching profession, encouraging them to concentrate on their basic obligations to students and their disciplines, assuring that judgments of professional performance would continue to be made on professional grounds, and creating an atmosphere favorable to academic freedom in research, the classroom, and as citizens for both nontenured and tenured faculty (AALS, 1994, p. 481). In 1975, under pressure from women and minority faculty, it adopted a resolution of support for affirmative action within its member institutions. Women's caucuses within professional research associations and learned societies also provided outlets for expanding the influence of women's scholarship in the humanities and the social sciences and their power base within their disciplines (Bloland & Bloland, 1974). In education, standing committees on the role and status of women and minorities in educational research sought greater representation and voice through similar means.

Teacher Education under Attack

Conservative Critiques. As noted earlier, the political conservatism of the 1980s manifested itself in a plethora of attacks on public education. SCDEs that prepared the bulk of the nation's teachers were not immune to this criticism in the many reports emanating from commissions, task forces, and private foundations. The politically inspired rhetoric of *A Nation at Risk* (National Commission on Excellence in Education, 1983) presaged a new era of school reform in which excellence replaced equity as the primary objective of school critics. In this banking model of education, control of the reform agenda became centralized in state and federal agencies, further eroding the autonomy of the largely female teaching staffs in American public schools. In 1986, the Holmes Group, a coalition of research university deans, and the Carnegie Forum, a foundation-sponsored panel, turned their attention to teacher preparation programs. They concurred on the need for several changes: the elimination of undergraduate degrees in education and the implementation of rigorous master's degrees in pedagogy, the adoption of differentiated certification and licensing, and the employment of master or lead teachers in the school redesign process. Clark observes that state-based initiatives ignored the reform agendas of privately funded commissions and task forces "with the exception of an increased emphasis on an academic major and school restructuring," focusing instead on teacher testing, alternative routes to certification that bypassed SCDEs, and mandated limits on credit hours in the teacher education curriculum (1992, p. 2). Between 1987 and 1994, responding to the critiques of reform groups, three major changes occurred that would ultimately affect SCDEs and their faculty: (1) The National Board for Professional Teaching Standards (NBPTS) was established for the purpose of developing national licensing examinations for the advanced certification of qualified teachers, (2) the Interstate New Teacher Assessment and Support Consortium (INTASC) developed a set of standards for beginning teachers to serve as a framework for the systemic reform of teacher preparation and professional development, and (3) NCATE revised its accreditation criteria, incorporating INTASC principles on pedagogical studies in its twenty standards and sixty-nine indicators, part of a trend toward performance-based teacher preparation and licensing (NCATE, 1994). Four of NCATE's twenty standards related to professional education faculty, reaffirming the traditional paradigm for hiring, promotion, and tenure of faculty whose teaching, scholarship, and service demonstrate that they are qualified teacher scholars and actively engaged in the professional community (p. 12). Faculty workload standards expanded the assumption that faculty service should include "curriculum development, advising, administration, institutional committee work, and other internal service responsibilities" (NCATE, 1994, p. 13).

Establishment Critiques. Goodlad, in his five-year study of SCDEs, firmly criticized research universities for contributing to the erosion of state support for teacher education and for tenure-track faculty appointments in teacher education programs by using resources to promote research agendas and staffing teacher education programs with entry-level and temporary faculty. He faulted faculty, whose interests were far afield from both teacher education and collaboration with public schools, for the low prestige and recognition given to teacher education with the result that "temporary faculty do the bulk of teacher preparation" (1990, p. 78). As is so often the case in higher education, comprehensive and regional institutions, perceiving SCDEs as "cash cows" to be regularly milked in times of resource scarcity, followed the lead of research universities. The consequent erosion of tenure-track faculty in regional and comprehensive SCDEs that account for the preponderance of teacher education programs has contributed to the fragmented paradigm. Goodlad does not address the fact that women constitute the majority of this part-time, non-tenure-track workforce in teacher education, being employed as instructors, lecturers, and supervisors to teach and to supervise administrative and student interns and clinical placements. These individuals may be retired teachers or school administrators seeking part-time employment or doctoral recipients unable to obtain full-time positions. In any case, they operate outside the mainstream of departmental decision-making, frequently teaching evening, weekend, or off-campus courses, with little direct guidance or supervision, and no possibilities of tenure-track appointments. Indeed, one of the reasons that fewer than half of all SCDEs are NCATE-accredited is directly related to its tacit policy that at least one-half of the faculty have full-time status. Since many of these schools rely heavily on adjunct faculty, this criterion acts as a disincentive to seek NCATE approval.

Federal/State Critiques. The adoption of Goals 2000: Educate America Act of 1994 as the centerpiece of the Clinton agenda reinforced this message with its emphasis on a top-down model of improving education through national tests, national "world-class standards of excellence," and a national program for teacher education reform (National Education Goals Panel, 1995). The most recent reform report, *What Matters Most: Teaching for America's Future* (National Commission on Teaching & America's Future, 1996) builds on the concept of national goals by linking INTASC standards, NBPTS licensing, and NCATE accreditation as the most appropriate means of recruiting, preparing, and retaining excellent teachers. This report is more focused on gaining the support of state boards of education, echoing Goal 4 of the Clinton agenda, that SCDEs strengthen teacher preparation and professional development programs. In its endorsement of NCATE accreditation for quality control of teacher education, the report's authors observe that "the other side of the accreditation coin [is] that weak teacher preparation programs should be shut down" (p. 70). Unfortunately, only oblique references are made to teacher education faculty or to the larger administrative and governance structure in which SCDEs are situated. Gender, race, and social class are also missing from arguments supporting extended teacher education programs without suggesting how women and minority candidates should be subsidized in two years or more of part-time graduate study plus a one-year internship in public schools. While teacher tenure is theorized, a reference to changing ground rules is embedded in the observation that "tenure for teachers makes sense only when offers of continued employment are based on evidence of competence" (p. 55). New York State is the first state to endorse this recommendation, and as of 2003, all teachers will be required to fulfill 175 hours of continuing education every five years as the basis for recertification (Regents Task Force on Teaching, 1998).

Undoubtedly, a major shift in attitudes toward tenure is taking place. States, as well as professional associations and schools, are reevaluating tenure policies and conducting studies of faculty employment policies and practices in relation to the demands of their changing fields. In designing standards for the assessment of research productivity, teaching effectiveness, and service within the professional community, professional schools link this process to broader efforts of accrediting agencies to redefine faculty roles and rewards in the professions. In SCDEs, studies of faculty employment policies are also directly related to external demands for reform in the recruitment and preparation of teachers. Educators have responded to external pressures with their own sets of recommendations. In designing higher standards for assessing research productivity, teaching effectiveness, and university and community service, they have linked this process to state and agency efforts to increase the level of difficulty for teacher licensing and for certifying and credentialing professionals in other school- and nonschool specializations, that is, administration, counseling, and teaching exceptional populations. These efforts to elevate the status of SCDEs and move them from the margins to the center of university decision making have originated in institutional and disciplinary proposals to strengthen schools and schooling.

The Union Response. Both the AFT and the NEA have reiterated their support of academic freedom and tenure. In releasing its report, *The Vanishing Professor*, the AFT extends Goodlad's critique of SCDEs to all higher education, echoing his complaint about "the erosion of full-time tenure-track faculty positions and their replacement by a growing and exploited army of part-time and other non-tenure-track faculty" which it calls "the most dangerous trend in higher education today" (AFT, 1998, p. 1). The facts amassed by the AFT convey the gravity of the situation: part-time faculty rates in all higher education institutions have grown 266 percent in the past twenty-five years while full-time faculty have increased by only 49 percent.

If this trend continues, the AFT forecasts that part-timers will overtake full-timers by the academic year 2001. Between 1975 and 1995, the proportion of full-time faculty on term contracts increased from 19 to 28 percent; by 1995, 51 percent of new full-time faculty were appointed off the tenure-track (pp. 1, 2). The AFT also cites an *American Demographics* report of a 30 percent decline in new faculty appointments between 1991 and 1995. According to the AFT, early retirement buyouts of full-time tenured faculty at both the University of California (UC) and the City University of New York (CUNY) have become "the principal method for reducing the number of full-time tenured faculty" (p. 3). Indicative of the trend toward differentiated staffing in the UC system, graduate students account for 58.2 percent of all faculty, part-time adjuncts for 11.6 percent, non-tenure-track for 8.9 percent, and full-time tenure-track or tenured faculty for only 20 percent (p. 2). The AFT also reports that CUNY experienced a 21 percent decline in full-time faculty in the past decade (1987–1997) although total student enrollment rose 8.4 percent (p. 3).

The NEA Policy Statement on Academic and Intellectual Freedom and Tenure in Higher Education also expresses concern that "the excessive use of academic appointments on temporary, nontenure track, and/or multiple long-term contracts undermines academic and intellectual freedom, governance and educational quality" (p. 2). It defines tenure as "the expectation of continuing, indefinite, and/or permanent appointment in the institution, granted subsequent to the probationary period and extensive, objective peer and institutional review. The focus should be the institution. . . . Academic due process is usually part of a system of faculty self-governance and evaluation that has been established by faculty by-laws, constitutions, and collective bargaining contracts" (ibid.). This replacement of tenure-track faculty with a non-tenure-track and part-time teaching force strengthens the notion of a fragmented paradigm. In an autobiographical essay, Katherine Kolb, an adjunct instructor of foreign languages, articulates the dilemma faced by women faculty whose personal circumstances delay their entry into the academic job market, bringing them face to face with the reality that traditional assumptions about teaching and research further marginalize adjunct faculty.

> We adjuncts embody the dichotomy between teaching and research that is characteristic of the profession. And we do so in a way that accentuates the split between them. Whereas the two supposedly coexist harmoniously in college teaching, with teaching fed by research that feeds back into writing, in our case the cycle is in constant jeopardy, if it operates at all. No one expressly forbids our addressing the wider community, but no one expects it of us either. . . . Whereas regular faculty members can be promoted and the untenured tenured on the basis of publications and awards, there is nothing in the adjunct position to measure or reward progress. (1997, p. 99)

Gender and the Faculty Reward System

Traditional constructs for awarding tenure have tended to rely on assessments of the quality of faculty research, teaching, and service to the university community. As I found in my research on women faculty, in the majority of academic fields, women are less likely to gain tenure or to receive professional recognition for their research (Glazer-Raymo, 1999). Concern about the disproportionate weight given to research and scholarship, particularly in research universities, has resulted in a movement throughout the 1990s to reframe definitions of scholarship and to assign greater rewards to teaching and community service.

One of the most influential documents in both professional and academic disciplines emerged from the Carnegie Foundation for the Advancement of Teaching. In *Scholarship Reconsidered* (1990), Ernest Boyer proposed a paradigm for expanding the definition of scholarship to recognize and reward four dimensions: discovery, integration, application, and teaching. This approach resonated within the academy as institutions sought to respond to budget cuts, legislative mandates, and student needs. Admonitions that faculty workloads be increased, remedial programs be eliminated, and staffing be differentiated into clinical, part-time, and non-tenure-track positions, focused greater attention on the criteria for awarding tenure. Although Boyer and other critics referred to teaching and research as a "false dichotomy," evidence of the conflict between these two faculty roles has been endemic in a system that assigns greater status and prestige to those who do original research than to those who teach, design curricula, and collaborate with schools.

The Fragmented Paradigm

A subsequent Carnegie report, *Scholarship Assessed* (Glassick, Huber, & Maeroff, 1997), acknowledged the persistence of the research-teaching dichotomy, referring to it as a "fragmented paradigm" that fails to clarify how faculty are to be judged worthy of continued employment. Askling and El-Khawas (1997) also looked at the complexity and fragmentation of academic roles in their review of international data on faculty in fourteen countries. They question the underlying assumption of autonomy embedded within the research-teaching-administration model of the profession in the United States and other western nations. Their extended model adds two elements that acknowledge increasing role differentiation—academic management and leadership and special support activities related to such external mandates as quality assurance. This model has implications for women faculty in SCDEs as it contributes to the segmentation of academic work and the difficulty of meeting departmental, school, and institutional expectations for tenure and promotion. The fragmented paradigm is particularly applicable to SCDEs in view of the number and variety of their programs and the applied nature of the field. Goodlad found that on no campus was teacher education regarded as a highly scholarly activity but rather as a service to be provided. Nowhere was it organized or supported as a mission in its own right. "Rather, it took second place, at best, within an organized unit fitting the conventions of the institution as a whole" (p. 273). He observed that if the institutional research mission continues to dominate the tenure and promotion process rather than the activities required of teacher educators, then teacher education's weak status will persist.

My own review of faculty contracts in SCDEs in three private universities and one public multicampus system revealed few differences in the three major categories or sets of criteria for professional evaluation of candidates for promotion or tenure. These contracts each require evidence of research productivity, teaching effectiveness, and service to both the university and the larger educational community. However, the nature and extent of commitment to each of these aspects of faculty work tends to reflect the character of the institution (public-private, union-AAUP, doctoral-comprehensive) rather than education as a field of study. Four factors magnify the problem of redefining faculty roles in SCDEs: the multidisciplinary nature of field, the divergent visions of scholars and practitioners in its many specializations, the preoccupation of external arbiters with its credentialing and certifying role, and the ambiguity of the service function. In her analysis of faculty contracts in SCDEs in four land-grant universities in chapter 3, Lincoln's findings also support Goodlad's research, that tenure criteria are almost entirely based on the research mission of the institutions and on disciplinary and academic concerns whereas the activities that are central to teacher education—supervision of student experiences, work in professional development schools, or in the larger community—receive less emphasis and fewer rewards.

In research universities, where doctoral education provides the capstone experience, greater weight tends to be given to the quantity and quality of faculty research including publications in peer-reviewed journals, presentations at professional meetings, supervision of doctoral dissertations, and intellectual contributions to the discipline. In comprehensive institutions, where preservice teacher education predominates, effective teaching assumes greater importance and carries more weight. In teaching institutions where faculty are more likely to have twelve-credit hour workloads each semester, assessments of faculty performance seek sustained evidence of teaching effectiveness, determined through a variety of mechanisms—student evaluations, peer observations, and teaching portfolios.

Women Faculty Roles

Although tenure and promotion policies in regional colleges and comprehensive university SCDEs refer to teaching competence as an absolute condition for those whose primarily responsibility is teaching, it is ironic that faculty whose clientele are current or future teachers find it difficult to define what is meant by "effective teaching" in higher education. Women faculty are taking an active role in defining the criteria for evaluating the pedagogy of their colleagues and for implementing such innovative ideas as teaching portfolios, peer observations, and other mechanisms. This is proving to be a complex and contentious task as my interviews and observations in three SCDEs disclosed.

Interviews with women faculty revealed that efforts to modify tenure and promotion criteria are engaging both tenured and untenured colleagues in a highly reflective process about their own pedagogy. This process can be especially stressful in comprehensive universities, which have always considered themselves primarily teaching institutions, but have limited their assessment of pedagogy to the completion of student evaluation forms and peer reviews of untenured faculty. In one department of curriculum and teaching in a comprehensive institution, the personnel committee recommended a "thorough evaluation of the quality of the candidate's achievements in each of three areas"—Teaching, Scholarly Productivity, and University/Professional/ Community Service. To assess faculty teaching, it proposed the use of course and teacher evaluations, peer evaluations of teaching, student comments (written and oral) regarding teaching and advisement, course outlines, assignments, and tests. With respect to course evaluations, an area of some contention among faculty, it further proposed that "the focus . . . be on the pattern of response over a period of time and over different courses rather than the ratings in a single course or semester [and that] scores . . . be examined in view of the type of courses taught, the course enrollment, other information from students, peer observations, and information provided by the candidate in respect to the content, goals, and objectives of the course."

In another comprehensive university, an ad hoc faculty evaluation committee in its school of education recommended that all probationary faculty be required to compile an annual teaching portfolio for purposes of documenting teaching effectiveness and improving the quality of teaching and that tenured faculty also participate in this exercise as a form of continuing professional development. It proposed several items for inclusion in the portfolio: evidence of curriculum development, course information, and assessments of effective teaching from students, peers, and department chairs. The resolution ultimately approved by the faculty was scaled back to permit teaching portfolios for untenured faculty as an optional requirement only in each department's personnel guidelines.

As part of a realignment of faculty roles, women faculty are now rede-fining what it means to teach and learn in a feminist classroom (Maher & Tetreault, 1996; Ropers-Huilman, 1998; Gore, 1993). In the process, they are questioning the accepted paradigm through which faculty roles are also de-fined—teaching, research, and service. They are conducting this exercise in the context of a social change framework, one that challenges the power/ knowledge relationships that have sustained higher education throughout much of this century. As I found in my research on faculty tenure, in the majority of academic and professional fields, women are less likely to gain tenure, receive recognition for their scholarship, be promoted to tenured full profes-sors, and earn comparable economic rewards.

Meanwhile, hostile politicians, seeking to hold the line on escalating budgets, criticize what they perceived as the high opportunity costs of faculty workloads. Putative abuses are held up to public scrutiny as the norm rather than the exception. By 1994, twenty-three states were exercising greater in-tervention into workload standards, productivity, and classroom contact hours. For example, Ohio adopted a law directing all faculty in its public universities to devote 10 percent more effort to undergraduate teaching (Committee C, 1994). In October, 1999, an appeal challenging the constitutionality of this law was rejected by the Ohio Supreme Court, demonstrating the role of the courts in upholding changes in professional workload standards. At the same time, university administrators attempt to balance productivity mandates with reduced budgets and rising costs. In its analysis of faculty expectations, pri-orities, and rewards, the AAUP Committee C on College and University Teaching, Research, and Publication observed that "faculty feel caught in a ratcheting up of expectations to teach more, but continue to be evaluated primarily on publication, as these institutions continue to see faculty research as the road to institutional prestige and success" (p. 36).

Women Faculty as Agents of Change

A new paradigm for tenure is evolving, one that is based on a reformu-lation of the teaching-research-service model for evaluating faculty perfor-mance. Many factors are contributing to this paradigmatic change. Economic considerations relate to the overabundance of Ph.D.s in many academic fields and the consequent competition for tenure-track appointments, the need to cut budgets and the temptation to accomplish this task by replacing full-time faculty with graduate students, adjuncts, and short-term contractual appoint-ments. Political factors relate to legislative and trustee demands for greater productivity in the academic workforce, more flexibility in faculty appoint-ments, greater leverage in dealings with faculty bargaining agents, and, in the case of teacher education, the adoption of measures to redefine and strengthen its missions and purposes. Boyer's efforts to expand the meaning of scholarship has motivated learned societies and professional associations to redefine the meaning of scholarship, raise the quality of teaching, and promote university-school-community partnerships. Conferences on changing faculty roles and rewards and disciplinary and professional statements on faculty work in twelve fields exemplify the practical involvement of scholars in this process (Diamond & Adam, 1995).

Women, who are now entering the professoriate in increasing numbers, express concern about their prospects for earning tenure in a changing academy. In analyzing the tenure debate, the following questions need to be addressed: Can tenure be exchanged for other more immediate benefits? Can we design alternatives to tenure within the new paradigm that is evolving? Or should there be more equitable stop-the-clock tenure policies for women faculty, reduced teaching loads to enable untenured faculty to conduct research, and other mechanisms to assist women in managing constraints and opportunities? Will these have the support of boards of trustees, presidents, and provosts in research and teaching universities?

The current climate of reform in which faculty and administrators are actively collaborating to redefine the nature and rewards of faculty work is the appropriate time to engage in a dialogue of the situation of women and people of color and to confront the issues revealed by the data. SCDEs that now prepare master teachers for mentoring roles in K–12 schools might extend this practice to their own faculty, developing new models for the induction and support of women faculty and administrators, increasing pathways to leadership by identifying and promoting more women candidates, giving them greater access to research grants, adopting partner and spousal relocation programs, and appointing chairs who are agents for change rather than protectors of the status quo.

In his conceptualization of the professions, Freidson observes that "professions are divided internally by specialization and intellectual orientation into segments and by differences in interest, power, and prestige connected with the clientele being served" (1994, p. 144). He contrasts the relatively autonomous and powerful professions of law and medicine with their long traditions, distinct public images, and homogeneous systems of professional training over which they exercise significant control and the aggregate of professions such as teaching in which rank-and-file practitioners operate in different spheres from researchers and administrators. While he foresees the advent of greater external control of the status professions, he views governance of practice institutions and the relationship of working professionals to each other and to clients as essential to their continued strength and viability. Experience suggests, however, that from a feminist perspective autonomy and hierarchy, both of which are equated with specialized expertise, are incompatible concepts. It is evident that in SCDEs where women are the majority of students and faculty, numerical equality has not resulted in greater autonomy and status within the profession. The issues have become more ambiguous as the paradigm for rewarding faculty performance shifts from a model based on the triple premises of research, teaching, and service to a variety of models that encompass multiple and changing expectations in all three categories. As the ground rules change, practitioners, policy makers, and the professoriate have a great deal at stake in arriving at a thoughtful solution. In the meanwhile, this book provides a resource for opening up and expanding that dialogue in schools, colleges, and departments of education.

Notes

1. See Glazer-Raymo for comparable data on women in the professions of medicine, dentistry, pharmacy, law, business, architecture, and library science (1999, pp. 101–139).
2. Gender queuing theory refers to the persistence of sex segregation in the labor market and how power and privilege shape the composition of various occupations; see Reskin & Roos (1990) for an extended discussion of this phenomenon.

References

American Association of Colleges for Teacher Education. (1994). *Briefing Book 1993*. Washington, DC: Author.
American Association of University Professors. (1976). "Endorsers of the 1940 statement of principles on academic freedom and tenure." *AAUP Bulletin*, 62(3), 301–302.
American Association of University Professors. (1996, March–April). "Not So Bad: The Annual Report on the Economic Status of the Profession." *Academe*, 82(2), 14–22.
American Federation of Teachers. (1998). *The Vanishing Professor: An AFT Higher Education Report*. Washington, DC: American Federation of Teachers. <http://www.aft.org/higheduc/professor.html>.
Askling, B. & El-Khawas, E. (1997). *The Academic Profession: Evolving Roles in Diverse Contexts*. Unpublished paper presented at Association for the Study of Higher Education, Albuquerque, New Mexico.
Association of American Law Schools. (1994). "Report of the AALS special committee on Tenuring and the Tenure Process." *Journal of Legal Education* 42(4), 477–507.

Babco, E. L. (1997). *Professional Women and Minorities: A Total Human Resources Data Compendium.* 12th ed. Washington, DC: Commission on Professionals in Science and Technology.

Bensimon, E. M. & Marshall, C. (1997). "Feminist post-secondary policy analysis: Feminist and critical perspectives." In C. Marshall (ed.), *Feminist Critical Policy Analysis: A Perspective from Post-secondary Education.* London & Washington, DC: Falmer Press.

Bloland, H. G. & Bloland, S. M. (1974). *American Learned Societies in Transition: The Impact of Dissent and Recession.* New York: McGraw Hill.

Boyer, E. (1990). *Scholarship Reconsidered: Priorities of the Professoriate.* Princeton: Carnegie Foundation for the Advancement of Teaching.

Carnegie Task Force on Teaching as a Profession. (1986). *A Nation Prepared: Educating Teachers for the Twenty-First Century.* Washington, DC: Carnegie Forum on Education and the Economy.

Clark, D. L. (1992). "Leadership in Policy Development by Teacher Educators." In H. D. Gideonse (ed.), *Teacher Education Policy: Narratives, Stories, and Cases.* Albany, NY: State University of New York Press.

Clifford, G. J. & Guthrie, J. W. (1988). *Ed School.* Chicago: University of Chicago Press.

Committee C on College and University Teaching, Research, and Publications. (January–February 1994). "The Work of Faculty: Expectations, Priorities, and Rewards." *Academe,* 80(1), 35–48.

Diamond, R. M. & Adams, B. E. (1995). *The Disciplines Speak: Rewarding the Scholarly, Professional, and Creative Work of Faculty.* Washington, DC: American Association for Higher Education.

Freidson, E. (1994). *Professionalism Reborn: Theory, Prophecy, and Policy.* Cambridge, UK: Polity Press.

Glassick, C., Huber, M. T., & Maeroff, G. I. (1997). *Scholarship Assessed: Evaluation of the Professoriate.* San Francisco: Jossey-Bass.

Glazer, J. S. (1997). "Affirmative Action and the Status of Women in the Academy." In C. Marshall (ed.), *Feminist Critical Policy Analysis: A Perspective on Post-Secondary Education* (pp. 60–73). London: Falmer Press.

Glazer-Raymo, J. (1999). *Shattering the Myths: Women in Academe.* Baltimore & London: Johns Hopkins University Press.

Gore, J. (1993). *The Struggle for Pedagogies: Critical and Feminist Discourses as Regimes of Truth.* New York & London: Routledge.

Henke, R. R., Choy, S. R. & Geis, S. (1996). *Schools and Staffing in the United States: A Statistical Profile, 1993–94.* Washington, DC: U.S. Department of Education, Office of Educational Research and Improvement.

Kirschstein, R. J., Matheson, N., & Jing, Z. (1997). *Instructional Faculty and Staff in Higher Education Institutions: Fall 1987 and Fall 1992.* Washington, DC: U.S. Department of Education, Office of Educational Research and Improvement.

Kolb, K. (1997). "Adjuncts in Academe: No Place Called Home." *Profession* (pp. 93–103). New York: Modern Language Association of America.

LaNoue, G. R. & Lee, B. A. (1987). *Academics in Court: The Consequences of Faculty Discrimination Litigation.* Ann Arbor: University of Michigan Press.

Maher, F. A. & Tetreault, M. K. T. (1996). *The Feminist Classroom.* New York: Basic Books.

Marshall, C. (ed.). (1997). *Feminist Critical Policy Analysis: A Perspective from Post-Secondary Education.* London & Washington, DC: Falmer Press.

McCarthy, M. M. & Kuh, G. D. (1997). *Continuity and Change: The Educational Leadership Professoriate.* Columbia, MO: University Council for Educational Administration.

National Commission on Excellence in Education. (1983). *A Nation at Risk: The Imperative for Educational Reform.* Washington, DC: Author.

National Commission on Teaching & America's Future. (1996). *What Matters Most: Teaching for America's Future.* New York: National Commission on Teaching & America's Future.

National Council for Accreditation of Teacher Education. (1994). *NCATE Refined Standards.* Washington, DC: Author.

National Education Association. (1998). *NEA Policy Statements: Academic and Intellectual Freedom and Tenure in Higher Education.* Washington, DC: National Education Association. <http://www.nea.org/he/policy.html>.

National Education Goals Panel. (1995). *The National Education Goals Report: Executive Summary.* Washington, DC: Author.

Regents' Task Force on Teaching. (1998). *Teaching to Higher Standards: New York's Commitment.* Albany, NY: The University of the State of New York, State Education Department.

Reskin, B. F. & Roos, P. A. (eds.). (1990). *Job Queues, Gender Queues: Explaining Women's Inroads into Male Occupations.* Philadelphia: Temple University Press.

Ropers-Huilman, B. (1998). *Feminist Teaching in Theory and Practice: Situating Power and Knowledge in Poststructural Classrooms.* New York: Teachers College Press.

Snyder, T. & Hoffman, C. (1996). *Digest of Educational Statistics.* Washington, DC: U.S. Department of Education, Office of Educational Research and Improvement.

Snyder, T., Hoffman, C., & Geddes, C. M. (1997). *Digest of Educational Statistics*. Washington, DC: Department of Education, Office of Educational Research and Improvement.

The Holmes Group. (1986). *Tomorrow's Teachers*. East Lansing, MI: Author.

Tyack, D. & Hansot, G. (1985). *Managers of Virtue; Public School Leadership in America, 1820–1980*. New York: Basic Books.

Weis, L. (1997). Gender and the Reports: The Case of the Missing Piece. In C. Marshall (ed.), *Feminist Critical Policy Analysis: A Perspective on Primary and Secondary Schooling* (pp. 73–90). London: Falmer Press.

Wilson, R. (June 12, 1998). "Contracts Replace the Tenure Track for a Growing Number of Professors." *The Chronicle of Higher Education*, XLIV (40), A12.

CHAPTER 9

Graduate Student Socialization and Its Implications for the Recruitment of African American Education Faculty

JAMES SOTO ANTONY AND EDWARD TAYLOR

Despite decades of progress in gaining access to educational and professional opportunities, African Americans remain vastly underrepresented as faculty members in schools and colleges of education, particularly within predominantly white institutions. Nationally, African Americans make up only 7 percent of the faculty in schools and colleges of education—a figure that is highly inflated by their proportion as faculty within historically Black colleges and universities (NCES, 1990a; NCES, 1997a; Vining Brown, 1991). Although this rate of participation is meaningful, it is dramatically out of parity with African Americans' representation as students in the nation's educational system, and with their numbers among those pursuing doctoral degrees in the field of education (NCES, 1990a; Myers, 1998).

The paucity of African American faculty in schools and colleges of education has been, as in other disciplines, commonly attributed to the short supply of qualified candidates attaining the requisite graduate training for a faculty career. While this attribution has face validity, particularly for disciplines where there is a relatively lower rate of minority graduate student matriculation, the situation in education—which, among all fields, enjoys the largest participation rate of minority graduate students (Barbett & Korb, 1997)—appears to be more complex. The fact is, among African Americans who earn a doctoral degree, nearly 40 percent do so in education, making them the second largest racial group, behind European Americans, doing so (Barbett & Korb, 1997; NCES, 1990a).

Alternative explanations for the paucity of African American faculty are beginning to emerge. For example, Mickelson & Oliver (1991) found that many highly qualified African American applicants for open faculty positions were disregarded because they did not graduate from certain

189

prestigious programs. In a different study, Smith (1996) found that these, and other structural barriers, fuel the faulty perception that strong minority candidates for faculty positions simply do not exist, giving undue credibility to an educational pipeline-insufficiency attribution for low faculty diversity.

Certainly, rehabilitating how searches are conducted and increasing minority student participation in graduate school are important steps toward diversifying faculty ranks. However, these elements alone are increasingly being viewed merely as partial solutions (Antony & Taylor, 1998; Mickelson & Oliver, 1991; Myers, 1998; Smith, 1996; Taylor & Antony, in press). This is primarily because, despite being a leader in conferring doctoral degrees to minority students, education also produces the fewest number, relative to other fields, of minority doctoral degree recipients who aspire to pursue an academic career (National Research Council, 1990; Vining Brown, 1991).[1] This leads to an important question—How does the graduate school experience influence minority doctoral students to aspire or not aspire to careers in academia?

This paper emerges from the standpoint that education departments can better understand the complexities of increasing faculty diversity only by first critically examining what is occurring during graduate school that inhibits so many strong minority doctoral students—in this case, African Americans—from aspiring to, and ultimately pursuing, a faculty career. Specifically, we explore how African American doctoral students' conceptions of a professorial career are formed and shaped by their interactions with, and observations of, faculty and the faculty culture (i.e., through the professionalization and socialization process), and how these conceptions ultimately shape their aspirations to become education professors. Our data illustrate how African American students typically come to view their personal values (politically, philosophically, ethically, and intellectually) as incompatible with those they observe to be subtly promoted or actually promulgated by education faculty members and the faculty culture. Our data also demonstrate the extent of awareness these students have for how minority professors are regarded in academe. As we will show, for some, the decision to not pursue a faculty career stems from a self-perceived lack of fit—borne out of perceived value incompatibilities—with an academic career. For others, the decision to not pursue an academic career represents a disidentification with an academic career they feel would be characterized by the continual threat of being reduced (by others in the academy) to the stereotypes commonly attributed to minority professors. In light of our findings, we provide recommendations intended not only to improve our ability to encourage students of color to pursue academic careers, but also to help these students become professionalized into academic careers. Moreover, we provide recommendations that address how faculty mentors can help students of color develop strategies for reconciling the inevitable challenges associated with being an

African American academic—challenges that too often become impassable barriers to pursuing an academic career.

Background

The selection of any career takes place over an extended period of time and involves several decisions that typically are not made through a completely rational or purposive process (Bess, 1978). According to classical career-choice research, individuals are seen as "drifting" into occupations through a process of elimination rather than explicitly choosing them (Bess, 1978). Building on this earlier research, more recent occupational choice research reveals that a search for a fit between aspects of a given career and the characteristics and values of an individual considering that career are the cornerstones of the career choice process. In this literature, such fit or match is seen as the impetus for choosing or persisting in a career. Conversely, a lack of fit or match is the catalyst for an individual to change his or her mind and pursue another career (e.g., Antony, 1996, 1998a, 1998b; Fenske & Scott, 1973; Hansen, 1997; Holland, 1966; Zacarria, 1970). Moreover, occupational satisfaction, achievement, and stability are viewed to be a function of the congruence between the values, outlooks, and personality characteristics of an individual and those typically found among others in the prospective career (Antony, 1998a; Hansen, 1997; Holland, 1966; Zacarria, 1970). Therefore, for doctoral students to aspire to a faculty career, they must not only have the requisite training but must also feel the career fits who they perceive themselves to be, what they hold as personal values, and why they entered the field in the first place. This training, and the determination of person-career fit, are largely the result of the professionalization and socialization that occur during the graduate school years.

Unlike nonprofessional careers, faculty careers require formative education (Pascarella et al., 1987) and socialization that can be gained only in graduate school. Many researchers have shown that the firm commitment to an academic career usually takes place through the professionalization and socialization process in graduate school (Bess, 1978; VanMaanen, 1983). According to Bess,

> Professionalization is the process by which students learn the skills, values, and norms of the occupation or profession, while socialization . . . refers to the process of adopting the values, norms, and social roles which constrain behavior in an organizational setting such as a graduate school or the college or university where faculty are employed. (p. 292)

Other researchers have drawn a similar distinction (i.e., merely learning skills, values, and norms versus adoption of those elements) between professionalization and socialization (e.g., see Becker, Hughes, & Strauss, 1961; Bragg, 1976; Friedman, 1967; Tierney & Rhoads, 1993). Despite this important difference, professionalization and socialization do share many traits. In particular, both are continuous and social learning processes (Bess, 1978). Moreover, by elaborating upon the work of Bragg (1976), professionalization and socialization can be viewed as different parts of the same five-stage continuum. Specifically, the processes of professionalization and socialization both require: (1) observation—the identification of a role model(s); (2) imitation—the "trying on" of a role model's behavior; (3) feedback—the evaluation of the "trying on" of behavior; and (4) modification—the alteration or refinement of behavior as a result of evaluation. Socialization distinguishes itself from the process of professionalization by requiring a fifth stage, internalization or adoption—the incorporation of the role model's values and behavior patterns in the individual's self-image. Traditional notions of advancement into an academic career hold that the learning of academic culture and norms (i.e., professionalization) is necessary to form academic career aspirations. Additionally, adoption of academic culture and its associated norms has traditionally been seen as necessary for the successful pursuit of an academic career (Becker et al., 1961; Bragg, 1976; Friedman, 1967).

Recent theoretical evidence suggests that the acculturation demands associated with an expectation of adopting the mainstream culture and norms in order to succeed are problematic for populations of color (Fordham, 1988; Ogbu, 1990, 1993; Tierney, 1992). One of the reasons for this is that the academic culture and its norms are typically associated with European American and, increasingly, Asian values and sensibilities (Fries-Britt, 1998). As such, academically capable African Americans must reconcile how valuing academic and scholarly accomplishment—a precursor to adopting academic cultural norms—fits with their racial identity. Oftentimes, these students are challenged by their African American peers as "acting White" or not being Black enough, as if "academically-capable Black" were an oxymoron (Fries-Britt, 1998).

Ogbu (1993) argues that, in response to these tensions between academic ability and racial identity, these minority students develop a cultural frame of reference and identity that is opposed to the majority culture. Ogbu views this disassociation as the mechanism for many minority students' lower academic achievement. According to Fries-Britt (1998),

> [Even though] critics of Ogbu argue that his framework blames the victims for underachievement because they are "choosing" an oppositional identity or cultural frame of reference, which means they could choose to interact in the majority culture and develop other "positive" mechanisms for survival . . . evidence continues to emerge suggesting that gifted Blacks experience the judgement by other Blacks that they are "acting White" and/ or they think they are better than their peers because of their academic interests. (p. 559)

Certainly, issues of race and culture are factors to be considered in the experiences of Blacks who achieve academically (Fries-Britt, 1998). Summarizing
this point more succinctly, Cooley, Cornell, and Lee (1991) assert that the
difficulty Black students have in integrating their racial identities with their
academic capabilities can typically be traced to situations that reinforce (or
suggest to Blacks) that an intrinsic association between academic capability
and the majority race exists (as cited in Fries-Britt, 1998).

Additional empirical evidence highlighting the effects of having to reconcile personal accomplishment with stereotypical notions of race and achievement has been presented by other researchers and theorists. A particularly
relevant example can be found in the experimental work of Claude Steele,
who has developed a theory (parallel in many ways to Ogbu's notions) called
stereotype threat and domain disidentification theory (Steele, 1992; 1997;
Steele & Avonson, 1995). This theory, formulated to partially explain the
experiences and underachievement of African Americans in the domain of
school and women in the domain of math, illuminates the deleterious effect
of having to attend to the stereotypes of inferior intellectual ability that exist
for women and African Americans.

According to the theory, to sustain school success good feelings about
one's self depend in some part on good academic achievement. Students who
meet this requirement are seen as highly identified with academic activities
and the schooling domain. Unfortunately, for highly identified individuals, a
psychological barrier called stereotype threat can arise if the individual is
engaged in an activity for which a negative stereotype about his or her group
applies (Steele, 1997). As an example, school-identified African Americans
face the continual psychological barrier of possibly being reduced in the
minds of others to the unfortunate stereotype that Blacks are academically
inferior, instead of being seen as academically capable. Likewise, regardless
of their proven math ability, math-identified women have been shown to face
the continual threat of being reduced in the minds of others to the stereotype
that women are less capable in mathematics (Steele, 1997).

Research has clearly shown that, under stereotype threat conditions, test
performance and academic achievement suffer because anxiety (and its associated patterns of behavior) increase and the confidence necessary for good
performance decreases. Hampered achievement in turn can be self-threatening
because the individual is performing poorly in a domain from which they
derive a great deal of self-worth. This threat to the self, when chronic, can
pressure disidentification with the domain—a reconceptualization of the self
and of one's values through the removal of the domain as a self-identity,
making it less relevant in self-evaluation (Steele, 1997). Accordingly, in offering
a retreat from caring about the domain, disidentification, by undermining
achievement and motivation in the domain, too often has the deleterious
outcome of dropout. Traditionally, stereotype threat and domain disidentification

theory has been used to explain academic underachievement, particularly on standardized tests, and to a lesser extent, attrition from college. However, we have argued in other work that this theory can be extended as a framework for explaining the underattainment of professional careers among highly ambitious, highly identified African Americans (Taylor & Antony, in press).

Extant literature makes clear that the threat of being reduced by others to the stereotypes commonly associated with African Americans in an educational context can be an uncomfortable experience, motivating a reconceptualization of the self. Ogbu and Steele conceptually agree that students of color are pressed to redefine themselves. The former theorizes that students of color, in reaction to criticism from minority peers, develop an academically opposed frame of reference and identity. The latter sees student redefinition of the self as happening through disidentification with the academic domain, a result of performance anxiety that stems from attending to stereotypes about minorities in similar situations. In either case, students are responding to discomfort caused by the perceptions others have about minorities and academic achievement and accomplishment. Another potential discomfort for students of color is the expectation that, to successfully pursue an academic career, academic culture and norms must be subscribed to or adopted at the expense of their own values and sensibilities. Whether, and how, each of these discomforts is invoked for African American doctoral students through the professionalization and socialization process is unclear, and is therefore examined in this study. Moreover, the ultimate impact of these discomforts on the formation of academic career aspirations is also explored.

The Present Study

Open-ended interviews with twenty African American education doctoral students (14 women) were conducted during the spring and summer of 1997. Colleges of education at six Research I universities (4 public, 2 private) around the country were identified. Eight students were attending west-coast universities, six were in east-coast universities, three were from a southwestern institution, and three were from a midwestern institution. These institutions were selected for their status as leading departments in the field of education and for their strong reputations and rich history in developing doctoral students who go on to become faculty in schools and colleges of education. The names of African American doctoral students were obtained from the respective student personnel offices, and letters were sent inviting students' participation in the project.

Each of the participants had, at one point during their graduate career, expressed an interest in pursuing an academic career. Many had attended specialized workshops, seminars, or programs to encourage students of color to pursue academic careers. Prior to entering graduate school, each of the students had worked with noted faculty members and showed an interest in, and aptitude for, conducting research. As such, each student we interviewed had received multiple offers of admission into well-respected graduate programs, and most of the students received full financial support through a combination of fellowships and research assistantships, with several of the students we interviewed having received Spencer Foundation fellowships or awards. Fourteen of the students we interviewed were predissertation students either in their second year (4 students), or in their third year (10 students). The remaining six students were at the dissertation stage (2 in their third year, 2 in their fourth year, 1 in the fifth year, and one in the sixth year). All six of these students projected finishing their dissertations within two years of the date of the interview.

Traditional research methodologies, such as surveys and graduation rate data, although important, may limit understanding of the dynamics of relationships between students and faculty. Malaney (1988) suggests that qualitative, ethnographic studies have been overlooked in the field of graduate education research, especially ongoing and longitudinal investigations. Nettles (1987) and Stanfield (1994), noting that the quality of life for minority students has been underexamined, also calls for more qualitative research. Moreover, because oral interviews represent the most comprehensive way for people of color to articulate holistic explanations of how they construct their experiences and realities (Stanfield, 1994; Stage & Maple, 1996), we conducted face-to-face semistructured interviews with each participant.

Each interview continued until it was mutually agreed that the information was comprehensive. We sought to gather data that would allow the analysis to go beyond the mere reporting of experiences to provide insight into student's perceptions, relationships, circumstances, and choices. Each interview began with demographic information, including age, marital status, number of dependents, full-time/part-time status, their year in the program, department affiliation, and intent to pursue an academic career. Students were then asked to describe their educational history, how they made the decision to apply to graduate school, how they chose their particular institution, and why they chose education as a field of study. Their experiences in the doctoral program were explored, particularly their interactions with faculty, including their adviser. Specifically, students were asked to discuss how faculty interacted with them and the degree to which their professional and career aspirations were encouraged or hampered. Finally, they were asked to assess their ultimate career aspirations; whether or not they considered the professoriate as a goal and why; what they knew about faculty careers; and where they gained this information.

Participants' responses were transcribed and coded into general categories. During this process, utilization of the above-described five-stage professionalization/socialization continuum emerged as an organizing framework for our analyses and for our presentation of data throughout this paper. In particular, the five-stage continuum of professionalization and socialization, with its emphasis on the observation, emulation, and adoption of faculty culture, behaviors, and values, is useful for dissecting the graduate school experience. This framework allowed us to examine how interactions with faculty members and the academic culture of education departments influence students' self-assessments of fit with the academic career. It also allowed us to explore whether, in order to successfully to pursue an academic career, students perceive an expectation to internalize or adopt the academic culture and norms and, if so, how this perception influences their academic career aspirations. Most important, this framework allowed the treatment of participants' words as "thick description" of how the impact of graduate school professionalization and socialization experiences ultimately influence the formation of academic career aspirations.

Results

Positive Faculty Relationships and Professionalization as Precursors of Students' Attitudes toward Academic Careers

The importance of making connections with faculty has long been demonstrated in the research literature as a crucial element for ensuring student success. For example, higher-education scholars have clearly shown that involvement with faculty is directly related to higher levels of persistence and achievement among undergraduates. Likewise, doctoral students benefit from such involvement by learning the key pieces of information necessary for success—through a process of professionalization. Much of this information deals with graduate school or departmental culture and the language, issues, and behaviors valued by those in the fields for which the student is training.

For some faculty, the mentoring relationship involves presenting information formally, or in a structured manner or setting, to students. Other faculty members impart information through less formal channels. Some faculty members use collaboration on research projects as the mechanism for interacting with students, whereas others interact with students outside of the research context. Many faculty members expect students to go through a process of self-discovery, providing explanations and assistance only during times of need or confusion. In any form, mentoring by faculty is crucial for success. Like this student, most of the students we spoke to learned from others about the importance of connecting with a potential faculty adviser early on, one who would provide strong support and who could ensure proper professionalization:

There was this one professor, during my master's program, who put the idea in my head about pursuing a doctorate . . . I guess he just saw something in me. And he said, "Maybe you should think about the University of Greenland," where he used to teach and where [a professor whose work the student really admired] taught. He gave me the professor's home phone number and said, "Give him a call, tell him who you are, tell him you're a student of mine. He knows who I am." Surprisingly, it did not go as badly as I thought it would . . . and it all kind of just snowballed after that.

Other students had similar experiences, displaying great sophistication during the graduate school application process by contacting potential mentors in advance. Many students also obtained from pregraduate school mentors information about individual faculty members who were empathic and helped students of color succeed. As such, several of the students we interviewed applied selectively to graduate programs where specific minority faculty, or other nonminority faculty noted for their interest in issues pertaining to race or ethnicity as well as being noted for their success in mentoring students of color, taught:

During my master's degree work, we read all of Dr. Widermere's stuff. So knowing he was at Bayline University . . . and that I could go there and kind of learn from the source, so to speak, served as the draw, I guess . . . to learn under him.

I decided to apply to this program because I heard of Dr. Packard. She was a major factor in my decision.

So, to work with him would help me tremendously. I think the role model issue, but particularly from him, being an African American male. I, you know, you don't see young African American males with Ph.D.s in education talking about these issues, so I mean, I always have kind of looked up to him and learned a lot from him. So that made a big difference. Seeing someone doing something that you would like to do one day.

Those students who did not apply selectively to graduate programs, or who did not have specific faculty mentors who they sought to work with, were paired with faculty by the department. Much as when students made selective choices of faculty mentors, many departmental faculty-student pairings also led to mentoring relationships that these students felt worked quite well.

This place is a good fit for me because I've seen individuals here who have been able to really respond to my needs . . . My advisor is totally aware of my position . . . and that's what I am totally grateful for.

I think the factors are in place in terms of having, ah, you know, role models, mentors, things of that nature. Those things are in place right now, which I think are conducive to me growing in the way I want to.

Regardless of how students are paired with faculty, when students feel that they are able to connect with supportive mentors, there is great satisfaction. Moreover, students who connect with exceptional faculty mentors are likely to filter negative information about graduate school and academe, and take a positive outlook on faculty work, even in light of evidence that suggests it will be difficult at times, as these two students illustrate:

> Coming in, my whole perception was that, I kept hearing a lot that the politics involved in the academy are too difficult for people of color to survive as academics. If you want tenure, you have to put up with a lot of things. And it was a lot of hearsay that was affecting my decision to not want to go the faculty route. Um, but just being here, talking with my advisor . . . I think my whole position in this now is the work kind of rises above any politics that may take place . . . I guess I was realizing that my contribution would make a difference.
>
> In a faculty position, I would not only be able to influence people in the institution, but also outside. I worked in another sector for many years, on and off, and I really didn't feel I could affect people directly. Usually you are marginalized in that sector. True, that can still happen with faculty. However, my advisor says there are other meetings, other journals. You may not get published in the mainstream, traditional, functionalist journals. But hopefully, the different humanist, and subjective and qualitative journals will appreciate the work that I'll do.

As illustrated in these examples, the professionalization process aided in students' development of perceptions about academe. These students gained much information from faculty mentors that allowed them to process their observations and the discussions they had with fellow students. In particular, students were quick to acknowledge that the faculty route would present unique challenges to them as African Americans. However, they were able to draw upon the experience and advice of their faculty mentors to see viable ways of reconciling the tensions present in the faculty career so that they could pursue those careers.

Professionalization Occurs in Spite of Poor Faculty-Student Mentoring Relationships

Clearly, doctoral students who enjoyed supportive relationships with advisers were armed, through the professionalization process, with the tools and information to be able to maintain their interests in pursuing a faculty career. This professionalization not only included information that was relayed by faculty to the students, but also involved faculty incorporating students in research, giving them the skills and resources needed to present at conferences, and setting expectations for them to get involved in the department and in the professional associations. The product of this form of professionalization was oftentimes a boost in the students' confidence in being able to be a professor. As one student describes, these experiences made a world of difference:

> You know, presenting, being a participant in classes and doing some other key things. One of those key things would have been, I sat on a faculty committee. I also sat on a committee that was interviewing candidates for faculty positions. I saw myself—I said, "I could see myself sitting here, you know, talking about my areas of interest, what I've done, why I've done it, how I think it is important." Ah, it just seemed like something that I would enjoy . . . there are certain parts of it that don't fit in terms of the way I see myself. But just the [hiring] process . . . seeing that let me know this is something I could do.

As illustrated by the student's comments above, being able to pursue a career as a professor while acknowledging the challenges that would stem from being African American in a career environment that lacked substantial diversity was a byproduct of the professionalization received by supportive faculty.

In the absence of a supportive faculty mentoring relationship, students' understandings of the rules and values of academe, and their opinions of academic careers (all potential outcomes of professionalization) are too often shaped by sources other than a faculty mentor. As this student maintains, negative feelings about academe are typically the result of information gained through a different kind of professionalization—one rooted in student conversations, personal observations and interpretations of faculty behavior, and personal observations and interpretations of how faculty of color are treated in the academy:

> I think my experience is somewhat unique. I don't know, I guess I've just been somewhat fortunate to be given opportunities. I rarely talk to other African American students around the country who have been given these opportunities. I think if you don't get those experiences, you can oftentimes take a lot of your own perceptions of what being a faculty member is like and kind of run with them and never have them challenged by any other, um, position, because you never get that opportunity.

Additional evidence supports the idea that those students who felt their faculty mentoring relationship was less than ideal, or did not live up to their expectations, were more likely to form opinions about the academy that are rooted in observations and personal interpretations, rather than direct contact with faculty mentors. These two students, who acknowledged having nobody on the faculty to turn to for advice or assistance, illustrate the point:

> I know I have the skills, but question whether or not I have the stamina. I've just heard too many horror stories about how hard it is for African American

women. And, I've never been able to produce good work when I've been under
a lot of stress or strain . . . it would be difficult to survive unless you become
like the professor I heard about who just stole work from her graduate
students . . . because she was so frantic about getting tenure.

Do I want to go into academics? If so, what are . . . the sacrifices I am
willing to make to get there? I think everybody deals with these issues, but
particularly minorities because there is a host of other added issues. And we
[fellow minority students] have watched faculty of color . . . we see what they
go through. And we watch that very closely and we talk about it, you know?

What these comments show is that students develop an awareness of the
values and priorities of academic education that, though valid, is not balanced
(or even countered) by the experiences and interpretations of faculty mentors
who they trust and admire. Upon being asked why students of color are
underrepresented as faculty, one student asserted that students of color typically only hear or see the bad things. According to this student, nobody ever
tells students of color that, despite the difficulties, personal sacrifices and
problems associated with being a person of color in the academy, academic
work can be very good work. In his mind, students of color should be mentored
and told that in faculty positions:

you're not set up, you're not structured from nine to five, sitting at a desk
everyday. So there's flexibility. And if one is on the tenure track, and be it five
or seven years, one obtains tenure, that's security that can't be matched by too
many other positions. So, that's important. And finally, there is a lot of influence and power in faculty positions. To think that you could be in one of those
positions of power to try to drive the changes that you think should occur in
education . . . that's a very appealing message few students of color receive.

Socialization and Acceptance of Academic Values: Implications for Choosing a Faculty Career

As Ogbu and Steele conceptually agree, students of color are pressed
during the schooling process to redefine themselves in order to either fit in
or avoid being reduced to stereotyped characterizations of students of color.
Both theorists argue that students of color respond to discomfort caused by
the perceptions others have about minorities and academic achievement by
disassociating from academics. Ogbu theorizes that students of color, in reaction to critique from minority peers, develop an academically opposed
frame of reference and identity. Steele sees student redefinition of the self as
happening through disidentification with the academic domain, a result of
performance anxiety that stems from attending to stereotypes about minorities in similar situations.

Along these lines, many of the students we interviewed who did not connect with a mentor experienced great disillusionment with a potential faculty career. These students felt that in order to succeed as an academic, sacrifices needed to be made. They saw an expectation of needing to subscribe to or adopt academic values at the expense of their own, something that would turn them into the stereotypical minority who has sold out. Implicit here is the idea that, without selling out, they would merely be reduced, in the eyes of other academics, to the stereotypical minority who has not been professionalized or socialized properly—the minority who just cannot play the game the way it was intended to be played. These four students illustrate the point:

Many people spoke to me about pursuing a faculty career. It was a tremendously exciting idea, to explore new ideas, to be creative, to pay tribute to a body of knowledge, to be a part of the academy. Reality set in when I began to see that the Ph.D., like anything else, is a game, it's a process. Like when people say, "jumping through hoops"—it's more than just doing what's required and a little bit more. It's also accepting a certain ideology. And that was difficult for me.

And you look at who's been successful and who hasn't . . . and what kind of sacrifices they've made, because there are faculty here who, I think, have been successful, but have done it in a way that a lot of us [fellow minority students] agree we wouldn't do. . . .

[As a member of this scholarship committee] I've watched while they've picked the other students that were going to be funded . . . and the one tenured minority professor on the committee makes compromises that I wouldn't make. As a professor of color, you have an added responsibility . . . to shake things up a bit . . . and to point out when other people are coming from a limited standpoint. Also, one of the other professors on the committee is a white woman . . . who has had . . . very little experience with minorities. And we're choosing the . . . six or seven . . . fellows, but I think four of them were minorities. And she says, "Well, do you think this cohort looks a little bit too minority?" And nobody said anything! And mind you, last year, all the selected fellows were white. In fact, the whole stack of files we had to select from . . . all white . . . so I said, "Well, was last year's cohort too white?" Nobody else was gonna say anything. I mean, this minority professor on the committee certainly wasn't going to say anything. . . .

There are faculty that seem to have . . . bought into the system a little bit more than I would. And you see it, and I think this also comes from their training. But you see it in the kind of work they do, you know, where there's a faculty member who, for example, might be studying minority aggression from a . . . perspective that . . . buys into the idea that something is wrong with these kids and as a result, perpetuates stereotypes. People will hold this person up as a great . . . scholar . . . but to me, the research does damage. She makes compromises that I wouldn't make.

In short, these African American students were unable to see how, without coopting themselves, they could reconcile the inevitable challenges, demands, and sacrifices associated with being a minority academic in order to successfully pursue an academic career.

In other cases, African American students were, despite the challenges, able to see a way to work as an academic without coopting their values or ethnic identities. Once again, the difference was having a faculty mentor against whom students could bounce ideas, who was able to balance students' own interpretations with experiences and views the students might otherwise not receive:

> A senior faculty [mentor] showed me this big grid and it said there were this many Ph.D.s in a year... the percentage of all the Ph.D.s that were black males... was like a fraction of a fraction of something. And so that was a message. And I guess I saw it as a positive message because look, I have an opportunity to do this... I want to try and use this opportunity to help people...
>
> I'm very aware of some of the politics in the sense that a lot of our research—my research in particular—may not be valued... in the literature. For me, this is a big issue... [but] I've talked to [mentors] about navigating the tenure track... with that type of support, I'm really in a good spot.

Toward further illustrating the pivotal role that sensitive, caring, yet honest mentoring can play in helping students of color maintain their faculty career aspirations in the face of adversity, one student's comments are particularly revealing. During the interview, this student, who enjoyed exceptional faculty mentoring, had been describing her fears about being a faculty member of color—fears largely stemming from the anxiety of having to attend to many issues, having to deal with poor treatment, and having to respond to a variety of negative influences. Upon being asked how she would reconcile the difficult issues and negative influences that sometimes came with being a faculty member of color in the academy, this student responded:

> All of these [difficult] issues are a part of my decision to go into the faculty. I'm trying to go in with my eyes open.... And I think people have started to help me... I've been very fortunate to be exposed to [faculty] who are not afraid to share their mistakes, which has been a major help. I'm primarily talking about other African Americans that have opened their lives to me, taken the time... and I look to them for that. I value their opinions. I value what they share. So that's the best way to answer the question about those influences.

Discussion

The evidence provided here begins to paint a picture of how crucial it is for African American students to have professionalization experiences shaped by caring and supportive faculty mentors who understand the pressures and anxieties of students of color. This type of mentoring not only helps students build important academic skills and gain crucial experiences, but also helps students place their difficulties (both current and future) against a larger context. Specifically, students are able to respond to their fears and anxieties about being a future faculty person of color by conversing with their mentors. More to the point, they use mentors' experiences and perspectives as a counterbalance against the deluge of information—typically gleaned through personal observations and discussions—that otherwise would indicate that a faculty career is not for them.

Students who did not have this type of mentoring were at a disadvantage. Specifically, those without this form of support found themselves being professionalized through other means. In short, students who lacked mentoring never received the message that their supported counterparts heard in one shape or form—that despite the real, and oftentimes oppressive, difficulties and challenges of being an African American in academe, the work of a faculty member can be good, balanced, and rewarding.

The unsupported students, lacking the filter of the experienced mentor, saw only those aspects of the academic culture that require too much personal and familial sacrifice. These students were primed to pay particular attention to those aspects of the academy that abuse faculty of color; those aspects that demand students of color to acculturate in order to succeed in graduate school and, later on, as academics. Such conditions, no doubt, can lead a promising student of color to become uncertain whether an academic career is for them. Sadly, this is what we found. Among those students who had support, every single one expressed enthusiasm—even if guarded—about tackling a faculty career. Among those students who lacked support, there was a uniform ambivalence toward academic education, and a nearly unanimous feeling that a faculty career would lead them down the path of becoming a sell-out— someone who has made too many personal sacrifices in order to become a professor. Unlike their supported counterparts, those students who lacked the support of a mentor were unable to find a happy and healthy medium between keeping true to themselves and their own values, and surviving in a system that they felt invariably promotes contrary values.

In this chapter, we provide initial evidence for a preliminary model—one that represents the dynamic system of interpretation that informs graduate students' career decision making. We propose that this dynamic system of interpretation is the psychological space within which students must reconcile their personal values; their ethnic identities; the reverence, power and responsibility they give to the field of education; their observations of negative aspects of the faculty/academic culture; and their conversations with peers. The catalyst for decision making in this dynamic system of interpretation is their conversations and interactions with faculty mentors. As such, those students who have positive, caring, and honest mentoring that acknowledges the challenges of being a person of color in the academy, emerge from this dynamic system feeling capable of pursuing a faculty career. Those without this level of support emerge from this dynamic system of interpretation in fear of having to sacrifice in order to become education faculty. These students are unable to reconcile the incompatibilities between their own values and those required for success as a member of an education faculty. It is our hope that the evidence presented in this paper points to an opportunity for schools and colleges of education to rethink the impact that education professors' mentoring can have on minority students' career plans.

Conclusion

African American graduate students, in this sample, were highly domain identified, and brought to the table not only impressive academic credentials but deeply internalized beliefs about their ability to contribute to the traditional research, teaching, and service goals of universities. In addition, they exhibited strategies for resisting disidentification borne from years of experience. Although pervasive and disheartening, the operation of stereotype threat served as a primary motivator in guiding research interests. Because (in students' views) much of educational theory, research, and practice about minority children has been generated by European Americans in ways that have problematized and marginalized African Americans, they were highly motivated to challenge and expand existing paradigms. Their sense of mission was palpable. The desire to improve education for African American children, to be their voice, and to represent their needs and concerns was tied directly to research interests. Respondents preferred research that integrated theory and practice and were openly skeptical of faculty whose projects appeared to be self-serving rather than community-serving. Such faculty were described as "hit-and-run" academics, who would go, for example, into an urban setting, win the trust of students and teachers, and get data and publish it with no feedback or benefit to the school or children.

In all cases, students understood that the desire to connect research and service could potentially have a paradoxical effect. Many of these students were intent on pursuing an African American research agenda, even if mainstream journals did not particularly value (or want to publish) their work. They understood that if their research projects were difficult to fund, progress toward tenure was endangered. Nonetheless, there was widespread unwillingness to compromise essential values, even if it meant lost opportunities at top tier universities. What was fascinating was that, in some cases, this commitment would inhibit academic career aspirations. In other cases, students were able to hold this commitment to values without forgoing their plans to pursue an academic career. This latter group of students, unlike the former, was prepared—as a function of the sort of socialization and mentoring they received—to pursue an academic career without feeling that they would have to sacrifice their values and identities. These students felt that they could be faculty and still have a chance to improve schooling for African American children, all while resisting the stereotypes too commonly applied to the work of African American scholars, or to these scholars themselves.

Our analysis of these data also offers some early support of Steele's framework for higher education and some insights into the successful socialization of African American graduate students in education. And although this study was not designed for the purposes of generalizing results to all African American students at all research universities, we believe our data contribute to a larger understanding of complex phenomena with an eye toward generating potentially powerful ideas for others to consider and study. In particular, we believe that institutions of higher education should be encouraged by the presence of dynamic, enthusiastic, highly capable, and motivated African American doctoral candidates. These students possess the potential to reinvigorate both theory and practice in education. Specifically, these students can influence the production of the culturally relevant pedagogy necessary for an increasingly diverse student body. However, these students' presence also signals the immediate need for departments to confront some age-old tensions.

The first tension is the traditional distance between service and research. Many faculty members in education model a considerable separation between the two; these students, however, operate within a value system that says research *must* be of service. The challenge is for faculty members to understand this mind-set and begin to capitalize on the opportunity not only to bridge the gap between theory and practice, but to make their own work more relevant and exemplary. A second tension is embodied in the question, Whose responsibility is it to mentor graduate students? There are long-standing issues in many departments as to whether the responsibility is primarily individual (i.e., the adviser) or collective (i.e., the faculty's). Our data suggest that African American students benefit from a collective approach. Students realize that often the sole African American faculty member must act as "Hercules" for all the minority students and that such expectations are untenable. There is no strong evidence to suggest that mentoring must come from gender- and race-matched faculty. In fact, senior faculty members, who are usually White males, generally have more experience and resources. Recipients of their support appeared particularly well socialized. Their potential to contribute, however, must be weighed against the evidence that some White mentors (unknowingly or not) exacerbate stereotype threat for African American students through inattentiveness, or through damaging socialization practices.

One final note rooted in theory is in order. Steele proposes that schooling for African Americans can be improved through institutional strategies that reduce stereotype threat. In particular, he suggests that there are ways in which programs can be designed to assure students that they will not be cast in the shadow of negative stereotypes, where individual characteristics can surmount group membership. "Wise schooling" (Steele, 1997, p. 624; Taylor & Antony, in press) practices include strategies designed to reduce the threat of negative racial stereotyping that can undermine student performance. Such practices have been shown, in early results, to improve academic performance for groups negatively affected by stereotyping, such as African Americans and women in math and science (Steele, 1992; Steele & Aronson, 1995). Examples of such practices include: (1) optimistic teacher-student relationships, where teachers make their confidence in students explicit; (2) challenging, rather than remedial expectations and academic work, which builds on promise and potential, not failure; (3) stress on the expandability of intelligence, that skills can be learned and extended through education and experience; (4) affirmation of intellectual belonging; (5) emphasis on the value of multiple perspectives; and (6) the presence of role models of people who have successfully overcome stereotype threat.

In terms of our data, a wise schooling model of successful socialization could serve departments and institutions that are attempting to reduce stereotype threat and other obstacles that have kept African Americans from seeking academic careers. Analysis of individual programs could reveal current or prospective weaknesses. Strategies for mitigating the impact of unhealthy departments or academic units could then be devised. For example, institutions with very few African American students could compensate with a committed group of faculty members, a benevolent travel fund for conference attendance, and e-mail accounts. Those with very few (or even no) African American faculty could similarly counterbalance by matching students to adviser by research interests, or by fostering interdepartmental relationships with faculty of color. Potential mentoring relationships could be pursued by the department in a formal way and not place this burden on students. Given the impact socialization and mentoring have on the academic career aspirations of the students we interviewed, wise schooling strategies appear to represent an approach that is consistent with our findings. As such, we believe that the effects of wise schooling practices upon influencing the academic career aspirations of minority students offer a compelling avenue for future inquiry.

Notes

Correspondence regarding this article may be addressed to the authors at: University of Washington, College of Education, Educational Leadership and Policy Studies, Box 353600, Seattle, WA 98195-3600. This research was funded in part by grants from the Institute for Ethnic Studies at the University of Washington, and from the Boeing Foundation's Endowment for Faculty Excellence. All views expressed are those of the authors and do not necessarily represent those of the granting agencies.

1. We readily acknowledge that career decision-making is complex and that there are many lucrative or otherwise attractive administrative alternatives to faculty careers available to doctoral degree recipients in education. However, others have clearly shown that even in these alternative administrative positions, African Americans are, as in academe, grossly underrepresented (e.g., see NCES, 1997b; Smith, 1996).

References

Antony, J. S. (1996). *Factors Influencing College Students' Abandonment of Medical Career Aspirations.* Unpublished doctoral dissertation. University of California, Los Angeles.

————. (1998a). "Exploring the Factors that Influence Men and Women to Form Medical Career Aspirations." *Journal of College Student Development,* 39(5), 1–10.

————. (1998b). "Personality-Career Fit and Freshman Medical Career Aspirations: A Test of Holland's Theory." *Research in Higher Education,* 39(6), 679–698.

————. & Taylor, E. (1998). *Graduate Student Socialization and Its Implications for the Recruitment of African American Education Faculty.* Invited presentation at the conference: "Keeping Our Faculties: Addressing the Recruitment and Retention of Faculty of Color in Higher Education," Minneapolis, MN.

Barbett, S. F. & Korb, R. A. (May 1997). *Enrollment in Higher Education: Fall, 1995.* National Center for Education Statistics, Report No.: 97-440, Washington, DC: Office of Educational Research and Improvement.

Becker, H. S. et al. (1961). *Boys in White.* Chicago: The University of Chicago Press.

Bess, J. L. (1978). "Anticipatory Socialization of Graduate Students." *Research I Higher Education,* 8, 289–317.

Bragg, A. K. (1976). *The Socialization Process in Higher Education.* Washington, DC: ERIC/AAHE Research Report No. 7.

208   JAMES SOTO ANTONY AND EDWARD TAYLOR

Cooley, M. R., Cornell, D. G., & Lee, C. (1991). "Peer Acceptance and Self-Concept of Black Students in a Summer Gifted Program." *Journal of Education of the Gifted*, 14, 166–177.

Fenske, R. & Scott, C. (1973). "College Students' Goals, Plans, and Background Characteristics: A Synthesis of Three Empirical Studies." *Research in Higher Education*, 1, 101–118.

Fordham, S. (1988). "Racelessness as a Factor in Black Students' School Success: Pragmatic Strategy or Pyrric Victory?" *Harvard Educational Review*, 58, 43–84.

Friedman, N. L. (1967). "Career Stages and Organizational Role Decisions of Teachers in Two Public Junior Colleges." *Sociology of Education*, 40(2), 120–134.

Fries-Britt, S. (1998). "Moving Beyond Black Achiever Isolation: Experiences of Gifted Black Collegians." *Journal of Higher Education*, 69(5), 557–576.

Hansen, L. S. (1997). *Integrative Life Planning: Critical Tasks for Career Development and Changing Life Patterns*. San Francisco, CA: Jossey-Bass.

Holland, J. L. (1966). *The Psychology of Vocational Choice*. Waltham, MA: Blaisdell.

Malaney, G. D. (1988). "Graduate Education as an Area of Research in the Field of Higher Education." In J. C. Smart (ed.), *Higher Education: Handbook of Theory and Research, Vol. IV* (pp. 397–454). New York: Agathon Press.

Mickelson, R. A. & Oliver, M. L. (1991). "Making the Short List: Black Candidates and the Faculty Recruitment Process." In P. G. Altbach & L. Lomotey (eds.), *The Racial Crisis in Higher Education* (pp. 149–165). Albany, NY: State University of New York Press.

Myers, S. L. (1998). *The Crisis of Minority Faculty: Under-Representation in Higher Education*. Paper presented at the Annual Meeting of the American Educational Research Association, San Diego, CA.

National Center for Education Statistics. (1990a). *A Descriptive Report of Academic Departments in Higher Education Institutions*. Washington, DC.

National Center for Education Statistics. (1997a). *National Survey of Post-Secondary Faculty, 1997*. Washington, DC.

National Center for Education Statistics. (1997b). *Public and Private School Principals in the United States: A Statistical Profile, 1987–88 to 1993–94*. NCES 97-455, Washington, DC: U.S. Department of Education.

National Research Council. (1990). *Survey of Earned Doctorates*. Washington, DC.

Nettles, M. (1987). *Financial Aid and Minority Student Participation*. Princeton, NJ: Educational Testing Service.

Ogbu, J. U. (1990). "Overcoming Racial Barriers to Equal Access." In J. I. Goodlad & P. Keating (eds.), *Access to Knowledge: An Agenda for Our Nation's Schools* (pp. 59–89). New York: The College Board.

———. (1993). "Differences in Cultural Frame of Reference." *International Journal of Behavioral Development*, 16, 483–506.

Pascarella, E. T. et al. (1987). "Becoming a Physician: The Influence of the Undergraduate Experience." *Research in Higher Education*, 26(2), 180–201.

Smith, D. G. (1996). *The Pipeline for Achieving Faculty Diversity: Debunking the Myths*. Paper presented at the annual meeting of the Association for the Study of Higher Education (ASHE), Memphis, TN.

Stage, F. K. & Maple, S. A. (1996). "Incompatible Goals: Narratives of Graduate Women in the Mathematics Pipeline." *American Educational Research Journal*, 33(1), 23–51.

Stanfield, J. H. (1994). "Ethnic Modeling in Qualitative Research." In N. K. Denzin & Y. S. Lincoln, (eds.), *Handbook of Qualitative Research* (pp. 175–188). Thousand Oaks, CA: Sage.

Steele, C. M. (1992, April). "Race and the Schooling of Black Americans." *The Atlantic Monthly*, 68–78.

———. (1997). "A Threat in the Air: How Stereotypes Shape Intellectual Identity and Performance." *American Psychologist*, 52(6), 613–629.

———, & Aronson, J. (1995). "Stereotype Threat and the Intellectual Test Performance of African Americans." *Journal of Personality and Social Psychology*, 69, 797–811.

Taylor, E. & Antony, J. S. (in press). "Wise Schooling and Stereotype Threat Reduction: Successful Socialization of African American Doctoral Students in Education." *Journal of Negro Education*.

Tierney, W. G. (1992). "An Anthropological Analysis of Student Participation in College." *Journal of Higher Education*, 63(6), 603–617.

———. & Rhoads, R. A. (1993). *Faculty Socialization as Cultural Process: A Mirror of Institutional Commitment*. ASHE-ERIC Higher Education Report No. 93-6. Washington, DC: The George Washington University, School of Education and Human Development.

VanMaanen, J. (1983). "Doing New Things in Old Ways: The Chains of Socialization." In J. L. Bess (ed.). *College and University Organization: Insights from the Behavioral Sciences*. New York: New York University Press.

Vining Brown, S. (1991). "The Impasse on Faculty Diversity in Higher Education: A National Agenda." In P. G. Altbach & L. Lomotey (eds.), *The Racial Crisis in Higher Education*, (pp. 149–165). Albany, NY: State University of New York Press.

Zaccaria, J. S. (1970). *Theories of Occupational Choice and Vocational Development*. Boston, MA: Houghton Mifflin.

Conclusion

So What Now? The Future of Education Schools in America

ARTHUR LEVINE

- Three years ago, I assembled an advisory counsel composed of smart, creative, and influential people whose advice I trusted. At the first meeting I asked them what they thought of education schools. A former college president, now a leader in the philanthropic community said she was "not convinced the country would be any worse off if they all closed tomorrow." A Wall Street executive and former Ivy League college board chair said, "perhaps Teachers College was just the best of a bad breed."
- In the past several years, I have met with a number of governors. Rarely have those conversations failed to include criticism of higher education with particular blistering reserved for education schools.
- When I first started as president of Teachers College, I found the heads of national foundations sometimes expressed doubts about education schools as questions. More often now, they offer the same criticisms as facts.
- I was sitting on a World Bank advisory panel along with the current or former education ministers or subministers of four countries. During a discussion of a Third World literacy project, the chair of the group, apropos of nothing, said education schools are terrible. The other three ministers nodding in agreement. Then upon realizing I was in the room, they apologized.

This chapter asks why all these people are saying such horrid things about education schools. It also discusses what we need to do about these criticisms and what will happen if education schools fail to act.

211

The Case against Education Schools

The grievances against schools of education have at least three different roots. The first is long-standing and its elements have been mentioned in many of the preceding chapters. Education is a low-status profession and the schools that prepare educators share the very same mantel. The reasons are familiar:

- Education schools are poorly regarded by their university brethren and reside near the bottom of the academic hierarchy, but they are "coach class" to universities and therefore tolerated.
- The historical roots of education schools are noncollegiate, coming out of the normal school movement, giving education schools a less-than-prestigious pedigree in the university world.
- Education is a traditionally female profession, which in a male-dominated culture is a stigma. Moreover, education schools attract a student body that is comprised disproportionately of first-generation college, low socioeconomic status, women, minorities, and lower academic achievers.
- Educators are not well paid and in a society that valuates the importance of work and workers by salary. This is a minus. I don't know how many times I have been told that "teachers do not work hard," only nine months a year and "anyone could do their job."
- Education school alumni are in the main incapable of supporting their schools in the same fashion as graduates of medical, law, and business schools, so education schools remain one of the most underfunded in the university.

What all this says is that educators and education schools have been looked down upon in the United States historically. But a persistent lack of esteem does not explain the recent amplification of anger, criticism, and calls for action regarding them.

The second root of the current criticism of colleges is the school on reform movement that has been going on for the past decade and a half since the release of the *Nation at Risk* report. Americans have a tendency not to respond to their doubts and discontent on a continuing basis, but rather to store them up and periodically announce that there is a crisis in some aspect of American life. We then issue multitudinous reports on the problem, affix blame, mobilize the nation's resources to end the crisis, form a cornucopia of reform groups, experiment like crazy with approaches to the problem, and legislate randomly at all levels of government. Finally, we do not so much resolve the crisis as get bored with it and move on to the next one.

This is what is happening in education today. Every thirty years with the predictability of a metronome a reform movement of this type sweeps through education. This is why the 1963 James Koerner quote with which Bill Tierney begins this book is so reassuring. It describes an era that is familiar, a set of conditions that are a carbon copy of the present. It sounds like business as usual. Indeed, much of what is happening today occurred in the past reform movement as well. Then as now, the media was filled with reports of low student and teacher achievement; voluminous commission reports indicting education and education school were issued; philanthropic dollars poured into educational reform; government rhetoric and actioo-soared some under the banner of education importance, and the political right wing transformed complex educational issues into simple ideological tests.

Such movements have had the effect of magnifying the historic grievances against education schools. Underlying them is a sense that education is broken and needs to be fixed. The traditional education school response has been denial, followed by a frenzy of effervescent activity, a wave of innovation, and a small number of signature activities associated within a particular movement.

The current reform movement certainly explains the escalation of criticism of education schools and the sense of urgency for change. And if history is any guide, it also leads one to believe that with the passage of the movement, things will revert to normal with education schools simply being held in low esteem.

The third and final root for the current criticism is unique for our generation. Our society is undergoing profound changes—economic, demographic, technological, and global. Change of the magnitude we are experiencing today is rare. When it occurs, as it did in the industrial revolution, it has the effect of leaving our social institutions behind. The result is that these institutions, created for a time that no longer exists, do not fit the current era. They appear to have stopped working. Today we have this feeling about many of our social institutions—government, health care, manufacturing, the family, and education, to name a few.

In contrast to the reform movements, the need in the present time is not to repair a cherished institution that is currently broken. It is to rethink and redesign the institution to serve a changed society. This is an enormously hard task, quite different from tinkering, because what actually occurs is the passing of a familiar world as a new world is being born. It is far easier to see what is being lost then what is coming into being. To name the new era, to recognize its contours, is the work of historians decades later, not those living through the change.

Unlike the rising levels of doubt and criticism that occur in a reform movement, those in a time of quick and dramatic change do not fade away.

They persist until the existing institution adapts to the new social realities or is replaced.

What adaptation means is elusive. There is no golden era to return to. Our society is in motion; the pace of change seems to be accelerating, not stabilizing. Which of today's social changes do existing institutions follow—the demographic, economic, technological, global or some combination? How does an institution adapt to them? It is a guessing game. In a very real sense, it is this third root that will drive the future of America's education schools.

A Future for Education Schools

The chapters by Bill Tierney, Jeannie Oakes, Mary Kennedy, and Yvonna Lincoln focus on the fundamental issue facing education schools in the current era: What are they supposed to accomplish? What is the purpose?

Recently, I attended a meeting of the heads of a number of national education schools. The topic of what research is most important was being discussed. One head said he had become increasingly pragmatic in recent years and felt the most important research answered the question of what works. Another dean disagreed, favoring more theoretical, less practice-oriented research. A heated discussion followed with a third dean saying when the new superintendent of schools from Detroit calls, we need to be able to answer the question of what can he or she do. Another dean said, "This is not our job," and laughed adding, "if you consider it yours, I wish you luck." This brought the response "Does your legislature think it is as funny as you do that your school has nothing to say to urban educators in your states's largest cities?" Then came comments calling for the adoption of school systems by education schools; the rejection of the idea, pointing out that business schools did not adopt Amtrack when it was failing; and a counter that medical schools did not ignore AIDS because it was too difficult.

The simple fact is that the purpose of education schools today are blurred and confused. As noted in the previous chapters, education schools cannot decide whether they are arts and science colleges or professional schools. They are torn between theory and practice, the disengagement within the ivory tower and emersion in the field. They are even uncertain of their primary audience and patron—Is it the university or the education profession that are making demands upon education schools?

At the end of the day, some education schools choose the incestuousness of marrying the field and others the irrelevance of becoming cloistered behind the academy walls. Most have attempted to straddle at least rhetorically. Initiatives like UCLA's Center X described by Jeannie Oakes are unusual.

Bill Tierney is correct in saying different education schools will select different approaches. And the handwriting will continue.

But at bottom what is missing, and essential today, is an authentic and definite mission for education schools. Liberal arts colleges have this. Community colleges have this. Research universities have this. Medical schools and law schools have this. Education schools do not.

Sarah Turner's chapter describes the mission of education schools. For me it boils down to five activities:

1. conducting research on the critical issues facing education;
2. preparing the next generation of educators;
3. educating current leaders and professionals in the field;
4. leading and shaping the public dialogue in education; and
5. improving practice in educational institutions.

If education schools did these things and did them well they would answer their critics and more important, begin to create the education system we need for tomorrow.

And it is not "pollyannish" to think education schools can do this. Agriculture schools provide an excellent example of what is possible. If the activity statement above were changed such that the word "agriculture" was substituted for "education" throughout, it would be a reasonably good statement of the mission of agriculture school.

In the first decade of the twentieth century, Charles Van Hisc, the President of the University of Wisconsin, was able to boast to his legislature that his university had invented the cow, putting one hundred million dollars in the state coffers. What Van Hisc meant was that his agriculture school engaged in important research on critical issues relating to cows and dairy production. They educated the state's future farmers, giving them the most up-to-date knowledge and skills to ply their trade. They educated current farmers providing short courses, best practices, and instruction via extension. They educated the legislature, farmers' organizations, and commercial enterprises about essential future directives for agriculture. And they improved practice through experiment states to demonstrate the latest research. The result is that the unity increased the quality, efficiency, and quantity of dairy and cow production.

This, it seems to me, is an excellent description of the work that education schools should be doing. Perhaps our greatest error has been attempting to model ourselves after graduate schools of arts and sciences rather than other professional schools like engineering, medicine, and agriculture, which have achieved eminence in research, teaching, and service to their fields.

What would education schools look like if they were modeled after such schools? Two issues raised in the previous chapter might be worth revisiting—the research agenda and the faculty profile.

Research

The research agenda would shift. It would become far more field- or practice-based, employing a more interdisciplinary and less specialized approach to research. A number of the chapters in this volume explain the obstacles to such a charge. But there might also be resources to encourage it. Government and foundation dollars are available in unprecedented numbers. The utility of such research might also build supportive alliances with government and practitioners strong enough to counterbalance opposition within the academy.

The audience for research would have to expand. Not only would publicity be targeted at other academies, but the pressing need would be to get it into the heads of practitioners and policy makers.

The time frame for review and publication of research would have to be dramatically reduced. Today most of our research is two years old by the time it is published. To make that research useful to practitioners and policy makers, it would have to be made available within weeks. This would necessitate a redesign of peer review.

New methods of dissemination would also be required. Practitioners and policy makers do not read academic journals. Actually, academic contributors of journal articles are declining too. By the time articles are published, they are very out of date and the information is too old. The Internet and popular media will have to become far more prominent in research dissemination.

Hard research questions need to be asked too. In his chapter, Phil Hutcheson talks about the continuing importance of academic freedom. As he notes, it has never provided full protection for faculty during politically turbulent times like the McCarthy era or the Vietnam War. But it is important to recognize that the academy has also limited freedom of inquiry. Education schools tend to be rooted in the institutions of education—schools, teachers, and administrators—more than the children these institutions are supposed to serve. After all, the institutions pay the education school bills, not the children. This has discouraged schools of education from studying topics with the potential to upset the existing order—privatization and vouchers, unions, and nonpublic education to name a few. These topics demand serious research today, particularly if education schools want a voice in the national dialogue in education.

Faculty Profile

The chapters by Hearn and Anderson, Anthony and Taylor, Tierney, and Glazer-Raymo describe the current state of the faculty in education schools and the pressing need in terms of clinical, part-time, minority, and women faculty. The adoption of an agricultural or professional school model does not address most of these issues directly. It does make the issue of clinical faculty moot. They could be essential. Given the structure of education as a practice field this would very likely increase the number of minority and women faculty. The need to increase the number of women and minorities; particularly in senior posts in education schools, is a fact no matter what model education schools chose to follow.

Beyond clinical faculty, there would also need to be research professors in the educational equivalent of agriculture experiment stations. Part-time faculty would grow as particular facets of practice were brought into the curriculum and apprenticeships expanded. Faculty with a focus on pedagogy and technology would be added to the mix as education schools developed electronic extension activities. The short of it is that the variety of professional positions with and without tenure, full and part-time, would multiply. These positions would be located on- and off-campus in colleges and universities, schools, communities, and the air waves. And the expectations or rules governing academic excellence would need to become less unified in the manner suggested by Ernie Boyer or as Yvonna Kennedy showed is beginning to occur on some campuses.

If Education Schools Fail to Act

What I have suggested is one approach that education schools could take to address the very real and mounting doubts and criticisms about their performance both inside and outside the academy. I would be less than candid if I did not say it is the direction I hope they will choose. I am the president of an education school, so I am realistic enough to know that the proposed changes will not be easy. The pitfalls are documented throughout this volume.

But the indisputable fact is that doing nothing is not a choice. If education schools do not rethink and redesign themselves for the future, government will step in and do it for us, delegating issues ranging from faculty workloads and curriculum and professional development requests to outcome standards for graduates and admission requirements for entrants. A growing number of states are also preparing alternate routes to the education profession that bypass education schools. This means that if education schools do not reform themselves, government will either do that by itself or replace them.

And the profit-making sector, entering higher education at an unprecedented rate, is eager to share our studies. Increasingly, higher education is being perceived as the next health care, a 225-billion-dollar industry, characterized by high cost, low productivity, low use of technology, and poor management; ripe for a hostile takeover.

We live in a time when the largest private university in the United States, the University of Phoenix, is fully accredited and traded on NASDAQ. Kaplan, Inc. has an on-line law school. Business entrepreneurs Michael Milken and Larry Ellison are creating a for-profit on-line university. Venture capital firms are eagerly exploring the education market and Wall Street firms are developing education practices. New profit-making firms are entering the education market everyday.

It is an industry in which education stocks have done well; the cash flow is high; customer growth has been the norm often making long-term commitments of two to four years; worldwide markets are booming; the industry is countercyclical, producing its highest revenues during bad economic times; and it is highly subsidized by government grant and loan programs.

The private sector has the advantage of faster decision making, more disposable capital to invest, and a greater entrepreneurial spirit than most colleges and universities. Recently I visited the publisher Simon and Schuster. They explained to me they were no longer in the book business. They were now in the information or knowledge business. When I asked what this meant, I was told they were in the education business (providing teacher education and professional development to 12,000 schools via satellite television and Internet). They said they wanted to put the Simon and Schuster brand name on teacher professional development. I was shocked. I asked where the content came from, expecting them to tell me colleges and university faculty. No, they hire their own full-time content people. I asked about degrees and credits. They were still working on that.

In the years to come, the competition to hold onto our own business and our own statements is going to be fierce. The advantages we now hold will be temporary reputation, history, and brand name; content and intellectual capital; and accreditation and certification. The record is clear in showing that the profit-making sector can with effort secure all these things.

And, on top of all of this, nonprofit knowledge organizations are beginning to converge. That is, museums, libraries, symphonies, public broadcasts, and colleges are all starting to produce exactly the same services and products. All of us are now in the education business and professional development programs for education is going to be a the staple for most.

Given the circumstances, I cannot really think of a good reason why education schools should not rethink what they do.

About the Contributors

William G. Tierney is the Wilbur-Kieffer Professor of Higher Education and Director of the Center for Higher Education Policy Analysis at the University of Southern California. He holds advanced degrees from Harvard and Stanford Universities and a B.A. from Tufts University. Some of his books include *The Responsive University: Restructuring for High Performance, Promotion and Tenure: Community and Socialization in Academe* and *Building Communities of Difference: Higher Education in the Twenty-First Century*.

Jeannie Oakes is Professor of Education and Associate Dean in the Graduate School of Education and Information Studies at UCLA, where she directs Center X—Where Research and Practice Intersect for Urban School Professionals. Dr. Oakes has written extensively about the inequalities in U.S. schools and the progress of equity-minded reform. Her most recent book, *Becoming Good American Schools: The Struggle for Civic Virtue in Education Reform* (San Francisco: Jossey-Bass, 2000), follows the progress of educators across the nation who are attempting to eliminate inequalities in their schools.

John Rogers is the Director of Research at Center X at the UCLA Graduate School of Education. He received his undergraduate degree at the Woodrow Wilson School at Princeton University with a minor in African-American Studies. He received his Ph.D. in Education from Stanford University. His areas of research include teacher education, the history of urban school reform and college access programs.

Mary M. Kennedy is a professor at Michigan State University. Her scholarship focuses on the relationship between knowledge and teaching practice, on the nature of knowledge used in teaching practice, and on how research knowledge and policy ideas contributes to practice. She has published two books addressing the relationship between knowledge and teaching and has won four awards for her work.

Yvonna S. Lincoln is Program Director and Professor of Higher Education at Texas A&M University, where she teaches courses in college teaching, qualitative research methods, and university administration. She is the coauthor, editor or coeditor of seven books in qualitative research methods, evaluation theory or organizational theory, and the former president of both the American Evaluation Association and the Association for the Study of Higher Education. Her current research interests include public perceptions of higher education, and their impact on state support of research universities.

Sarah E. Turner is an Assistant Professor of Education and Economics at the University of Virginia. In addition to work on the labor market for teachers, she has written on the effects of federal financial aid policy, the changes in the return to college quality, and differences between men and women in the choice of undergraduate major. She received her Ph.D. in economics from the University of Michigan in 1997.

James C. Hearn is Professor of Higher Education, Chair of the Department of Educational Policy and Administration, and Interim Director of the Postsecondary Education Policy Studies Center at the University of Minnesota. His research and teaching focus on policy, organization, and finance in higher education.

Melissa S. Anderson is associate professor of higher education and coordinator of the higher education program at the University of Minnesota. Her recent research is in the areas of research misconduct, graduate education, ethics in science and engineering, academic-industry relations, and faculty demography.

Philo A. Hutcheson is associate professor of educational policy studies at Georgia State University, where he also serves as faculty coordinator of the higher education doctoral program. His recent publications include a chapter coauthored with Linda Buchanan, "Re-Considering the Washington-DuBois Debate: Two Black Colleges in 1910–1911" in *Southern Education in the Twentieth Century: Exceptionalism and Its Limits*, ed. Wayne Urban (New York: Garland Press, 1999), as well as "McCarthyism and the Professoriate: A Historiographic Nightmare?" in *Higher Education: The Handbook of Theory and Research*, vol. 12, ed. John C. Smart (New York: Agathon Press, 1997).

Judith Glazer-Raymo is professor of curriculum and instruction at Long Island University where she is concerned with the connections between research, policy, and practice in teacher education. For the past decade, she has been conducting international studies of the role and status of women in higher education and in the professions. She is the author of *Shattering the Myths: Women in Academe* (Johns Hopkins University Press, 1999) and co-editor of the forthcoming reader, *Women in American Higher Education: A Feminist Perspective* (Pearson, 2000).

James Soto Antony (Ph.D., UCLA, 1996) is Assistant Professor of Higher Education, and Affiliate Assistant Professor of Multicultural Education, both at the University of Washington. Professor Antony's research focuses on identifying the factors that influence aspirations to, and success within, professional occupations, with a special focus on minorities pursuing college faculty careers.

Edward Taylor (Ph.D., University of Washington, 1994) is Assistant Professor of Educational Leadership & Policy Studies, and Affiliate Assistant Professor of Multicultural Education, both at the University of Washington. Professor Taylor's research employs critical race theory to examine policies and programs servicing disenfranchised groups in secondary and post-secondary settings, and the construction of race-based policy.

Arthur Levine is the President of Teachers College and Professor of Education. His scholarly interests include the history of higher education, college students and multiculturalism and university leadership. He received his undergraduate degree from Brandeis University and his Ph.D. from State University of New York, Buffalo.

Index

Abdal-Haqq, I., 132
Academic freedom, 5–6; assumptions about, 37–41; challenges to, 152; commitment to, 6; dismissal cases, 153–157; disparate views regarding, 152; external pressures and, 161; gender and, 159–160; infringements on, 6; morality and, 39–40, 55n2; professors of education and, 151–162; protection of, 151; research and, 36; sustaining, 37; tenure and, 32, 41, 60, 152, 153; threats from public pressure, 34; women and, 6
Adam, B.E., 183
Adamany, D., 100
Addams, Jane, 9
Affirmative action, 11, 20, 174
African Americans. *See* Minorities
American Association for Higher Education, 152–153, 174
American Association of Colleges of Teacher Education, 80
American Association of University Professors, 5, 80, 135, 152, 154, 155, 156, 157, 173
American Educational Research Association, 18, 174
American Federation of Teachers, 170, 174, 177, 178
Anderson, Melissa, 5, 125–143, 216
Antony, James, 6, 84, 189–206, 216
Aronson, J., 193, 206
Askling, B., 179
Association of American Colleges of Teacher Education, 173, 174
Auerbach, J.S., 128

Baldwin, R.G., 126
Barbett, S.F., 189
Bartley, W.W.I., 38
Barton, P.E., 36
Becker, H.S., 192
Bell, D., 38–39
Benjamin, E., 126
Bensimon, E.M., 169
Bess, J.L., 61, 191
Bloland, H.G., 174
Bloland, S.M., 174
Blue Sky Committee, 74
Book, C., 44
Borrowman, M.L., 48
Bowen, W.G., 116
Boyer, Carol, 136
Boyer, Ernest, 17, 18, 52, 64, 69, 179, 183
Bragg, A.K., 192
Breneman, D.W., 100
Bronner, E., 80, 142
Browne, D., 44
Bullough, R.V., 137, 138, 139
Bush, Robert, 130
Byrne, J.P., 100
Byse, C., 61

Calderhead, J.A.M.R., 44
California State University, 13
California Subject Matter Projects, 20
Carnegie classification, 107, 121n2
Carnegie Commission, 158, 159
Carnegie Corporation, 130
Carnegie Forum, 175
Carnegie Foundation for the Advancement of Teaching, 179

SUNY series: Frontiers in Education
Philip G. Altbach, Editor

List of Titles

Excellence and Equality: A Qualitatively Different Perspective on Gifted and Talented Education—David M. Fetterman

Class, Race, and Gender in American Education—Lois Weis (ed.)

Change and Effectiveness in Schools: A Cultural Perspective—Gretchen B. Rossman, H. Dickson Corbett, and William A. Firestone (eds.)

The Curriculum: Problems, Politics, and Possibilities—Landon E. Beyer and Michael W. Apple (eds.)

Crisis in Teaching: Perspectives on Current Reforms—Lois Weis, Philip G. Altbach, Gail P. Kelly, Hugh G. Petrie, and Sheila Slaughter (eds.)

The Character of American Higher Education and Intercollegiate Sport—Donald Chu

Dropouts from Schools: Issues, Dilemmas, and Solutions—Lois Weis, Eleanor Farrar, and Hugh G. Petrie (eds.)

The Higher Learning and High Technology: Dynamics of Higher Education Policy Formation—Sheila Slaughter

Religious Fundamentalism and American Education: The Battle for the Public Schools—Eugene F. Provenzo, Jr.

The High Status Track: Studies of Elite Schools and Stratification—Paul W. Kingston and Lionel S. Lewis (eds.)

The Economics of American Universities: Management, Operations, and Fiscal Environment—Stephen A. Hoenack and Eileen L. Collins (eds.)

Going to School: The African-American Experience—Kofi Lomotey (ed.)

Curriculum Differentiation: Interpretive Studies in U.S. Secondary Schools—Reba Page and Linda Valli (eds.)

The Racial Crisis in American Higher Education—Philip G. Altbach and Kofi Lomotey (eds.)

The Great Transformation in Higher Education, 1960–1980—Clark Kerr

College in Black and White: African American Students in Predominantly White and in Historically Black Public Universities—Walter R. Allen, Edgar G. Epps, and Nesha Z. Haniff (eds.)

Critical Perspectives on Early Childhood Education—Lois Weis, Philip G. Altbach, Gail P. Kelly, and Hugh G. Petrie (eds.)

Textbooks in American Society: Politics, Policy, and Pedagogy—Philip G. Altbach, Gail P. Kelly, Hugh G. Petrie, and Lois Weis (eds.)

Black Resistance in High School: Forging a Separatist Culture—R. Patrick Solomon

Emergent Issues in Education: Comparative Perspectives—Robert F. Arnove, Philip G. Altbach, and Gail P. Kelly (eds.)

Creating Community on College Campuses—Irving J. Spitzberg, Jr. and Virginia V. Thorndike

Teacher Education Policy: Narratives, Stories, and Cases—Hendrik D. Gideonse (ed.)

Beyond Silenced Voices: Class, Race, and Gender in United States Schools—Lois Weis and Michelle Fine (eds.)

The Cold War and Academic Governance: The Lattimore Case at Johns Hopkins—Lionel S. Lewis

Troubled Times for American Higher Education: The 1990s and Beyond—Clark Kerr

Higher Education Cannot Escape History: Issues for the Twenty-First Century—Clark Kerr

Multiculturalism and Education: Diversity and Its Impact on Schools and Society—Thomas J. LaBelle and Christopher R. Ward

The Contradictory College: The Conflicting Origins, Impacts, and Futures of the Community College—Kevin J. Dougherty

Race and Educational Reform in the American Metropolis: A Study of School Decentralization—Dan A. Lewis and Kathryn Nakagawa

Professionalization, Partnership, and Power: Building Professional Development Schools—Hugh G. Petrie (ed.)

Ethnic Studies and Multiculturalism—Thomas J. LaBelle and Christopher R. Ward

Promotion and Tenure: Community and Socialization in Academe—William G. Tierney and Estela Mara Bensimon

Sailing Against the Wind: African Americans and Women in U.S. Education— Kofi Lomotey (ed.)

The Challenge of Eastern Asian Education: Implications for America—William K. Cummings and Philip G. Altbach (eds.)

Conversations with Educational Leaders: Contemporary Viewpoints on Education in America—Anne Turnbaugh Lockwood

Managed Professionals: Unionized Faculty and Restructuring Academic Labor—Gary Rhoades

The Curriculum (Second Edition): Problems, Politics, and Possibilities— Landon E. Beyer and Michael W. Apple (eds.)

Education/Technology/Power: Educational Computing as a Social Practice— Hank Bromley and Michael W. Apple (eds.)

Capitalizing Knowledge: New Intersections of Industry and Academia—Henry Etzkowitz, Andrew Webster, and Peter Healey (eds.)

The Academic Kitchen: A Social History of Gender Stratification at the University of California, Berkeley—Maresi Nerad

Grass Roots and Glass Ceilings: African American Administrators in Predominantly White Colleges and Universities—William B. Harvey (ed.)

Community Colleges as Cultural Texts: Qualitative Explorations of Organizational and Student Culture—Kathleen M. Shaw, James R. Valadez, and Robert A. Rhoads (eds.)

Educational Knowledge: Changing Relationships between the State, Civil Society, and the Educational Community—Thomas S. Popkewitz (ed.)

Transnational Competence: Rethinking the U.S.-Japan Educational Relationship—John N. Hawkins and William K. Cummings (eds.)

Women Administrators in Higher Education: Historical and Contemporary Perspectives—Jana Nidiffer and Carolyn Terry Bashaw (eds.)

Faculty Work in Schools of Education: Rethinking Roles and Rewards for the Twenty-First Century—William G. Tierney (ed.)

FACULTY WORK IN SCHOOLS OF EDUCATION

SUNY series

FRONTIERS IN EDUCATION

Philip G. Altbach, Editor

The Frontiers in Education Series draws upon a range of disciplines and approaches in the analysis of contemporary educational issues and concerns. Books in the series help to reinterpret established fields of scholarship in education by encouraging the latest synthesis and research. A special focus highlights educational policy issues from a multidisciplinary perspective. The series is published in cooperation with the School of Education, Boston College. A complete listing of books in the series can be found at the end of this volume.